Economy and Society of Laos

A Brief Survey

Joel M. Halpern

Monograph Series
No. 5

Southeast Asia Studies
Yale University

Second Printing 1966

Library of Congress Catalog Card No. 64-8763

distributor
The Cellar Book Shop, 18090 Wyoming, Detroit, Michigan 48221

Printed in U.S.A.

PUBLISHER'S NOTE

The response of the academic community and others interested in Southeast Asia to our publication of Professor Joel M. Halpern's Government, Politics, and Social Structure in Laos: A Study of Tradition and Innovation (Monograph Series No. 4, 1964) has encouraged us to publish the present companion volume. Like its predecessor, the present work brings together several earlier studies by the author which were issued for a very limited circulation and hence are by and large inaccessible to interested readers. Like it, too, the study published here represents the results of careful field work and wide reading in government reports and monographs not readily available in this country. We are grateful to Professor Halpern for having undertaken the additional labors that made republication in the present form possible, and we are confident that Economy and Society of Laos: A Brief Survey will be accorded as merited a welcome as his earlier work in this series.

H. J. B.

PREFACE

Like the preceding monograph in this series, the present study is based on field data and basic statistical materials obtained in the course of the year 1957, spent as a field representative for the American aid mission in Luang Prabang in northern Laos, and in 1959 during a second visit as a consultant to the RAND Corporation. In addition to field work, several years of intermittent research have been devoted to going through available literature and consulting individuals who have worked in Laos.

Essentially, this is an attempt to integrate what is known about northern and central Laos from a socioeconomic point of view. Documentary, and especially statistical, materials pertaining to Laos are extremely imprecise. In view of current political conditions future field studies in depth do not appear probable, but it is hoped that some will be possible before present ways of life are altered too drastically. This monograph, like its predecessor, is a background study rather than an up-to-date survey. Aside from some summary data and brief reference to the current refugee situation, no attempt has been made to deal with the present aid programs (American, French, Colombo Plan, and United Nations). Certain side effects of the large-scale American military aid program are, however, discussed. By the time this monograph reaches the reader the political situation doubtless will have again changed. But far-reaching social and economic changes obviously occur more slowly and hopefully some of them will benefit the peoples of Laos.

While this study is based primarily on the author's field experience, a considerable amount of supporting data has been drawn from the reports of other anthropologists working in Laos during the 1950s. Specifically, William Smalley made available some of his field materials pertaining to the Khmu of the Luang Prabang area; Linwood Barney's study of the Meo of Xieng Khouang was useful; Howard Kaufman, Georges Condominas, Tsuneo Ayabe, and Keiji Iwata have done valuable studies in the area of former Vientiane province; and there was much helpful information in the reports of B.H. Duclos, FAO consultant to the Lao government.

The works of all these investigators are cited in detail in the text since, with the exception of Ayabe's and Iwata's studies which have been published in Japanese, none are easily available. The contributions of Kaufman and Barney and English translations of Ayabe and Iwata were issued for limited circulation in the author's Laos Project Papers (see the bibliography) and those of Condominas and Gaudillot in even smaller mimeographed editions in Paris. There is a significant French literature on Laos for the colonial period, but only those sources bearing directly on economic and demographic problems have been cited in this monograph (see Laos Project Paper No. 22 for a relatively complete list of French sources).

The author's own observations, incorporating some materials of Kaufman and Smalley, first appeared in 1958 as "Aspects of Village Life and Culture Change in Laos," a report prepared under a grant from the Council on Economic and Cultural Affairs, New York, and then in expanded and revised form as Laos Project Papers Nos. 3, 4, 9, 11, 17, and 19. The assembly of these materials as Laos Project Papers was aided by a grant in the summer of 1960 from the Asian Studies Program of the American Council of Learned Societies and by grants during 1959-61 arranged by the Faculty Research Committee at the University of California.

In the course of the circulation of different versions of this study numerous helpful comments have been received from Lao, French, British, and American scholars and officials. Aram Udol served as my interpreter in 1957 and Kamron Inthanoochai in 1959; university graduates from Udom and Chiengmai respectively, they not only helped as interpreters but also conducted interviews of their own, thereby supplying valuable perspective on my personal field notes. I particularly want to acknowledge the kind assistance of the Reverend G. Edward Roffe of Vientiane, whose extensive knowledge of Lao language and culture is perhaps unique among Westerners, the interest and comments of the distinguished Thai anthropologist Phya Anuman Rajadhon, and the many suggestions of Pierre-Bernard Lafont, associated at that time with the Ecole Française d'Extrême-Orient in Laos. Rose Kerewsky was indispensable in helping to prepare the original Laos Project Papers. My wife, Barbara K. Halpern, shared the field experience and performed the affectionate albeit trying labor of rendering the manuscript and statistics presentable. The responsibility for the end results, however, is mine.

Brandeis University
September 1964

JOEL M. HALPERN

CONTENTS

CONTENTS (continued)

CONTENTS (continued)

LIST OF PLATES

Vientiane, Saravane, and Champassak provinces were subdivided in 1964, creating the additional provinces of Borikhane, Wapikhanthong, and Sithandone respectively.

ECONOMY AND SOCIETY OF LAOS

A Brief Survey

I

POPULATION AND ETHNIC DIVERSITY

Geography and Climate

Landlocked Laos, bordered on the north by China, the east by Vietnam, the south by Cambodia, and the west by Thailand and Burma, covers an area of approximately 91,000 square miles, making it somewhat smaller than the state of Oregon or the British Isles. Here dwell, according to the most optimistic estimates, two to three million people or at most an average of thirty-three persons per square mile.[1] In the most heavily populated area of Laos, the Mekong river plains along the Thai border, the population density may reach 180 per square mile. This figure is not quite half that of the average for the whole of India (326 in 1954) or for a Thai village (320) near Bangkok (Sharp 1953: 24). Compared to these areas, most of the Laos countryside is relatively empty (see Table 1). The topography of Laos provides a partial explanation, since most of the country, particularly the northern part, is mountainous.

The Annamite mountain chain forming the eastern frontier with Vietnam plays an important role in conditioning the climate of the country. There are two distinct seasons, a wet period from May through October and a dry one from November through April.[2] About two-thirds of the 100 to 150 rainy days in a year occur in the rainy season, with the amount of precipitation outside the wet season only about 20 per cent of the total annual rainfall. The rice crops in both the paddy fields and the upland clearings are, of course, dependent on this rainfall pattern. Luang Prabang province, along with most of northern Laos, is one of the drier areas of the country, receiving annually approximately 40 to 80 inches of rainfall, while the Bolovens plateau area in southern Laos has well over 150 inches of rainfall in its central portions.

During the height of the rainy season crops may be damaged, overland transportation is rendered hazardous if not impossible, and air traffic suffers disruption to some degree, but river transportation improves with the rise in the river levels. Relative humidity is high, often reaching 90 per cent even when it is not raining. During the wet season winds are predominantly from the southwest and during the dry season from the northeast. In late April, prior to the onset of the rains, temperatures reach the maximum for the year, the actual high varying significantly with altitude. Once the rains begin temperatures drop slightly, although the driest months of the year, January and February, are also the coolest. These winter months are frequently chilly in northern Laos, presenting a problem to all but the more prosperous inhabitants as most of the people lack adequate clothing and shiver around fires in the early morning and evening. There is a considerable incidence of pneumonia during this season.

From November to March the plains and valleys are foggy until late morning. In the area around the royal capital of Luang Prabang, a small basin surrounded by mountains, planes frequently cannot land until the haze burns off around noon. Some observers have linked an all-day haze from March through May to the burning of forest clearings which occur at this time. Although the fires are clearly visible and give off a fair amount of smoke, most geographers doubt that swidden burning is of sufficient extent to have any real meteorological effects.

Population

Commenting on the population figures for Laos is a complicated undertaking in view of the limited reliability of the few available statistics. With the present division of the country and accompanying conflict it would appear unlikely that more serviceable statistics will soon be available. No complete official census has ever been undertaken. Those figures that do exist were collected largely by untrained local officials during the French colonial administration and many French and Thai sources specifically emphasize their limited value.[3] While Laos was a French colony one of the chief uses of these figures was for tax rolls and obviously such figures should be interpreted with extreme caution. But this does not mean that they cannot be credited, particularly where a certain internal consistency exists and the figures follow a logical trend. As a further check, it is also possible in certain cases to compare data from Laos with analogous areas in neighboring Thailand and other countries in Southeast Asia.

The only figures for the population of Laos prior to the establishment of the French protectorate are from the census of King Oun Huan, son of the famous Fa Ngoum, traditional founder of the Lao kingdom of Lan Xang. This census, undertaken in 1376, recorded 300,000 Lao-Thai males between eighteen and sixty years of age and 400,000 non-Thai. From this a population total of three million inhabitants can be derived, but it is of limited utility for comparison with contemporary figures because the precise boundaries of the kingdom at that time have not been defined. These figures are also obviously very approximate, and there is doubtless a wide margin of error. But from what is known of the relatively complex political organization existing at that time it seems reasonable to assume that a population of approximately this size existed in the general area now occupied by Laos (Pietrantoni 1953). Significantly this is also somewhat less than the size of the Laotian population today.

In the absence of a validated census for Laos, various means have been used to estimate population density. One recent observer gives a figure of 19 per square mile and judges 8 per cent of the land to be cultivated (Lafont 1959: 9, 11). About sixty years earlier Reinach estimated the population density to be 4.7 per square mile and stated that 12 per cent of the land was cultivated with one-third of the total land surface potentially cultivable. He felt that the country was capable of supporting 26 to 30 inhabitants per square mile (Reinach 1901: 92-93). Current estimates of population density in Laos range from 15 to 33 per square mile, which indicates that, taking even the most modest present estimate, a tripling of the population relative to the total land area in a little less than half a century has occurred.

Another way to view population concentration is to compare the population densities of similar geographic regions with differing amounts of arable land (see Table 2). On this basis we find that the Mekong area, though heavily populated, nevertheless has a lower density than the average for the Asian tropics and that despite a threefold increase in population Laos remains one of the most sparsely settled countries in Asia.

In 1900 the population was estimated at approximately half a million, increasing to about two million by 1960. Changing boundaries further complicate the estimates. From what is known of population dynamics in predominantly agricultural and tropical countries analogous to Laos, it seems logical to suppose that the population grew at an increasing rate under French control. There are several reasons for this assumption. First, even if the birth rate remained constant during the more than half century of French rule, it was a period of imperial peace and Laos was free of the debilitating wars with Thailand and her other neighbors that had taken such a toll of the population, e.g. during the early nineteenth century when the Thai decimated Vientiane and removed a large portion of the population of that area to the other bank of the Mekong.

In addition the French established a health service. Even assuming that it was not too effective on the local village level, particularly among the scattered mountain peoples, the fact is that hospitals and clinics were established in the major towns, large numbers of rural patients were treated, and inoculation campaigns begun, doubtless affecting the death rate, especially in those relatively densely populated plains surrounding the major towns (see Table 3). The large-scale malarial spraying campaign conducted in the last few years by the government of Laos may also have had a significant effect on population increase, as malaria is a major cause of death (Halpern ed. 1961: No. 10). Since World War II similar developments have been documented for other areas where DDT spraying dramatically decreased the death rate from malaria.

With regard to the internal distribution of the population, there is a noticeable variation between the hilly northern provinces and the central and southern ones, the latter having a considerable area (for Laos) of rice-bearing plains bordering on the Mekong. The northern provinces have for the most part about half the population density of the central and southern ones. Although the population density appears to have increased about 50 per cent in the past fifteen years, the relative distribution by provinces has remained approximately the same.

This historically observable pattern of provincial population distribution is closely correlated with village size, the most densely populated provinces also having the largest villages. These differences are particularly striking in comparing Vientiane, Attopeu, and Xieng Khouang: in the case of Xieng Khouang 88 per cent of the population is concentrated in villages of less than 200 inhabitants, while in Vientiane only 42 per cent of the population is found there (see Table 4). In Xieng Khouang only ten villages are listed as having a population of over 300 or less than 1 per cent of the total compared to over 13 per cent for Vientiane. Vientiane, Savannakhet, and Champassak, with an average village population of over 200, are also the three most densely populated provinces at 22 persons per square mile. Similarly, Khammouane, Nam Tha, Phong Saly, Sam Neua, and Luang Prabang all have a population density of less than 16 and an average village size of less than 130 persons (see Table 5).

If we look at the ethnic composition of the first group of provinces, we see that all are at least 80 per cent Lao-Tai, while in the second group only Khammouane has a majority of Lao-Tai in its population (Phong Saly and Sam Neua have practically no Lao villages, although they do have Tai groups).

Ethnic Origins

Two salient geographic facts -- the sparse, scattered population and the mountainous terrain -- are most forcibly impressed on the traveler making a plane trip north from the administrative capital of Vientiane to the royal capital at Luang Prabang. Circling over Vientiane one sees the town stretched out along the Mekong, surrounded by rice fields with occasional small patches of forest. Leaving the Mekong plain the land abruptly changes to rugged mountains cut by narrow valleys. The observer looking closely at the settlement pattern below can discern almost a textbook illustration of ethnic stratification and economic-geographic adaptation to the land based on varying degrees of altitude.

Lao officials divide the population into four groups: Lao-Lu or valley Lao; Lao-Tai or tribal Tai[4]; Lao-Theng or Lao of the mountain sides (instead of the derogatory term Kha); and Lao-Soung or Lao of the mountain tops (Meo and Yao). Implicit is an attempt to emphasize the unity of the country. These terms, however, are largely political and cannot erase the important cultural differences.[5]

Some scholars have claimed that the tribal Tai are representatives of an earlier form of social organization out of which the Thai (of Thailand) and Lao evolved. The Lao and tribal Tai do belong to the same general language group (see Table 6) and share a common origin in China, but there are also important differences. The tribal Tai, of whom perhaps the most important group in Laos are the Black Tai, are patrilineal, with a belief revolving around ancestral deities. There are also hereditary elite families in the villages and at one time they were organized into petty kingdoms, the last of which collapsed after World War II. By contrast the Lao and their associated subgroups are bilateral in their social structure, Buddhist, and without hereditary class groups within the village. Unfortunately there is insufficient information available for us to draw a rigid distinction between Thai-Lao and tribal Tai. For example, the Tai Lu in the area of Muong Sing bear many resemblances to the neighboring Tai Dam but unlike the latter are Buddhists albeit by adoption in recent times.

The Lao-Theng or Kha is the general name applied to the very diverse group of indigenous inhabitants who lack both a writing system and formalized political organizations beyond the village. Those few who are Buddhists have adopted the faith of the Lao relatively recently, a few have become Christians, but the majority are animists. In contrast to both the Lao and tribal Tai, whose economy is based largely on irrigated rice, the Kha with few exceptions cultivate slash-and-burn fields.

The Meo and Yao, although culturally distinct groups, share in common a number of important cultural traits. Like the Kha they are primarily slash-and-burn agriculturists, with the distinction that they dwell high in the mountains and raise opium as a cash crop. Both Meo and Yao have strong patriarchal influences in family and village organization and share a common origin in China, from which many of them migrated during the colonial period. Literacy in Chinese is also fairly widespread among these groups. Their religion has certain strong Confucianist and animistic influences. Their characteristic dress is another feature distinguishing them from other inhabitants (see Tables 7 and 8).

It is important to note, however, that the tribal distinctions being made here for Laos are by no means absolute and that, among many of the Khmu groups and Kha groups generally as well as among some of the Tai groups, a subgroup may be distinctive because of its progressive assimilation to Lao culture.

Migrations and Distribution

Reconstructing the patterns of migrations, the Khmu and other proto-Indochinese groups appear to have originally been widely distributed in both the mountains and plains. About eight centuries ago the valley-dwelling, wet-rice cultivating Lao-Thai appeared in Laos, migrating south in response to the expanding pressures of the Han Chinese. Later, largely during the past few centuries, the Meo and the Yao tribes moved in from Yunnan and Tonkin, engaging in shifting cultivation. The current ethnic stratification, then, does not appear to have very great historical depth. In general the Lao live along the rivers and in the valleys, the Tai in higher valleys. The Meo and Yao inhabit the mountains from about 2,000 to 5,500 feet while Lao-Theng groups are irregularly distributed in between on mountain slopes.[6] In the northern part of Laos the Tai and Lao are distributed along the Mekong and its tributaries (see Figure 1).[7] Turning to the eastern part of Indochina we find the Tai in the vicinity of the Tonkin plain and thence inland, the Tai Dam and Tai Kao in the highlands, and to the south the Tai Deng.[8]

The Tai Dam and Tai Kao are located to the north and east of Sam Neua in the former 4th Military Territory of Indochina. Generally speaking, the Tai Kao inhabit the north of this territory and are not an important ethnic group in Laos while the Tai Dam are found in the southern part, particularly in the area of Dien Bien Phu only a few miles from Phong Saly (Roux 1954: 364).

The Tai Neua or northern Tai inhabit the Mekong valley from Vang Vieng in Vientiane province to Sam Neua and on into part of the Salween valley. In 1918 they were estimated to number 600,000 (Seidenfaden 1958: 24-25). Up to recent times there are said to

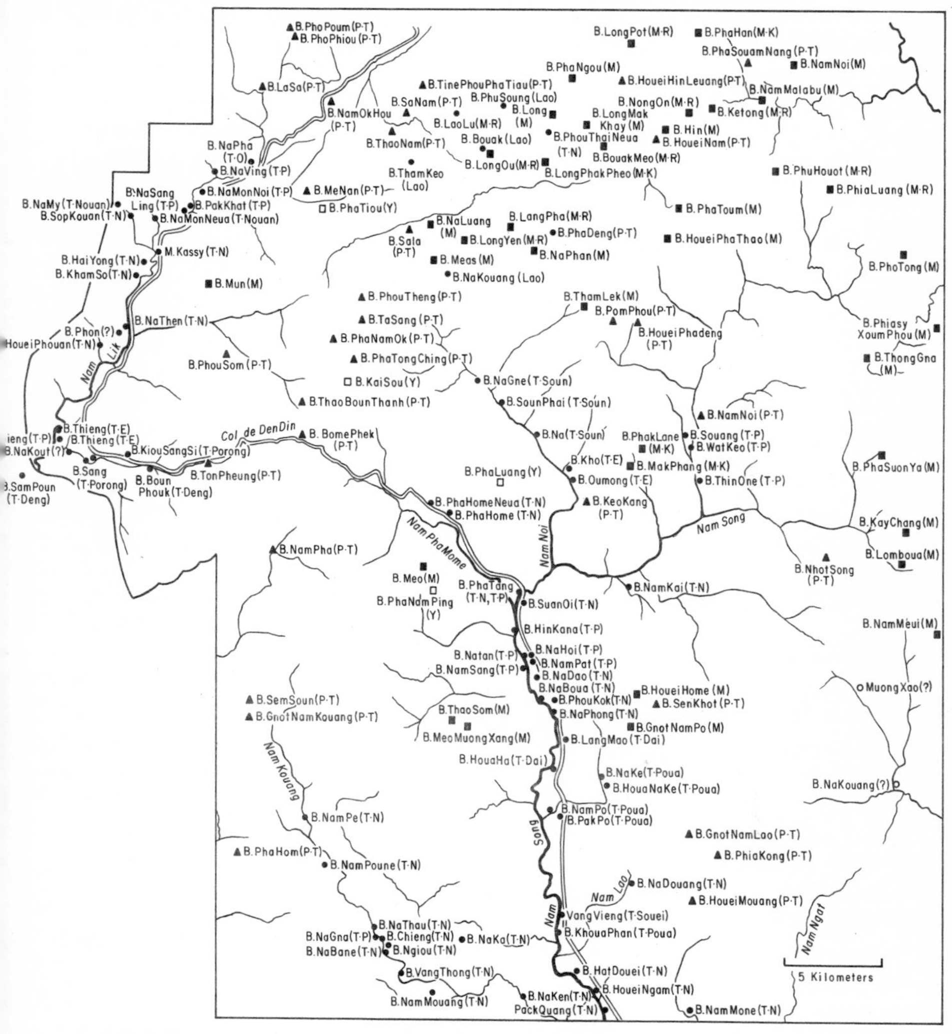

T·N–ThaiNeua, T·P–ThaiPouan, M–Meo (M·K–MeoKhao[1], M·R–MeoRai[2]); Y·Yao, P·T–PhouTheng

• Lao ■ Meo □ Yao ▲ PhouTheng

ETHNIC DISTRIBUTION IN THE VALLEYS OF THE NAM SONG AND NAM LIK

FIGURE 1

1 MeoKhao = White Meo
2 MeoRai = Striped Meo

From Keiji Iwata, "Ethnic Groups in the Valley of the Nam Song and Nam Lik," Laos Project Paper No. 15.

have existed 28 Tai Neua districts, some of which are thought to overlap with the Tai Lu of Sip Song Pan Na in Yunnan.

The Tai Lu, called by the Chinese Pa-vi or Shui Pa-vi, inhabit the twelve Pan Nas, eleven of which are situated on the west bank of the Mekong, the twelfth being Muong Sing in Laos.[9] Outside the Sip Song Pan Na there are many Tai Lu groups in places such as Chieng Tung in Burma, Chieng Rai and Lamphun in North Thailand, and the Nam Ou valley near Luang Prabang in Laos. The Lu of Lamphun are the descendants of prisoners of war taken 150 years ago when a Thai army invaded Chieng Tung in Yunnan. There are also a few hundred Lu in northern Tonkin. A 1918 estimate put the Tai Lu at over 350,000 in the Chinese-owned Pan Nas, with 50,000 more in Chieng Tung. Counting those in Thailand and Laos, the present total may easily be over 750,000 -- or almost equal to the number of Lao in Laos.

The Khmu are located mainly in the western part of northern Laos up to the Nam Leng, a tributary of the Nam Ou which joins the Mekong a few miles north of Luang Prabang, and are particularly numerous in the mountainous areas between Vientiane, Luang Prabang, and Xieng Khouang. The Khmu of the Nam Leng mark the northern limit of the Khmu on Lao territory with the exception of those in the area of Muong Sing.[10]

The Meo are distributed sporadically in northern Laos from Yunnan south to Phou Khao Quai but are concentrated mainly in Xieng Khouang.[11] The Yao are found in relatively large numbers in the northern part of the Tonkin plain and in the mountains to the west, as well as in northern Thailand; in Laos they are located chiefly in southwestern Sam Neua, around Nam Tha town, in northwestern Phong Saly, and to a lesser extent in the Luang Prabang and Vang Vieng areas. Their distribution is irregular and their villages are scattered.[12]

The Lao are the dominant group politically, economically, and socially. Their principal religious, linguistic, and other cultural affiliations are with the Lao of Northeast Thailand. A handbook on Thailand published by the Thai government on the occasion of the Ninth Pacific Science Congress in 1957 makes the following statement about the Lao:

> The Lao differ but little from the Thai, and are in reality as much Thai as are the Thai. The Lao do not call themselves Lao but Thai.[13] The Lao of Thailand are divided into two divisions: the Lao of northern Thailand, or Lao Phung Dam, and the Lao of eastern Thailand, or Lao Phung

> Khao (Black-bellied and White-bellied Lao). [The terms refer to the fact that the men of the former are closely tattooed from waistline to mid-thigh; this tattooing is absent in the latter.[14]] The Northern Lao inhabit the whole of Northern Thailand . . . In addition to the name Lao Phung Dam they are frequently called by their neighbors Lao Yuen or Thai Yuen. The Eastern Lao occupy a great part of the Khorat Plateau and the valley of the Mae Khong [Mekong]. There are also scattered communities of both these Lao divisions in Lower Thailand . . . The Eastern Lao can be divided into two language groups: the Lao Wiengchan [Vientiane] and the Lao Kao . . . most of the population of the three provinces of Prachin, Krabin and Nakhon Nayok are Lao Wiengchan, all originally prisoners of war deported to these districts just one hundred years ago[15] . . . The dialectic difference between Lao Wiengchan and Lao Kao is not great, but quite distinct to an observant ear.[16]

Clearly the distinctions to be made between the neighboring peoples of Laos and Thailand are largely political. That this is true of the tribal groups as well as the Lao reveals something of the nature of population movement in the area. Warfare is a significant cause and has brought important population movements both between countries and, as in Laos, within countries. Economic conditions can also provide the motivation. But in both cases the movement is almost always southward. This applies to all major ethnic groups.[17]

It has been observed with regard to the migration pattern of the Northeast Thai-Lao that villages moved as units after sending ahead some responsible citizens to scout the possibilities (Klausner 1959). The Lao village may change location every few dozen years and is also not too stable a unit, at least in the perspective of fifty years or more: tribal villages, which move every few decades, are even less so. It can be truly said that almost none of the rural villages in Laos are really permanent, the few villages in the Vientiane area that have existed for several centuries being rare exceptions. The tendency of the Lao and Black Tai to have more permanent villages than the Meo or Khmu stems from their dependence on irrigated rice culture. Such mobility of the population can be, and is, a major problem for map-makers, census takers, and government planners.

Ethnic Composition of the Population

In recent years it has become common when discussing the

problems of Laos to assert that the lowland Lao who control the government are not even a clear majority in their own country and that at least half of the people belong to tribal groups (see Table 9). Unfortunately, it is not possible on the basis of currently available information to furnish any detailed documentation on this point, a major complication being that the Lao and Tai are now listed together and not under separate categories as in statistics issued during the period of French rule. The political motivation for this is obvious: it places the Lao in a more favorable position. Yet on a personal basis the Lao sharply distinguish themselves from the Tai groups -- though acknowledging a closer relationship to the Tai peoples than to the Lao-Theng or Meo-Yao groups. The hierarchies of the various Tai groups were not integrated with those of the Lao. In fact, for the most part these Tai peoples could trace their origins to North Vietnam and without question some now residing in Laos feel themselves strongly drawn in that direction.[18] This feeling is intensified by their awareness that although some Tai do occupy government positions the Lao subtly discriminate against the Tai groups as a whole. It is also interesting that the inhabitants of the Tai Dam refugee villages near the towns of Vientiane and Luang Prabang appear to have integrated themselves into Laotian society after the pattern of the Vietnamese rather than the Lao, e.g. becoming craftsmen, vegetable gardeners, petty traders, and domestic servants -- occupations approximating those of the resident Vietnamese. These particular groups are also generally not Buddhist and share certain ritual observances with the Vietnamese.

The proportions of the total population in each of the major ethnic groupings remained relatively unchanged in the period 1911-42: the Lao went from 45 per cent of the total population to 44 per cent, the Kha from 32 to 30 per cent, and the Tai from 19 to 17 per cent according to the 1911 and 1942 figures respectively. Only the Meo-Yao figures differed appreciably, more than doubling -- from 2 to 5 per cent -- over the forty-year interval (see Table 9). There is a very plausible explanation for this -- many Meo-Yao groups may have migrated south into Laos from neighboring China and North Vietnam during these years, following earlier trends. In fact, interviewing of contemporary groups reveals an apparent migration in recent years from the provinces of the north bordering on Vietnam and China southward into Luang Prabang and subsequently into Sayaboury and Vientiane.

Trying to assess the validity of the proportions expressed for 1942-55 presents a number of difficulties. The figures show a spectacular jump in the Lao-Tai category from 61 to 74 per cent and a decrease in the Kha figure, with the Meo-Yao statistics remaining more or less constant. This reflects the absence of Phong Saly and Sam Neua from the 1955 calculations. Fortunately there are detailed statistics available for Sam Neua for 1936 which indicate a Tai population of approximately 68 per cent, rather close to the Lao-Tai average for all of Laos of 74 per cent for 1955 (based on the maximum population estimate). We may roughly assume therefore that the omission of this one province would not have made a great difference in the overall average if the percentage composition of the population had not greatly altered in the intervening nineteen years. But in the case of Sam Neua it must be remembered that the "Lao-Tai" are actually tribal Tai; there are virtually no Lao in the province. This leaves only Phong Saly, whose population was estimated at about 50,000 in 1955, or approximately 4 per cent of the total population of Laos.[19] One must look elsewhere for an explanation of the increase in the Lao-Tai component of the population of Laos.

In Table 9, we see that in 1942 in the Kingdom of Luang Prabang, which included much of northern Laos (principally Luang Prabang and Nam Tha provinces), the valley Lao constituted only 35 per cent of the population. In a survey conducted by the French authorities in 1950 in Sayaboury province, the Lao composed only 25 per cent of the population in Hong Sa district and 40 per cent in Pak Lay district. Together these two districts account for most of the populated area of the province, with 229 and 166 villages respectively out of a 1954 total of 523, or about 75 per cent, while the 1960 census figures give 76 per cent for Lao-Tai groups in the province. Recent estimates for Xieng Khouang based on an 88 per cent complete sample give 38 per cent Lao, some Tai groups being included in this figure. In Nam Tha province for 1953 the Lao were not significant. In Muong Sing district they comprised only the officials and their families, while the Tai (principally Lu) were 37 per cent of the population. In Nam Tha and Houei Sai districts the Lao were 2 and 6 per cent respectively, while the Tai were 44 and 40 per cent. In Sam Neua no Lao were officially listed by the French, while the Tai formed approximately 68 per cent of the population in 1936. In Saravane the Lao were 43 per cent of the population in 1938, while only 30 per cent of the population was Lao-Tai in Attopeu in 1955. This leaves the provinces of Khammouane, Vientiane, Champassak, and to a lesser extent Savannakhet as predominantly Lao. It is only in Vientiane province that the non-Lao-Tai peoples constitute a small minority.[20]

It is not without significance that with the exception of the province of Khammouane, all of the provinces bordering on the Democratic Republic of Vietnam and People's Republic of China contain only a minority of Lao. This has made close ties with the

Pathet Lao much easier for the DRV since the same tribal groups are found on both sides of the border.

Another important factor is underestimation of the population. The villages of the tribal peoples are much smaller and more scattered over mountainous terrain than the larger settlements of the Lao located in the valleys. Differences in village size on an ethnic basis reflect different geographic adaptations and land use. The Lao practicing irrigated or flood rice agriculture are able to have the largest, most permanent villages, while the Meo who live on the mountain tops appear to have the smallest and least permanent, with the Kha occupying an intermediate position in terms of geography, population, and permanence. In Luang Prabang province Meo villages of 200 or 300 do occur but are rare, while those with over 100 inhabitants are not unusual -- in marked contrast to the pattern of Lao and even Lao-Theng villages. An important factor not brought out in these figures is the occasional proximity of Meo villages to each other. For the most part Meo villages appear to be widely scattered in Luang Prabang, but certain ecological factors may cause concentrations. Thus on a plateau several hours' walk from Luang Prabang town there are estimated to be some 3,000 Meo living in villages with as many as 80 to 90 houses each. This clustering is due at least in part to the fact that the soil has a high lime content, making it good for growing opium. By contrast, Meo villages of 500 to 1,000 population are by no means unusual in Vientiane province (where Meo make up 12 per cent of the rural population) although these larger villages are less likely to be found in the north. It is also pertinent to note that the average size of villages in Laos has increased almost 50 per cent in the past half century, although it is impossible to say in any precise way exactly how this has affected the different minority groups. One might infer that, since the Lao villages are nearest the growing towns and are more and more becoming accessible by roads, increasing trade contacts may have tended to promote population concentrations. It is likely that for this reason the average size of the Lao villages has grown faster than the average size of those of the mountain peoples though at least some Meo villages -- such as those on the Xieng Khouang plateau -- have probably also shown increases.

The smaller size, dispersion, and hence greater inaccessibility of non-Lao villages were implicitly acknowledged in the 1959 five-year development plan of the Lao government. This official source states (apparently quoting a French report on the census of 1936) that the Lao-Tai were underestimated by a factor of approximately 15 per cent, the proto-Indochinese (called Kha or Indonesians in the report) by 40 per cent, and the Meo by 50 per cent.

Applying these figures to the proportions given in the 1942 census and extrapolating to a census figure of 2,000,000 we arrive at a figure of 820,000 (40 per cent) for the Lao, 320,000 (16 per cent) for the various Tai peoples, 680,000 (34 per cent) for the proto-Indochinese, and 100,000 (9 per cent) for the Meo-Yao. These figures are exclusive of other groups such as the Vietnamese, Chinese, Indians, and Europeans, who dwell in the towns. In fact, in most cases the Lao appear to be definitely a minority in the towns demographically speaking -- e.g. Pakse with its large Chinese and Vietnamese groups -- while in Vientiane, in addition to sizable communities of these two groups, there also appear to be more immigrants from across the river in Thailand than from Laos proper. According to Pietrantoni (1957: 230) in 1943 the Lao made up 61 per cent of the population of Luang Prabang town and only 41.5 per cent in Vientiane, with 16, 14, 10, and 11 per cent in Savannakhet, Pakse, Xieng Khouang, and Thakhek respectively.

Ethnically and linguistically, the point can be made as far as the rural and urban areas are concerned that Laos has no characteristic population groups that cannot be found in greater numbers in neighboring states. Phong Saly and Sam Neua adjoin the Tai-Meo Autonomous Zone of North Vietnam, and Phong Saly and Nam Tha border on the Tai Autonomous Region (Sip Song Pan Na) of China. Far greater numbers of Meo and Yao reside in North Vietnam and China than in Laos. A similar observation is possible with regard to the Tai peoples. The Lao population of Northeast Thailand amounts to approximately seven million, of North Thailand some five million. This situation is the source of a mild Lao irredentism though more important perhaps is the fact that the Thai annexed parts of Laos when France was weak, e.g. Sayaboury during World War II. As we have seen, the Kha constitute a great many individual tribal units which also overlap into North and South Vietnam, Cambodia, and Thailand.

Although it is of great significance that there are ethnic overlappings with North Vietnam and China, without doubt the most significant cultural relationships are with the Lao of Thailand. The borders with China and North Vietnam are for the most part in mountainous country that can be crossed but with difficulty, while the Mekong which marks the Thai-Lao border for much of its length is in no sense an obstacle since the Lao are a riverine people. In fact it encourages contact as the Lao like to fish and traverse the river to trade. By contrast, the many cultural differences -- in language, religion, ethos, and food habits -- between the Lao and their Chinese and Vietnamese neighbors are strongly felt. During recent battles the Royal Lao government talked darkly of "foreign" soldiers who use chopsticks and eat nonglutinous rice -- an oblique way of referring to the Vietnamese.

History provides several indications of the ancient origin of present migratory patterns. The population pressures generated by the Han Chinese evidently were the major reason for the Tai-Lao migrations which led to the founding of the Thai capital of Ayuthaya in 1350. A parallel situation during the preceding century probably caused the legendary migration of Tai-Lao people along the Nam Ou river to the present site of Luang Prabang (Hall 1955: 145). Both represented the end result of a long series of southward migrations (Wiens 1954: 113). During the pre-Chou period (prior to about 1000 B. C.) there appears to have been a belt of Tai people on the north bank of the Yangtze. Because tattooing has characterized the Lao people up to the present time, some scholars hypothesize a direct relation between the presence of this trait and the presence of Tai peoples in China. According to this hypothesis, a logical reason why during the Han period (200 B.C.-200 A.D.) tattooed people were found scattered over much of southern China but not in Yunnan and Kueichou would be that the Thai peoples had not yet migrated to the latter. The general picture presented by the historical records is that of a migration of related Tai peoples, first eastward from Szechwan, then south, and again west and southwest. These migrations continue today, the latest arrivals being groups of tribal Tai peoples who have crossed into northern Laos from Yunnan in their flight from the Chinese commune system.[21] As the Chinese complete their roads into Pathet Lao-held areas of northern Laos migrations can be expected to increase.

A similar pattern is discernible with regard to the Meo. During the last 500 or 600 years the Meo have been subjected to pressures by the Han Chinese, who have steadily forced them into marginal and mountainous areas and also pushed them southward. The Chinese undertook military campaigns against the Meo in 1698, 1732, 1794, and 1855, the result being a series of movements by the Meo, one of which was to the eastern part of Yunnan and northern parts of Vietnam and Laos. As indicated earlier, large numbers of Meo and Yao have entered Laos since the beginning of this century. This migration is confirmed by the present population estimates for the various ethnic groups. Whereas the other ethnic groups have approximately tripled since 1911, the Meo have increased over sixfold. Even discounting a greater degree of underestimation and confining ourselves to the official figures for 1911 and 1942, we see that in this period the Meo-Yao group more than tripled, while none of the other groups even doubled -- this despite the migration of certain groups from Laos into Thailand during the same period (Young 1961: 45, 58).

Urban Population

An important indicator of a country's social, economic, or cultural development is the extent of urbanization. Laos is one of the least urbanized areas in Asia even by the most generous estimates, with only 4 per cent of its population living in Vientiane, the only town with over 20,000 inhabitants (see Table 10). Yet it would be quite wrong to assume that Laos outside the administrative capital is composed exclusively of small villages, with a few oversize villages forming the provincial capitals. This is definitely not true in any general sense. The royal capital of Luang Prabang, official residence of the king, is certainly not a large village, as might be inferred by its population of some 7,600. It has a long history as an administrative center and the fact that it is also the residence of the chief Buddhist monk of Laos emphasizes its importance as a religious center. Luang Prabang has paved streets, a power plant, piped water, a hospital, and an airfield. In addition to administrative personnel there is a significant population of Chinese and Vietnamese engaged in commerce and crafts. The town is a major trading center, and only a minority of the population lives by agriculture.

No other town in Laos has the religious or ceremonial importance of Luang Prabang, but several are administrative and commercial centers. If 5,000 is set as a minimum population figure, we can include Savannakhet, Pakse, and Thakhek in this category.[22] This raises the question as to how to classify the remaining provincial capitals and towns of lesser importance. In reality most of them are minor administrative centers (muongs) containing, in many cases, the residence of the chao muong or district administrator, a lower court, a police post, a six-year school, perhaps an army company and a practical nurse, and usually a few Chinese merchants. With the exception of Nam Tha, Sam Neua, Phong Saly, and possibly Attopeu, where the only Lao are officials, most of the others are Lao villages where the majority of the inhabitants are farmers with trading sometimes a secondary occupation. Many of these towns, particularly in the south, have road connections; some are located along rivers; those not accessible in these ways may have a landing strip which can be used during the dry season. The provincial capitals of Attopeu, Nam Tha, Phong Saly, Sam Neua, and Sayaboury would fit in this category, being distinguished from other secondary towns by regular air service (at least during the dry season), usually a post and telegraph office, and often a military garrison. There may be other towns in the province which have an equal or greater commercial importance, e.g. Houei Sai in Nam Tha province. Yet by even the most conservative estimates at least

90 per cent of the population of Laos are peasants or tribesmen living in rural areas, engaged in agriculture or related occupations. Considering that a number of areas usually included in counting the population of the towns are predominantly rural in character, it would seem safe to assume that about 95 per cent of the people of Laos are either primarily or exclusively farmers, making it one of the most rural countries in the world.

The overwhelming importance of the Mekong is clearly demonstrated by the fact that all of the important cities of Laos are located along its banks -- from the trading post of Houei Sai in the north through Luang Prabang, Vientiane, Thakhek, and Savannakhet to Pakse in the south. Those towns located in non-Lao areas such as Sam Neua, Phong Saly, Nam Tha, Xieng Khouang, and Attopeu are all distinctly of secondary importance. The only town that does not fit into this clearly marked dichotomy is Sayaboury, but the river town of Pak Lay is almost as large even though lacking the administrative apparatus of a provincial capital. French administrators, of course, strongly influenced the development of the towns away from the Mekong and are largely responsible for the creation of Thakhek and Savannakhet.

Within the last thirty years population in most of the provincial capitals has about doubled, approximating the increase in the population of Laos as a whole (see Tables 11 and 12). Vientiane, which has approximately quadrupled, is the outstanding exception though most of the growth has occurred since the end of World War II and the emergence of Laos as a nation. The large-scale American aid program, by encouraging urban businesses and subsidizing the growth of government bureaus, the army, and the police, has greatly contributed to the growth of Vientiane and other towns as well. Not too surprisingly Luang Prabang was the most significant town in Laos at the beginning of the century and more than twice the size of Vientiane. The population of Luang Prabang seems to have remained remarkably stable since then. This cannot be said for towns such as Xieng Khouang, Savannakhet, and Saravane -- still small villages at the turn of the century -- which have in some cases increased more than twentyfold. On the other hand, several provincial centers have apparently increased at a somewhat slower rate than the population as a whole.

The towns of Laos are predominantly non-Lao in ethnic composition, an exception being Luang Prabang where Lao comprised an estimated 61 per cent in 1943.[23] But if the essentially rural areas usually considered within the town limits were excluded, it is likely that the percentage of Lao would fall even lower. In any case, in 1943 approximately 30 per cent of the "urban" population was Lao, the remainder being predominantly Vietnamese and Chinese. When comparing the growth of the Chinese and Vietnamese communities between 1921 and 1943 with the increase in the population of Laos as a whole, we find some impressive differences. In these twenty-two years the population of the country as a whole did not quite double according to the official figures, yet the population of the Chinese increased from approximately 500 to 4,000, or by a factor of eight, and of the Vietnamese from 4,100 to 30,700, or more than seven times. The total gain was approximately 30,000 for both groups during this period. This Chinese-Vietnamese population increase alone is almost sufficient to account for the total growth of the major towns during part of this period as given in Table 11. Although not all of these people settled in the major towns it is safe to assume that most did in view of the fact that the Chinese came principally as merchants, petty traders, and in some cases coolies, the Vietnamese as craftsmen, gardeners, or technicians and administrators recruited by the French for colonial government service.

Between 1943 and 1959 a number of important changes occurred, but as the pertinent statistics are not available we must attempt to ascertain the extent of these changes indirectly. Among the more significant has been the departure since independence of a large number of Vietnamese, particularly those who were in government service. As colonial administrators, the Vietnamese were very much resented by the Lao -- even more than other colonial officials because the Lao had a strong traditional basis for both fear and distrust of their more aggressive neighbors. Vietnamese truck gardeners in the area of Vientiane also left. Many were Catholics as the deserted churches in some of the villages around Vientiane testify. It should be noted, however, that the departure of the Vietnamese was not total and, with the recent growth of Vientiane, a number have emigrated from overcrowded Saigon to set up small businesses or take jobs in the various service trades. In 1957 approximately 90 more Vietnamese were entering Laos each month than were leaving, so that one could estimate the annual increase by immigration at about one thousand.[24]

The case of the Chinese is somewhat different since, unlike the Vietnamese, they were not involved in the government. They prospered greatly in commerce, as the increase in their population attests. According to some sources there was an increase of over sevenfold in the Chinese population in the sixteen years between 1943 and 1959, or proportionately equivalent to the increase which had taken place in the preceding thirty-one years.

Today Vientiane remains an important center for both groups, and the Vietnamese as well as Chinese communities in towns such as Pakse and Savannakhet are still strong. One of the difficulties in evaluating statistics for these groups, however, is that the Chinese and Vietnamese communities are composed not only of foreign-born individuals but also of many born in Laos, a distinction not made in the official statistics.[25] With the progressive diminution of the authority of the Royal Lao government to the area bordering the Mekong the presence of more and more Vietnamese and Chinese cadres in Pathet Lao-dominated areas approaches critical importance.

The Indian population, composed mostly of cloth merchants, has grown from 6 individuals in 1912 to some 957 in 1958. French and Americans also figure appreciably in the Lao urban population. It was estimated that in 1959 there were approximately 8,000 Frenchmen in Laos. Presumably this included the military garrison stationed at the Seno base. Large numbers of Frenchmen serve as military and civilian advisers to the government in various parts of Laos, and there are also many businessmen. Like the Chinese, Frenchmen in this category seem to have increased in recent years. Without a doubt there were more French in Laos in the late 1950's than during the colonial period.

As to Americans, almost all -- the only significant exception being a few dozen missionaries -- have been attached to United States aid or information programs. A reasonable estimate for 1959-60 was 500 including families. In addition a few hundred Filipinos worked in the American aid program or in the Philippines-sponsored rural medical program called Operation Brotherhood. Both Americans and Filipinos were post-World War II additions to the ethnic mosaic of Laos.

If one were to approach the question of Lao urban population composition on a formal statistical basis this might well be the end of the discussion, but it would be to overlook one of the most crucial groups -- the Thai and Thai-Lao from the northeast provinces of Thailand. This migratory element does not appear in the official French statistics in any meaningful way, in part because of French interest in emphasizing the integration of Laos with the other provinces of Indochina. But the few migration statistics that do exist must in any case be suspect in a country with only a small number of poorly supervised custom posts and an easily navigable river separating the two countries for much of their common border, particularly in the most populous regions.[26]

In discussing the migratory groups it is necessary to define terms, for distinctions between the Lao and the Thai-Lao are not readily apparent. First it should be noted that Thai businessmen coming from Bangkok to Vientiane in recent years as well as Thai students seeking jobs are certainly a small minority compared, for example, to the Chinese or Vietnamese. Also excluded from consideration here are the villagers and traders who live on opposite sides of the Mekong, crossing back and forth at will. Nor will we be concerned with the many Lao (elite as well as peasant) who temporarily leave their country for an education, a job, or a business venture in Thailand. Of more significance are the large-scale migrations, often of a transitory nature, of farmers and coolies from poor and overpopulated Northeast Thailand to the towns of Laos bordering on the Mekong, particularly to Vientiane. Here most of the samlaw drivers and coolies engaged in construction work (both men and women) are from the other side of the river. It is estimated that in 1959 there were 5,000 samlaws in all of Laos, of which a majority were probably operated by Northeast Thai-Lao in Vientiane who also monopolized this trade in Bangkok before it was banned there. In addition, many come to work in the villages around Vientiane at planting and harvest time. Within the last decade some of these farm workers have settled on the Vientiane plain, bought land, and formed Thai hamlets. Their cultural similarity permits easy integration (Gaudillot and Condominas 1959: 52-53).

As a result of joining the army or police some Lao have migrated to towns; in one particular case half the population of a Lao village moved en masse to Vientiane (Gaudillot and Condominas 1959: 101). With the exception of Xieng Khouang where a few Meo have settled in the towns, the non-Lao tribal peoples do not live in the towns. A partial exception are the Khmu who come to work as coolies in towns such as Luang Prabang but usually return to their own village in a few months. Conversely there are, however, some Chinese merchants scattered in certain of the larger Lao villages in the countryside.

The various ethnic groups described here are not rigid and unchanging. Through acculturation and some intermarriage there is considerable flexibility, and by these means the Lao, being the dominant group, have absorbed both tribal peoples (e.g. Smalley 1961b) and some members of foreign ethnic groups such as the Chinese and Vietnamese. Some Lao women have married Frenchmen (the reverse is also true but much rarer) and a number of Lao possess French citizenship. The political implications of these problems have been considered elsewhere (Halpern 1964b) and the economic aspects will be discussed here in subsequent sections.

II

THE NATURAL ECONOMY

Agricultural Activity

It is a commonplace that no understanding of the economy of nonindustrialized countries is possible without taking into account the existence and attitudes of the overwhelming mass of people who constitute the peasantry. The proportion of this group to other elements in the population will vary from country to country but for Laos, with its almost totally rural population, the statement acquires an absolute sense.

A rough division of agricultural activity in Laos can be made between two continuing traditions: the cultivation of wet rice in flooded fields and the cultivation of dry rice in forest clearings. The dominant pattern centers on the cultivation various kinds of glutinous rice (khao neo) as the major crop and of nonglutinous rice (khao chao) as a subsidiary crop. (The major exception is the reversal of this pattern sometimes found among hill peoples such as the Meo.) There is only one harvest a year, an important reason being the seasonal concentration of rainfall. Other factors which at present preclude two crops are the lack of adequate irrigation systems and the relative shortage of flat fertile land. [1] Hillside terracing is not practiced in Laos and, with valley land and river plains scarce, especially in the north, wet rice is cultivated there only on a restricted scale, typically in narrow valleys where the few population clusters consist of trade and administrative centers surrounded by wet-rice fields. In north and central Laos most wet-rice farming is dependent entirely on rainfall, the water being held in the fields by crude dikes. "Flood rice" has been suggested as a more accurate term in these circumstances (Gaudillot and Condominas 1959: 2, 114).

These paddy fields are known as na. Generally speaking the system of na cultivation permits a concentration of population with a concomitant tendency to centralized political structure, while those groups relying primarily on cultivation in burned-over forest clearings, or hai, as a rule form scattered, autonomous village communities.

The ramifications of these two types of cultivation are enormous and affect all aspects of the villagers' lives. Distinctions are not always clear-cut, but there is no doubt that the traditional authoritarian centralized political structures of the Lao and tribal Tai, in contrast to such diffuse forms of authority as exist among the Khmu and Lamet (and the Meo, but for different reasons), are directly related to their respective types of cultivation. The potentiality of wet rice agriculture to produce an exploitable surplus and permit the formation of relatively dense populations appears to be a key factor in this situation.

Agricultural Techniques

As there is general similarity in the procedure for cultivating paddy fields in north and central Laos, the following account of practices in Vientiane province by Kaufman (1961: 3-4) and Ayabe (1961: 6-7) provides a representative description. By late May, after the rainy season has begun to soften the ground, the paddy fields are plowed and harrowed with a wooden plow drawn by buffalo. Seedlings from the previous year's crop are soaked for four days and sown broadcast in an area prepared as nursery beds while small dikes are being built around the paddy fields. The young rice seedlings are ready for transplanting after anywhere from six to twelve weeks, depending on the type of rice. The arduous task of transplanting is usually done cooperatively, with small groups of people pulling the seedlings, cleaning the roots, and tying the young plants into small bundles to deposit in the corners of the fields preparatory to the actual replanting. By the end of August most work in the paddy fields is complete and delegated farmers begin their stay in temporary huts in the fields to guard the young crop from marauding animals. The rice matures in 150, 120, or 90 days according to the type used, the most common being the first, or heavy, variety. On larger holdings more than one type is grown in order to stagger the harvesting. Usually all harvesting has been completed by the end of December. Threshing, accomplished by beating the harvested plants against boards or by flailing them with sticks, is followed by milling in a foot-operated wooden mortar and pestle device. During the peak of the dry season in January and February the fields dry and begin to crack; the buffalo munch the remaining stubble.

Another account, quoted at length below, is by a Khmu in the Luang Prabang area and indicates both some regional differences and the extent to which some Khmu have adopted wet-rice techniques from the Lao:[2]

> The seventh month arrives.[3] Strip off bark, come home and twist it into rope. Twist rope for holding the clack on the buffalo's neck, twist rope for his noose, twist heavy rope to go around his neck for tethering him for the night, twist the tether rope, twist rope for the yoke, twist rope for attaching the yoke to the plow. Go and

look for the handle of the plow, go and look for the shaft of the plow, go and look for the wooden core of the plow blade. Mount the plow blade. Go and look for the other tools. When they have all been collected, assemble them. When they have all been assembled, cut the grass and stubble in the rice field. After it has been pulled up, throw away the grass and wait for the rain. When the rains come, go and clean out the seed bed. When it has been cleaned off and burned, plant the rice. When the rains come, go and build up the dikes, let water into the rice paddies, soak them until the earth is soft. After two or three days go and plow. When it is time to plow, plow around the edges first to build up the dikes. When the dikes have been fortified, plow the rest. If you want the paddy to be nice, force the plow in and make it cut deep. When the plowing is finished, soak [the fields] with water. Let the earth and the stubble become soft and decayed. Then go out and cultivate. Take a harrow and force it into the ground, lift it out, and force it in. When this is finished, smooth the surface. When it is all smoothed off, take the seedlings from the seed bed. If the transplanting is done early, the seedlings must be widely separated. If it is done late they must be close together. Put in a lot of paddy.[4] Now let the water in for two or three days, let the rice take root. When that is done, dam off the water, let the rice sprout and leaf out. Then let the water back in again until the time when the rice grows a pod. When it has grown a pod, stop the water until the rice is ripe. Allow the earth to become hard, then get the sickle and go cut the rice. To cut with a sickle, grasp a handful of rice, bend the stalks over and lay them out on the stubble. Then smooth them off and spread them out about one thickness deep. When the rice has been cut, quickly go back and tie up the rice stalks, carry them right back and put them on the threshing floor. When they have dried out, cut off the stalks and throw them away.[5] Take some wood and beat the earth to make it hard and flat. Then go and look for some buffalo dung. Spread it out and plaster it down, bring water and soak it. When it is soaked, let it dry out in the sun. Then carry in the rice and put it on the buffalo dung threshing floor. Lay out the rice and let the buffalo walk on it. When the buffalo have finished treading it out, shake the rice around to stir it up and throw away the rice straw. Then scrape up the rice and pile it together. Take a fork and spread the rice out and fan it. See that the wind blows. Throw the

> rice in the air. This is unpleasant. It irritates the skin. When the rice has been winnowed, measure it. How much is there? When it has been measured, carry it back to the village. Whoever has no buffalo has to rent one from someone else and return it after he has finished threshing.

The commonly used terms dry or upland rice cultivation and wet or lowland cultivation can be confusing. Upland or shifting field cultivation has been defined as a system characterized by a rotation of fields rather than crops, with cropping periods of from one to three years alternated with fallow periods of up to twenty years, sometimes more, but often as little as six to eight years. The forest is cleared by means of slash-and-burn (Pelzer 1958: 126).

An excellent monograph on the Lamet of Nam Tha (Izikowitz 1951), a group very similar to the Khmu and living in close contact with them, introduced the English dialect word "swidden." Although by no means universally accepted, this term has found increasing acceptance during the past few years in works dealing with tropical agriculture. The present writer finds it more exact than terms such as "burned clearing" and in this study swidden will be used interchangeably with the Lao "hai" to denote the type of dry rice cultivation based on the clearing of fields by the cutting and subsequent burning of the forest cover as practiced by the Khmu and Lamet, Meo, and some Lao in northern Laos.[6]

The following Khmu account (Smalley 1952) describes swidden agriculture as it dominates their yearly cycle of activities:

> The first month [December-January] go looking in the forest. Measure off the place where the rice field will be made. When it has been measured off, come back home, make charcoal, prepare [forge] knives. When the knives are made, begin to cut down the underbrush. Cut it down during the second month. When this is done, cut the heavy trees. Cut them and spread them out during the fourth month. From the fourth to fifth month, burn the forest and gather up the debris. When that has been done, sow the paddy. When the time to sow the paddy arrives, do it cooperatively.[7] The sowing finished go attend to other things in the fifth month. When the sixth month starts, go prepare the weeding tools. Go cut the grass and weeds. When the second weeding is finished,[8] it is the seventh month, going into the eighth. Then the men go and search for vines. The ninth month

> comes and then the tenth. They split rattan vines and make mats for spreading and drying the rice. They split vines and make baskets in which to store the husked rice. Then the men go out and make various kinds of traps -- spear trap, deadfall, pit trap with spikes. Go and look for meat and come back and eat it. The tenth month has already arrived. They make carrying baskets and harvesting baskets. They carry in wood and make the rice field hut. Some people harvest by cutting with a sickle and others by plucking the heads of the rice. They harvest the rice and go and step on it. When it is threshed they store it away. By this time it is the twelfth month. The first month comes. Take the rice and carry it home. . . .
>
> Some people who make upland rice fields do not have enough for the year. Such people are stupid, they really have no sense. They do not have the sense to raise enough rice to keep themselves alive. We do not have enough money to go and buy and sell.

The last few comments are interesting in that the chastising of poor Khmu probably reflects something of the acculturated status of the informant and his complex of cultural inferiority. His concluding statement is expressed in the first person, implying the generally impoverished position of the Khmu in the Luang Prabang area, who, unlike other Kha groups such as the Lamet, normally do not produce a rice surplus.

The variation in agricultural adaptation among the ethnic groups of Laos can be summarized by distinguishing three types of hai cultivation. First, among the Lao, hai agriculture functions as a supplementary form in areas where the na fields are limited, in periods of immigration and adjustment to new surroundings, or in times of forced and temporary displacement such as that caused by war. To a considerable degree this situation is paralleled among the tribal Tai peoples. The second form of hai agriculture is exemplified by the Meo; here it represents an ecological adaptation of limited time depth based on a pattern of extensive migrations in Indochina. However, if political and ecological conditions are favorable, the Meo are capable of readapting to na agriculture or using the two systems simultaneously. Finally, the indigenous tribal groups of Laos, exemplified by the Khmu and Lamet, appear to have been dependent exclusively on hai agriculture throughout their history so that learning to cultivate na fields with a plow is an historically new experience for them.

Associated with these differing ecological patterns and historical experiences are different levels of cultural development. Generally speaking the Khmu and Lamet are able to produce only limited rice surpluses. Their social structure does not possess any forms of unity beyond the village level, the number of their specialists is limited, and their position is one of submissive marginality to the dominant Lao. The Meo, although more migratory than the Khmu and Lamet, nevertheless appear capable of organizing on the extravillage level. Corn is an important subsidiary crop for the Meo and provides livestock feed while rice is generally preferred for human consumption. Corn is known to the Khmu and Lamet but does not appear to be developed as a livestock feed. Certainly it appears that hai agriculture as practiced by the Meo, who also have a well-developed livestock-raising economy, is able to support a more diverse economy and social life than the form in which it is practiced by the Khmu and Lamet. A precise comparison cannot be made, however, because of the importance of opium cultivation to the Meo economy.

Rituals Associated with Agriculture

Various means, sacred as well as secular, are taken to ensure the water supply and fertility of the crops. The sacred are connected with the dominant belief in phi or nature spirits which exists throughout Laos. In April, just before the rains, an elaborate New Year's celebration is held by the Lao, a prominent feature of which is reciprocal water dousing everyone gives everyone else.

On an auspicious day in the sixth month of the Lao calendar, chosen by consulting the proper sacred manuscript or a local astrologer, villagers make offerings of a boiled chicken, rice alcohol, and sometimes a pig to the protective spirits of the village. The phi are then beseeched to protect the villagers during their work, to keep destructive animals and insects out of the rice fields, especially the small crabs which can destroy the crop, and to provide adequate rain and a good harvest. In addition to this ceremony each worker presents an offering to the spirits of the fields, who live in the trees and in the rice fields (Sinavong 1963: 103). The belief in the efficacy of these phi is still very strong and the villagers have been known to refuse to work in certain fields if they think the spirits are angry.

In traditional Thai-Lao culture rice is not regarded simply as a food but as a sacred substance presided over by a guardian spirit. In many ways these beliefs are analagous to those connected with wheat and bread among European peoples or corn among the American Indians. A Thai ethnologist describes Me

Posop, the Rice Goddess, as the guardian deity of mankind who has the power to endow with health and wealth those individuals who take proper care of the rice, as well as to punish those who ignore or anger her by trampling over a paddy or leaving it in a damp place (Rajadhon 1956: 6).

A legend recorded in the vicinity of Luang Prabang purports to show the Lao why it is necessary to labor in the rice fields. A dissatisfied widow cursed the rice and told it to grow as high as it wanted to, saying that she no longer needed it. The rice did so and the grains grew to the size of pumpkins and entered the storage sheds of their own accord. She scolded them for so doing and ever since then the rice has been small and refuses to grow unattended (Lévy 1959: 172).

Among the Lao each stage in the cultivation of rice, after the initial planting, is accompanied by appropriate rituals. Formerly, when it came time to start work in the fields, the king turned the first ceremonial spade of earth since there was believed to be a degree of kinship between the royal family and the protecting spirits.[9] The rite of Lieng Phi Ta Hek ("feeding the Phi Ta Hek") is held at transplanting time. Altars for Phi Ta Hek, the leading spirit of the rice fields, are built in a corner of the paddy field to receive offerings of glutinous rice mixed with grains of paddy and shaped into ears of rice to symbolize abundance. Also placed on the altar are four banana leaves rolled into horns to contain betel. The transplanting starts after the recitation of chants that accompany the planting of the first seven shoots of rice (Sinavong 1963: 104):

> I plant the rice shoot; may you be green as the Thao.
> I plant the second shoot; may you be green as the grass of the ninth month.
> I plant the third shoot; may the gong of nine kam[10] be mine.
> I plant the fourth shoot; may the ninety thousand pounds of gold be mine.
> I plant the fifth shoot; may ninety thousand baskets of rice be mine.
> I plant the sixth shoot; may I have a wife to sleep by my side.
> I plant the seventh shoot; may a rare elephant saddled in gold and silver be mine.
> Glory! Prosperity!

The transplanting finished, further offerings usually of boiled chicken, alcohol, and cigarettes are made to Ta Hek to ensure protection of the fields. During the threshing, four guardian symbols wrapped in white cotton thread are placed on the threshing floor at the cardinal points to form a barrier against the possible entry of evil spirits who might make off with the rice.

A celebration known as Khoun Lane takes place in connection with the storing of the rice in raised storage sheds. At dawn the souls of the rice are informed that food is about to be presented and a meal is offered to the bonzes at the threshing ground before a gathering of the villagers. After the meal a bonze climbs on top of the rice pile and reads a traditional text. This recitation is followed by villagers calling together the souls of the rice where-ever they may have wandered. Taking a basket of hard-boiled eggs and other delicacies they walk through the fields intoning: "Spirit of the Rice, here are tubers for thee, here are the buds of the areca palm and good alcohol made from your grain. Spirit of the Rice, come down to earth! Come and preside over the festivities I am giving in your honor." The basket, which now carries the spirit of the rice, is brought back to the village by the owner to be suspended from a beam of the storage loft. The old women of the village come to welcome the Rice, speak familiarly to it and compliment it, all the while running the paddy through their wrinkled fingers. The owner brings a small figure made of straw and, just as a friend would be greeted on his return from a journey, the women tender the figure a sukhwan, tying white cotton threads on the straw wrists. The spirit of the rice is congratulated on having returned to the village, made welcome in the most affectionate manner, and begged never to leave the granary (Faure 1959: 153-54).

There is even a special rite for the re-opening of the storage sheds -- Boun Khay Pa Tou Lao, which is celebrated on the third day of the waxing moon of the third month. A platter of offerings for the souls of the rice is brought to the loft where, crouching and holding candles, the people recite: "Today is an auspicious day. We take you. We draw you out. When we eat of you, you shall still remain undiminished. May you always be plentiful." Then they tell the souls of the rice not to fear the rhythmic sounds and heavy weight of the pestles that will soon come to break up the rice (Sinavong 1963: 103-04).[11]

In recent years these rites have been modified. Bouns such as Khoun Lane and Khay Pa Tou Lao, which were formerly exclusively religious, have gradually tended to become profane -- more a time for relaxation and amusement than an occasion on which to pray and thank the spirits. Yet by no means has rice cultivation become a secular process, for great respect is still paid to the guardian phi of the rice fields and their altars can be seen frequently in the paddy fields of Lao villages. Bonzes continue to participate in the ceremonies, particularly those rites connected with harvesting and with ensuring a good yield the following year.

For the Lao, then, raising paddy rice is not simply an economic activity, subsistence or otherwise, but rather a way of life closely interwoven with the supernatural. Intensive wet-rice cultivation as practiced by the Lao and Black Tai is capable of yielding a surplus beyond the need of the farmers and thereby provides the basis for the establishment of an elaborate hierarchy of political and religious specialists, as reflected in the rituals described. In the case of the Lao prominent ceremonial roles are given to the Buddhist priests (and formerly the king with his ritual plowing); among the Black Tai these roles go to hereditary priests and leaders. Such specialization does not exist in cultures relying primarily on dry-rice cultivation.

The Black Tai usually live in upland river valleys and practice wet-rice cultivation utilizing rainfall and natural flooding of streams. Around Nam Tha some villages have simple water wheels which lift water into shallow canals leading to rectangular fields surrounded by low dikes. Water buffalo are used to pull plows with iron blades.

The beginning of the rice planting season is heralded by Lon Ton, a ritual to attract the spirit of the soil. Just before the rainy season, in a special field set aside in each district, the officiating priest, the hereditary official, and the villagers gather at the field and make offerings of food to the spirit of the soil, represented by a simple paper figure. Sometimes a small ball of rice is placed on the figure's mouth. After prayers for a good crop everyone partakes of rice wine before returning to the village for games and feasting.

After the rice has been planted there are private offerings of the first grains of new rice to family ancestors. During this period nothing may be given to a stranger in the village, who might "carry away the luck of the harvest." At harvest time more individual offerings are made to invite the spirit of the rice to come sleep in the granary for the winter. The village is again taboo and a public ritual with buffalo sacrifice is held in honor of Ten Luong, the supreme Black Tai god of the soil, and in sequence all the other gods and village spirits (Hickey 1958: 135, 145-47).

Rituals associated with dry-rice cultivation again point up the significance of religious practices. The following Lamet account is abridged from Izikowitz (1951: 212-15):

> When the families have come to a decision about which land to clear and which families are going to work together, the chopping and the clearing of the land can begin. First of all the implements, chopping knives and axes, must be seen to . . . the smithy is now put in order, and grindstones are brought forth, but before the smithy can be used, a sacrifice to the spirit must be made. Betel nuts, a little salt and one egg are used for the sacrifice . . . and one says, "Spirit of the pump, eat fruits, eat salt, eat an egg, see that the chopping knives are right. Don't let them be jagged."

Before the Lamet begin the actual sowing, festivals are held to honor the spirits of the village. Betel, a pig, and a hen are offered and, when the feast is over, the village astrologer chooses the day on which to start the sowing. Like the Lao and Khmu, the Lamet raise mostly glutinous rice but scattered in their swiddens will be a vegetable patch and small plantings of tobacco, chili, cucumbers, citronella grass, mint, eggplant, or various types of beans.

Early in September when the rains begin to let up, the rice is ready to be harvested. In common with other rice-cultivating peoples of Southeast Asia, the Lamet believe in the soul of the rice and make appropriate sacrifices but the concept of soul is, among the Lamet, reserved exclusively for rice and human beings and does not extend to other plants.

Like the Lao, the Meo erect small altars for the spirits in the rice fields and gardens, often offering sacrifices to these spirits on their way home from work in the fields or before leaving in the morning (Bernatzik 1947: 200).

There is no question that religious ritual connected with the rice crop is common to all the ethnic groups in Laos, forming an indispensable part of basic agricultural activities. It will be interesting to see to what extent these observances endure or, if abandoned, to what extent their abandonment affects related agricultural practices, which now give supernatural sanction to the work patterns of the villagers and help make their work in the rice fields part of a supernaturally ordained way of life. It is possible that once these religious activities cease, the prestige of agricultural pursuits may come into question in Laos (or vice versa) as they have in so many other areas of the world. These two developments appear to be closely related.

A Comparative Analysis of Hai and Na

It has been postulated that one-third of the total area used for agricultural purposes in Southeast Asia, including Malaysia, is farmed by shifting cultivators and that Indochina, a naturally forested area, has some fourteen per cent of its land cleared for agriculture and another fifty per cent modified by cutover practices and new savannah (Dobby 1954: 311, 349). As far as populations are concerned, it is estimated that about two and a half million people in Burma, of a total population of some nineteen million, are engaged in swidden farming and that almost a million people in northern and western Thailand depend primarily on shifting agriculture (Dobby 1954: 267-71). If the Lao who practice swidden cultivation either principally or as a supplement to wet-rice cultivation are added to the tribal peoples of Laos, most of whom are swidden farmers, it can be seen that swidden farming is of great significance to the majority of the people of Laos.

A basic distinction between the na and hai is, of course, the great difference in the population each can support. To cite extreme examples, the carrying capacity of irrigated land may be ten or more times as high as the maximum obtainable under swidden cultivation. A square mile of rice land in the Tonkin delta can support a population of from 1,000 to more than 3,500, while the same amount of land under hai cultivation can provide for only 18 to about 160 persons (Jin-Bee 1958: 114). Actually in Laos the highest population estimate (outside of urban areas) is 180 per square mile for the Mekong plain; this is just slightly above the maximum that can be supported by swidden agriculture according to the above figures. On the other hand, 4.6 persons per square mile, which is given for the Lamet (Izikowitz 1951: 38) is considerably under this minimum estimate. These contrasting figures are, of course, indicative of the fact that no systematic land use surveys have been made in Laos and suggest that there may be some overlap between the maximum population which can be supported by swidden agriculture (outside of Laos) and the relatively small population supported by the rather simple irrigated cultivation practiced in Laos. This possibility should not obscure the fundamental fact that irrigated rice cultivation is capable of supporting a much greater population than any form of swidden cultivation. This statement applies to valley or flat land because, although hillside terracing for irrigated rice fields does occur in some parts of Asia, it presupposes a more complex technological background than the peoples of Laos at present possess. Thus Khmu and Meo swidden agriculture on steep hillsides may represent the most efficient type of land utilization currently practiced in Laos (Smalley 1952).

The idea that hai cultivation is a labor extensive method of cultivation as opposed to the labor intensive features of na cultivation is not true in the absolute sense. Among hai cultivators clearing the field at the outset is certainly a labor intensive process, and labor is required to guard the fields from marauders in both cases. It appears, however, that hai cultivators are less concerned about weeds. Furthermore, hai cultivators do not have to go through the laborious transplanting process, or worry about the maintenance of dikes and irrigation systems. Fertilizer is already present in the wood ash, while both green and animal manures are used with varying degrees of frequency by na cultivators. The use of the plow and buffalo in na cultivation implies a greater capital investment, and therefore more associated labor, than do the hoe and digging stick of hai cultivation.

Hai Farming and Village Stability

The uplands of northern Laos are characterized by generally parallel mountain crests, with elevations of 4,000 to 6,000 feet, interspersed by small plains. All major settlements and the only na cultivation in the area are found in these small alluvial basins, which were formed where water erosion on less resistant rock hollowed out small circular pockets upstream from more resistant rock walls through which the stream has cut a narrow gorge.

How do such geographic limitations affect agriculture in the specific cases of the Meo, Lao, and Khmu? With the exception of the cultivators on the plain of Xieng Khouang and a few other small settlements, the Meo depend entirely on swidden agriculture of a type more extensive than that of either the Khmu or Lao, and in the area of Luang Prabang the Meo inhabit mountain areas exclusively, neither using the plow nor cultivating irrigated fields. As a rule, their fields are on steep mountain slopes.

In most areas where the conventional economy is followed, the Meo move every decade or so, i.e. once all land within walking distance of their village has been cut over. (Precise investigations remain to be done on this important point.) The Meo tend to migrate as family groups and, like the Lao, usually send out advance parties to scout the new locations. Quite extensive migrations may be involved. Meo in northern Laos recall moves from Xieng

Khouang to Luang Prabang, Sayaboury, and Vientiane provinces. For their main crops -- opium, rice, corn, tobacco, and vegetables -- a new site usually will be cleared each year although the same field may then be used for several years depending on the quality of the soil.

The Lao and Khmu (and the Lamet) have relatively stable villages as compared to those of the Meo, although here again precise comparative data is lacking.[12] The situation varies according to the size and location of the village, the land available for crop rotation, and the quality of the soil, particularly its suitability for opium cultivation in the case of the Meo. The location of the village relative to opium, rice, and corn fields can vary considerably. For example, at Kiouketcham, some sixty miles south of Luang Prabang on the Vientiane road, the opium hai are located about eighteen miles away. Part of the family goes there during the planting and harvesting seasons, erecting temporary houses near the fields. Rice and corn fields are located near the village. At other Meo settlements in the Luang Prabang area, and at some in Xieng Khouang, the situation is reversed.

Bernatzik states that opium fields may be cultivated for as long as twenty years, but if the opium does not grow well in the new site the village may move much sooner. A decision to move is by no means made lightheartedly and the actual moving involves great effort. Soil exhaustion is not the sole reason for migration. Historically the major motivation for the southward migration of the Meo appears to have been the political and demographic pressure of the Han Chinese.

In the movement of Meo from Xieng Khouang to Luang Prabang or within the latter province there are some cases in which nuclear families or even unmarried men have migrated, but possibly this situation is attributable to the extremely unsettled conditions in this area since the end of World War II. In Luang Prabang there are a number of settlements which have only a few households, although these may be temporary settlements awaiting the arrival of additional relatives.[13]

Upon arrival in a new area the Meo attempt not only to cultivate for their own use but to produce sufficient reserves so that those who follow will have something to eat.[14] After the first successful harvest at the new site, those who have remained behind move in bringing with them whatever can be transported, even the supporting posts of the old houses.

A basic criterion in the choice of a new settlement is altitude, since the Meo rarely, if ever, settle below 4,000 feet. This pattern has been changing in certain areas of Laos, but in those cases where settlement at lower altitudes occurs the Meo are sure to be involved to a great extent in a cash economy. Within the preferred altitude range the site is selected with great care and is usually on an incline. According to Bernatzik the Meo never build a new village on a plain, in a depression between peaks, or at the summit of a mountain but prefer a site just below the crest of a mountain range.

Unlike certain other upland peoples such as the Khmu and Lamet who move relatively short distances, the Meo and Yao may move from one province to another. The difference stems not only from the exigencies of opium cultivation but also from the demands of their relatively greater number of livestock. In addition, it is claimed that erosion is much greater at the high altitudes and steep slopes on which the Meo live (Lafont 1960: 187)

Cultivation Practices and Possible Evolutionary Stages

Since in Laos many Meo living on the Xieng Khouang plain or near towns such as Luang Prabang cultivate rice while those in the more remote regions appear to rely on corn, one is tempted to equate wet rice as a primary crop cultivated with the use of the plow as a "modern" phenomenon and the culture complex of hai agriculture, corn, and the digging stick as the "traditional" method.

Unfortunately the data does not permit any such generalization. In fact, the case of the Meo indicates the lack of a clear demarcation line between hai and na agriculture and the great ability of individual groups to adapt to ecological patterns. Two observers reporting on investigations about three decades apart both see the Meo in a stage transitional to irrigated rice cultivation.[15] The earlier investigator mentions both the plow and the hoe when speaking of corn cultivation and quotes from a prayer for the planting of corn. Another interesting point is that fields planted to corn or rice may also be used to grow opium, indicating the possibility of substitution from year to year. The more recent Xieng Khouang study reports nonglutinous rice cultivated in hai fields as the main food crop with corn looked upon as a reserve food, ranking third after rice and opium. A few Meo have begun to cultivate irrigated rice fields in the vicinity of Xieng Khouang town. A monograph on Sam Neua suggests that corn as opposed to rice cultivation may in certain cases be geographically determined by the altitude at which the Meo live.[16]

Among the Meo Bernatzik studied in northern Thailand (1947: 353-62), corn ranked eighth as a cultivated crop, after rice, opium, sugar cane, yams, cucumbers, radishes, and beans. Bernatzik also found the Meo abandoning the use of the plow, which had proved impractical on the steep and unterraced slopes, and turning to hai agriculture. Only a very few old Meo were still familiar with the use of a plow. When asked why its use had been abandoned, one replied: "The land on which we live, and even more so the regions we had to cross before we came here, were mountainous and stony and did not permit the use of the plow. In our old homeland there were certain regions where we could not use a plow. As time goes on, the old people die and the younger ones do not know how to use a plow anymore, and an old custom sinks into oblivion even where it might still be useful today." Bernatzik feels this tradition indicates that the Thailand Meo, rather than having imitated the use of the plow after contact with the Chinese and the Annamites on their migration, were already familiar with its use.[17]

It is reported for the Yao of Laos and Thailand, who cultivate the hai with the use of the digging stick, that rice is the main crop while corn is mainly for animal fodder.[18] In most reports dealing with the Meo and Yao corn is definitely a secondary food (occasionally for animals) except during hard times when the preferred food, rice, is not available. This suggests anew that reliance on corn may be an adaptation to living at high altitude. The minor importance of corn among the Thailand Meo studied by Bernatzik is probably linked to their relatively recent abandonment of plow-rice cultivation, though this appears to conflict with the proportionately greater importance of corn among the Xieng Khouang Meo. Chinese conditions and reports from Tonkin seem to indicate that the Meo are capable of cultivating irrigated rice fields but that their tendency to do so is controlled by economic and political factors.

The above descriptions pointedly show the flexibility of Meo economy and its ability to combine corn and rice cultivated in either hai or na of the glutinous or nonglutinous variety. This flexibility has very important implications for contemporary settlement programs, which we shall explore in detail subsequently. The preference of the Meo for the mountains may also be a rationalization of the economic and political pressures to which they have been subjected.[19] In certain areas, such as Kweichow and Hainan, the total Han agricultural economy has been adopted. (It is not clear for how long the Meo have known terracing and irrigated rice cultivation, although as we have seen Bernatzik and others claim it is an old pattern.)

The notable changes taking place among the Meo occur not against a background of "immemorial customs" but rather within a setting of constant innovation. Since cultivation practices vary historically, the settlement of the Meo (in Laos) in the valleys and their cultivation of irrigated rice fields is, then, not something new or unique in their history but rather a readaptation in a recurrent cycle of change as much influenced by political and economic factors as by demographic and geographic conditions.

Swidden agriculture as practiced by the Meo in Laos seems to be a cultural adaptation that may not have a very great time depth. Although Meo swidden practices are sanctified by religious ritual, this is not an indication of their constant usage but rather the incorporating or reincorporating of ecological patterns into their familiar universe of nature spirits and deities.

Among the Meo we do not have any neat dichotomy; as a matter of fact, coexistence appears to be common -- hai and na, digging stick and plow, corn and rice. This is not to say that the two methods of cultivation are not distinct, for they clearly are, but rather that they can alternate in time or be practiced simultaneously by the same people. It appears to be the techniques that change more than the crops (bearing in mind here that under the term rice are subsumed thousands of varieties).

Lao Swidden Farming: A Supplementary Technique

Swidden cultivators in Southeast Asia have been classified in three groups: those who are sedentary, living in substantial dwellings in permanent villages and constructing temporary houses near their swidden; those who have less elaborate houses in semipermanent villages that may be abandoned after one or two decades; and those who build a new house, simple in structure, as often as a new swidden is cleared (Pelzer 1958: 127).

Historically, swidden farming of the first type was important throughout much of Thailand as well as Laos and has been associated with the movement of Lao peoples from Laos into Northeast Thailand. An observer in 1910 wrote that it was probable that not more than half the delta of the Menam (in central Thailand) was under cultivation: any man could go into the jungle and, by burning off the long grass and bamboo scrub, clear for himself a space in which to plant his rice and, if he wished, claim as his own. It was equally simple to clear a new patch and abandon a former clearing (Thompson quoted in Benedict 1952: 7).

In the area of Ubol in Northeast Thailand the predominant

pattern is of small farmers (Lao) owning their own land. Originally they were settlers from the north who cleared the jungle and established villages. The practice of shifting cultivation appears to have gradually given place to na cultivation with definite field boundaries, but legal title deeds were issued beginning only in 1954 (Madge 1957: 51).

Aside from occurring historically, reversion to swidden farming can also take place in times of war or other disaster. The Frenchman, Captain Cupet, making an exploration in 1888 of the region northeast of Luang Prabang, found that much of the area had been devastated by the Hô and noted the remains of charred house pillars, gardens overgrown with brush, and deserted rice fields along the streams. The Lao found it impossible to continue their wet-rice farming because their buffalo had been killed and so took to swidden farming in the forest (Bartlett 1957: 352-53). Similar situations doubtless occurred in times during the war with the Vietminh and will continue until peace comes to the area. Many upland peoples have had to shift village sites a number of times (see concluding remarks on the current refugee problem, beginning page 134).

With regard to swidden farming among the Lao, estimates obtained within Luang Prabang province have ranged from villages in which there were no swiddens, the population depending entirely on na cultivation, to settlements in which only one house in thirty had a permanent rice field. Other villages yielded estimates of a tenth of the households having paddy fields while in an equal number of villages about a third used swiddens. One Lao swidden farmer said he used a cleared field for about five years before preparing another site; three years appears to be a more common figure.

Not a wide enough survey was conducted to present any coherent pattern over a sizable area. Even this observer's small survey does, however, present some interesting implications. First is that within a relatively small area (all the villages surveyed were within fifteen miles of Luang Prabang town) there may be a considerable variation in the basic type of agricultural economy. Some villagers claimed that although they preferred cultivating paddy fields it was impossible because of the recent lack of sufficient rainfall or, more important, because of a complete lack of or inadequacy of irrigation facilities. This applies to diked fields dependent solely on rain as well as those that utilize irrigation canals. One swidden cultivator maintained that if a way could be found to irrigate the paddy fields he and his fellow villagers who now cultivate hai would "return" to wet-rice agriculture.[20]

Although in certain villages only a minority of people work irrigated rice fields it does not necessarily follow that the others are completely dependent on their swiddens. For not only in the Luang Prabang area but throughout much of northern Laos the Lao villages are often trading centers for the surrounding mountain peoples. Thus some of the Lao, particularly those in the larger villages situated along the Mekong, earn a significant part of their living from trading.

The Lao feel that swidden cultivation carries less prestige than wet-rice farming. Some consider the latter less work since no weeding is necessary (although the opposite has also been reported). Villagers in the region of Ubon in northern Thailand are said to rely on swidden cultivation only when the yields are insufficient from the wet-rice fields. The amount of swidden cultivated depends on the labor available as well as the felt need (Klausner 1956). A general survey for Vientiane province states that approximately twenty per cent of the Lao farmers in that area rely on swidden farming. The villages surveyed were located mainly along river banks and near roads in the flat plain surrounding the town of Vientiane. It would be expected that the percentage of swidden cultivators would be higher in the mountainous north of the province (Kaufman 1961).

Khmu Transitions to Na

Among the Khmu, as among other mountain peoples, cultivating swidden is viewed as the norm, with working paddy fields an innovation. Wet-rice cultivation in the case of the Khmu in the area of Luang Prabang is definitely a culture trait borrowed from the Lao and as such is symptomatic of the extent of their acculturation. It is estimated that in one Khmu village about four hour's walk south of Luang Prabang town ten per cent of the farmers had paddy fields. This, however, was an exceptional case, not only in that it was a relatively prosperous village as Khmu settlements go but also in that there were a number of Christian converts who may have been more amenable to change.[21]

In Khmu villages surveyed by the present investigator, the percentage was much smaller. Often only the village headman and perhaps one or two others had wet-rice fields. In one village a day's walk from the royal capital a paddy field formerly owned by the Khmu tasseng has been lying fallow since his death because "people don't like to work in the na." Their explanation continued: "It is very expensive to buy a buffalo. Even if we do have a buffalo we must sell it if we need money, or we may decide to kill it for a festival. This leaves us with no buffalo to work the na, and we never have enough money to buy a new one. Besides, it is very complicated to drain and to dam and our yields are higher in the hai." It is further maintained that "mountain rice" tastes better.

Despite the factors making for cultural conservatism it seems likely that among the Khmu and other tribal groups cultivation of wet-rice fields will increase in the coming years as these groups become more Laotianized. The change in agricultural techniques is being actively encouraged by a number of Lao officials, and some government assistance has been provided. For example, a group of Meo at Phou Kao Quai near Vientiane received government gifts of buffalo to be used for plowing. In some cases tribal people reluctant to take the major step of moving their homes to the valley have begun to cultivate na, meanwhile living in temporary houses near the fields and returning to their mountainside villages when work is completed. This is the case of some Yao in the area of Muong Sing who received tools and seed from the government.[22]

Na and Hai Yields in Laos and in Neighboring Countries

How do Khmu and Lao rice yields from na and hai compare and how do these yields stand in relation to those recorded for Vietnam, for the Lao of Northeast Thailand, or for the Thai of the Bangkok plains? A word of explanation is advisable before citing the available figures, namely, that "yields" are variously calculated in these countries on the basis of hectares planted, amount of seed rice, or the labor of one family.

As shown in Table 13, there is a difference by a factor of approximately ten between the highest swidden yield for the first year of cultivation among the mountain tribes of central Vietnam, 2,300 kilos per hectare, and the lowest yield in na fields in Northeast Thailand, 225 kilos per hectare, and even lower figures are known in northern Laos. The best wet-rice yield for Northeast Thailand is still less than half the highest swidden yield cited for central Vietnam. Yet the average figure for Lamet swiddens is slightly above both the central Vietnam figure and the best wet-rice yield from Northeast Thailand. The maximum noted for the Lamet exceeds that of the wet-rice yield for Bang Chan on the Bangkok plain.

In Phong Saly we find averages of about 600 kilos of rice per hectare, but also in northern Laos averages of 2,020 for the Nam Tha plain and 1,755 and 1,600 for Muong Sai and Muong Ngoi districts in Luang Prabang province are reported. Great variation in yields exist for various villages surveyed in north, central, and southern Laos, ranging from almost 3,000 to a little over 300 per hectare. This, of course, reflects the differing fertility of land, the varying efficacy of irrigation systems, and the general level of economic development of the area, plus possible inaccuracies in the statistics themselves. But there does appear to be a regional difference. On the basis of surveys Champassak appears to have the highest average yield of any province (1,231), while in the northern areas of Phong Saly and Sam Neua the range is between 600 and 700.

As might be expected the yields in Laos fall considerably below those in neighboring Cambodia and Thailand. The average yield of all of Laos, 932 (1954), is almost 200 kilos per hectare less than the Cambodian average and 300 to 400 below that of Thailand. It should be noted, of course, that there is an overlap in terms of the high average yields of certain villages (see Table 14). The major problems in Laos, with respect to na cultivation, appear to be the lack of good irrigation systems, the mountainous terrain, and a lack of psychological motivation. Excess production is very difficult to market from certain regions and in some cases is fed to livestock because of prohibitive transportation costs. It is also possible that the extreme fragmentation of the land is a factor. Apparently the small holdings of the Lao farmers are often split into a few dozen plots; by contrast, in Thailand even the largest holdings are only split into a few sections. The fragmentation of the na fields in Laos may be a reflection of the limited area of flat land in the valleys. It seems likely that the hai lands are not so finely fragmented. If more detailed data were available for hai fields it is possible that the rice production in Laos might appear more favorable (see Tables 15 and 16).

It is interesting to compare these figures with respect to the claims of authorities of the Democratic Republic of Vietnam, who are proud of their efforts to raise agricultural productivity in the Tai-Meo autonomous area.[23] Even the "average" exceeds all the figures for the area and is surpassed only by Japan. The lowest yield cited is 2.7 tons. Here repeated water shortages are mentioned. This compares with a maximum of 1.5 tons recorded for a village on the Bangkok plain. Although it is obvious that the claims may have been exaggerated for propaganda purposes (they may also be paddy figures with a built-in 30 per cent over-estimate), still they cannot be ignored because obviously intensive use of labor, fertilizer, and careful planting techniques can produce impressive results, as Japanese yields indicate.

Implied but not clearly stated in the North Vietnamese data

is the shift from hai to irrigated rice culture. This would certainly be a logical step for the Communists since it is easier to control the production and distribution of concentrated wet-rice agriculture than of scattered hai plots. The fostering of cooperative, centrally controlled work groups is also important in this connection. Rice cultivation cannot, of course, be isolated from broader political developments. In Thailand and Laos, in contrast to North Vietnam, government participation and control in rice growing has been minimal.[24] But that the situation is far from ideal in the DRV is indicated by persistent reports in 1961 of famines in that country.

In agricultural reports on areas in the provinces of Luang Prabang, Nam Tha, and Phong Saly constant reference is made to water shortages and the lack of irrigation facilities or the inadequacies of existing ones. It is implied that if adequate water were provided almost all of these areas could become at least self-sufficient and others could export surpluses (Duclos 1959). If the irrigation problem has been solved by the intensive use of labor in the adjoining areas of North Vietnam, this would go a long way toward explaining the much higher yields there. But even the Communists do not claim to control the rainfall and they too admit the crucial problem of water shortages.

The data unfortunately do not include sufficient background information to permit any real conclusions about the relative productivity of wet rice and swidden-cultivated rice in Laos and Thailand. They do serve, however, to indicate the possibility that hectare for hectare in any given season swidden cultivation, at least in the first year, can be more productive. It is also possible that a greater return per hour of labor may be received from the hai. This point is reinforced by observations on the rejection by the Rhadé (a tribe of central Vietnam) of enforced adoption of wet-rice agriculture between 1920 and 1940.[25]

It must also be remembered that the yield begins to decline by the second year and may drop as much as eighty per cent by the third. Swidden is an extensive type of agriculture adapted to the mountainous terrain of the Meo, Lamet, and Khmu but lacking the long-term stability of intensive irrigated cultivation, which is capable of supporting much larger and more stable populations. Thus while a swidden may give a higher yield per hectare when new, it can support only a relatively sparse population because of its declining fertility.

A meaningful indication of productivity is found in the yields of household groups (see Table 17). Among the many factors here and elsewhere making for difficulty in accurate evaluations, one of the major ones is the lack of a uniform system of measurement, even within the same ethnic group. The Lao, for example, use terms such as touque, kalon, and wa; the Yao use mut; and the government uses the metric system.[26]

Estimates of total household rice production per year among Lao, Khmu, Meo, and Yao groups in northern Laos range from a little more than one metric ton to twelve among both hai and na cultivators. The largest na yield per household in one village in Luang Prabang district surveyed by the ministry of agriculture was 12,000 kilos (see Table 18), while in Bang Chan over half the households produced more rice than this (Thailand 1958: 133). However, the yields do compare with those from Pao-ao in Northeast Thailand, although it should be noted that this is considered one of the poorest areas of Thailand.

Despite the lack of precision, Lao agricultural statistics point up the problem that, generally speaking, the Lao farmer produces barely enough to feed himself and has relatively little if any rice to market. For example, in 1953 Bang Chan produced 193,594 tang of rice (about 2,090 tons); of this amount 52,548 were consumed as food, 20,264 as feed, and 7,682 as seed, leaving a marketable surplus of 113,100 tang (Janlekha 1955). It would be a very rare Lao village that could duplicate this achievement. Herein lies at least a partial explanation of the failure of the Lao farmer to supply the growing towns of Laos with rice and of the resulting necessity for Vientiane, and even a smaller town of less than 10,000 like Luang Prabang, to rely on imports from Thailand to feed the population. The case of Vientiane might be alternatively explained as adaptation to the fact that Thai towns with good transportation facilities are across the river, but in Luang Prabang the rice must be brought in by river barge over a distance of several hundred miles. Prior to independence these areas received imports of food by road from Tonkin.

Taken together, the evidence indicates that swidden agriculture compares favorably with irrigated rice farming not only in Laos but in some of the more productive areas of Thailand as well. The clearly marginal nature of all types of farming in Laos, and that of the Lao in Northeast Thailand as well, shows very definitely when compared to a major rice-producing area of Southeast Asia such as the central Thailand plain. The average rice production for the plain village of Bang Chan approximates the maximum yields from Khmu swidden or Lao paddies, while a substandard Bang Chan farmer producing largely for his own family would be considered fairly prosperous in Laos with the same production.

These differences are dramatically illustrated in the case of one Lao village headman; his yield of 12,000 kilos from three irrigated fields, based in part on the use of hired labor, approximates the 11,700 kilos for an average Bang Chan household.

Within Laos itself, the swidden yields per household seem to be similar to those from the paddy fields. This is almost to be expected, for in many cases in Luang Prabang province, Khmu swiddens supply the Lao traders in the valleys with a significant portion of their rice needs. According to available data, the Khmu yields from swiddens have a higher maximum than those of the Lao swiddens, a natural consequence of the fact that swidden farming is the primary Khmu technique while hai cultivation is at best a second choice for those poorer Lao who practice it. An important point here is that swidden land is free for the cultivating while na land must sometimes be rented.

Ecological Considerations of Swidden Agriculture

Lao government agricultural officials(i.e. the French experts employed by and presumably endorsed by the government) take a rather dim view of swidden farming in general. The following statement is taken from the 1956-57 *Rapport de Gestion et d'Activité du Service des Eaux, Forêts et Chasses du Laos:*

> It is no exaggeration to state that migratory agriculture constitutes the primary forestry problem in Laos. The forest mass almost completely shelters this practice to a more or less significant degree.
>
> Most of the cultivation practiced in the mountainous areas is done in the rays [hai]. This paradoxical situation is aided by the fact that while the amount of agricultural land in the plains is just about fixed and the forests retreat little due to [na] cultivation, in contrast, in the mountains a systematic deforestation dangerously menaces the forest cover.
>
> It is evident that the inverse situation would be the normal one.
>
> It is often stated that the rays give better yields than the [wet] rice fields. This is true for the first few years in good soil and after the burning of a 'good forest.' In addition one should consider that the yield calculated for an area is for a single year. In reality, however, during a period of ten years, for example, a ray of one hectare

cultivated for a period of two years requires five hectares. The actual yield, that is to say the production according to the total surface 'immobilized,' is then inferior to the [wet] rice field. One can roughly distinguish three types of rays in Laos, according to the methods used and their different effects:

1st, Exhaustive rays: These are the rays cultivated for long periods of time, particularly in the mountain regions of higher elevation by peoples of Chinese origin, typically by the Meo. These are the most disastrous. Actually the long period of cultivation literally exhausts the soil and reconstitution of the cover is almost impossible.

2nd, Subsistence rays with short rotation: These are cultivated in an attempt to assure an adequate rice harvest. The period of cultivation is fairly short, usually two years. The [vegetative] cover can be regenerated, but fire and accelerated rotations help to further the process of soil exhaustion. This type is practiced in the mountains by the Laotheng and sometimes at lower altitudes by the Lao.

3rd, Supplementary rays: Practiced everywhere by valley villages to produce additions to the harvest. The period of cultivation is generally short. Practiced less systematically, they are frequently made in more or less isolated parcels of land, which facilitates the reconstitution of the surface cover. Their area is very variable. In general, they increase after a period of poor harvests, and diminish when this problem lessens.

Because of the lack of basic statistics, it is difficult to evaluate even the area of the rays. One can nevertheless get an idea of the importance of this problem:

a. One can estimate the population of Laos at 2,000,000 inhabitants. The statistics of the Ministry of the Interior list more than twenty-six per cent as Laotheng and Meo.[27] One can consider that since the Lao population also practices rays, it is possible without exaggeration to say that two-fifths of the population makes some sort of rays. This gives us 800,000 inhabitants or 160,000 families. At one hectare of ray per family we arrive at the figure of approximately 160,000 hectares of rays.

b. One can also make an estimate based on the area of [wet] rice fields cultivated. This area is estimated at 700,000 hectares. If one estimates that the area cultivated in rays is one-third of that cultivated in [wet] rice, one arrives at the figure of approximately 230,000 hectares of rays, a figure quite different from the one above.

c. It is thus possible to estimate without exaggeration somewhere between 160,000 and 200,000 hectares of rays. We will not comment further on this figure. The annual destruction [of the forests] would be on the order of 50-100,000 hectares. This represents an area equivalent to Pakse.

Perhaps most important in these official comments is the great emphasis placed on preservation of the forests and the negative attitude toward hai cultivation as a whole even though its superior yields under certain circumstances are conceded. Such views do not contribute to a solution of the problem, for unless the Lao government is prepared to undertake moving all of the mountain peoples to the valleys hai cultivation will of necessity continue.

Also important are the conclusions regarding erosion and soil exhaustion. Implied in part is an intensive occupancy of the land so that the destruction is progressive and the forests do not rejuvenate, although the various data presented do not entirely support this view.

According to Izikowitz (1951: 208-09) who has made the only comprehensive study of a hai cultivating group in Laos:

> The Lamet . . . are not nomadized. Thus, when they have harvested they leave the swidden, and allow the forest to repossess the lost territory. Then they do not return to the same place until after from twelve to fifteen years.[28] Only then has the forest grown up to the extent that the land can again be used for cultivation. Thus it is easy to understand that the Lamet require vast regions for their disposition, and indeed, they have no lack of these. . . .
>
> A newly deserted swidden . . . covered with bush growth is called prim by the Lamet. There the forest gradually grows up again, and a young forest of this kind the Lamet call lau. Not until after twelve to fifteen years have the trunks grown to any considerable size and the undergrowth

> given way to the overshadowing trees. A forest like this is called klut, and is just the kind that is suitable for clearing.

Smalley (1961b: 11), describing the swidden situation among the Khmu, indicates that it involves a certain degree of order and planning:

> There is a definite system of rotation of fields. Decisions as to which fields are to be used in a given year are made on the basis of the length of time in fallowing, convenience, omens and consultation with the spirits. Although the swidden fields are not legally owned by anyone, the last village to have used a field is considered to have rights over it. . . . Someone using a field over which he does not have rights must pay a fine. . . . Among village members the swidden plots are assigned by group decision of the headman and elders.

Many investigators have stressed the fact that swidden agriculture can be practiced in such a way as to conserve forest resources.[29] Some claim quite positively that frequent fires actually promote the growth of certain types of forest. Historically most forest-living tribes have not been at all careful in extinguishing fires and, in fact, fires have been deliberately started among many nonagricultural peoples to make access to game easier and to promote the growth of wild seed plants. Therefore talk of fire simply as a negative ecological feature does not accord with its widespread usage, often intentional, throughout human history.[30]

Coordinating hai cultivation with modern forest management would admittedly be a formidable task for the government but the alternative, elimination of the hai system, would require the setting up of new communities at very high capital cost and there is a strong possibility that compulsion would have to be used to break up old cultural patterns.

Certainly swidden agriculture should not be regarded as a primitive, inferior type of agriculture to be abolished as soon as possible, but as an extensive type of land use in some ways well suited to the mountainous areas settled by the Khmu and Meo. As we have seen, a major drawback is that it can support only very limited populations. Another is that under conditions of rapid culture change, when population pressures increase and the people do not allow the forest to regenerate, the soils become exhausted and eroded at the same time. In Laos hai cultivation must be regarded as a complex series of interrelationships that must be considered in any solution of the country's basic agricultural problems.[31]

Generally speaking, northern Laos is a deficit area as far as rice production is concerned. During the late 1950's the Ministry of Agriculture, with the aid of funds and technicians supplied by the American aid mission, had begun to construct a series of small concrete dams to further irrigation and make possible two rice crops a year. The eventual goal was to make this region independent of rice imports from Thailand. But production is not the only problem: there is the persistent transportation problem. Wirtz (1958: 7) quotes a high official in the Lao Ministry of Agriculture who had been advocating an import duty on rice to encourage local production:

> If one estimates the population at 2,000,000 and the daily per capita consumption of rice at .5 kilos, the total consumption would be about 365,000 tons of rice annually. In the Annuaire Statistique du Laos (1951-52) the gross growth of land under rice cultivation rises from 386,000 hectares in 1951 to 585,800 hectares in 1952. It has been estimated that the present [1957] land under rice cultivation amounts to at least 700,000 hectares, yielding .7 tons of white rice per hectare, or a total production of 490,000 tons of rice if all fields were cultivated. There is also fairly large production of mountain rice. The Forest Service estimates its annual cultivation at 160,000 to 230,000 hectares, or about 200,000. Even if the ray yield doesn't exceed .5 tons of white rice per hectare, the total production would be 100,000 tons which, added to the estimated production of 490,000 tons from the [na] rice fields, would give a total production of 590,000 tons of white rice, against the consumption figure of 365,000 tons.[32]

In view of Laos' extremely underdeveloped transportation system, surplus in some areas and inadequacy in others is understandable. This, however, does not explain the drastic increases in rice imports during the 1950's. Two factors are involved: first, the growth of Vientiane and other towns after Laos gained her independence and, second, the American aid program, which because of certain currency restrictions and other regulations permitted importers to make a big profit on their transactions. The latter situation changed in 1958 with a currency reform that removed much of the motivation for excessive rice imports. Government interest in making Laos self-sufficient in rice production has produced certain projects designed to achieve this end, but evidently it will be some time before such measures become effective on a scale sufficiently broad to make a dent in the problem -- particularly in view of recurrent political and military conflicts.

Subsidiary Crops

The Lao of the Vientiane area generally do not plant a second crop in the idle rice fields, a condition existing primarily from lack of sufficient water and of implements for irrigation. Kaufman (1961: 51) adds:

> On several occasions informants stated their main reason for not growing vegetables was not lack of water, but the fact that poorer relatives constantly borrowed vegetables without repaying them, thereby making vegetable production quite unprofitable. Even farmers who do raise vegetables must supplement their diet with vegetables from the market at a monthly cost of about 200 kip [in 1957].

Where an adequate water supply is available, cucumbers and sometimes manioc and corn are grown in the paddy fields. Individual household compounds may grow some peppers, cucumbers, sugar cane, betel, and fruit trees. No compost or other fertilizer is used in either field or garden. In addition to the items mentioned above, some villagers grow eggplant and chili in their paddy fields. Gardens on the river banks are cultivated during the dry season and are particularly important in the vicinity of a town, since they supply the local market with fresh vegetables.[33] In some villages where people have been forced for one reason or another to give up their rice fields -- drought, breakdown of irrigation system, army confiscation -- increasing emphasis has been placed on gardens. A case in point is the Tai Dam village on the outskirts of Vientiane town, which has no rice fields as the men all work as traders, laborers, and craftsmen. The women there, assisted by children and older people, are engaged in intensive horticulture. Some residents of Luang Prabang who are not primarily farmers maintain small gardens on the banks of the Mekong and the Nam Khan, raising cucumbers, tomatoes, salad greens, eggplant, chili, onions, cow peas, a sort of spinach, bonarista beans, and peanuts.

In villages in central and northern Laos bananas are grown in nearby fenced-off areas; in more prosperous villages near towns these areas have barbed wire fences to keep out buffalo. Pineapple, cassava, mangoes, gourds, pomelo, papaya, yams, betel nut, sugar cane, and some coffee are also cultivated in small amounts. In every Lao village are coconut trees surrounding the houses and there are also quite often a few fruit trees within the pagoda compound. Although oranges are not grown in Luang Prabang district, they are raised in several areas within the province, particularly in the area of Nam Bac. Cotton is raised in certain Lao hai, separately from the rice, but has declined in importance in recent years as manufactured clothing has become more easily available.

In certain areas of northern Laos corn is an important supplementary crop and when the rice fails may become the primary crop, as is often the case among the Kha Ko of the Muong Sing area. The potato is also important here. It has been noted that in some villages in the area of Muong Noi (Luang Prabang province) where the people can raise only a three-month supply of rice, corn and manioc are cultivated extensively (Duclos 1959a: 5).

It is a common practice among the Khmu to plant small amounts of beans, cucumbers, and corn in the swiddens along with the rice. Other hai may contain chili, okra, citronella grass, and eggplant as well as occasional patches of onions, garlic, cabbage, and Chinese mustard. This casual gardening is supplemented by the gathering of roots, mushrooms, and bamboo shoots. Tobacco, cotton, and opium are also grown in small quantities.

For the Meo, glutinous and nonglutinous varieties of rice must be considered the main crop, though in times of rice crop failure the Meo in the Luang Prabang area turn to corn as a major human food. [34]

As it would hardly be correct to label opium cultivation among the Meo as a subsidiary activity, this important cash crop is discussed separately in the next chapter to emphasize its economic significance for the Meo. But in the opium fields the Meo also grow cucumbers, Chinese mustard, cabbage, and potatoes. Corn, raised mainly as feed for the horses and pigs, is usually grown separately. [35]

At the turn of the century Reinach (1901: 405) remarked of the Meo:

> If he stays in one place for any length of time he also produces, in addition to the maize and rice which form the basis of his food supply and the opium which he smokes, very fine eggplants, gourds, sweet potatoes and nonsweet potatoes, sorrel, green beans and all the French vegetables whose seeds are given him.

Tea is a secondary crop of the Lamet, grown in plots in the woods. In and around Lamet villages are small fenced-in garden patches where a few vegetables are raised. There are also enclosures for fruit trees -- typically, mango, tamarind, lemon, orange, tangerine, and pomelo. In addition, every family has a banana grove, which, as among the Lao, is enclosed to keep out the pigs, who are fond of the stalks. The gardens are tended mostly by old men and children who do not go to the swiddens (Izikowitz 1951: 257-60).

Gathering is an important supplement to the economies of all these groups, who rely on forest products such as roots, tubers, and fruits particularly in the period when food is short before the rice harvest matures. For the Khmu forest products are significant trade items. When there has been a bad harvest collecting becomes almost a necessity for survival.

It is difficult to assess the relative importance of the different subsidiary crops. Gaudillot and Condominas (1959: 3, 28-30) cite statistics for a village near Vientiane, where an average family holding was 2.1 hectares. Here about 80 hectares were devoted to rice, 34 to tobacco, and 28 to sugar cane. Official government sources for 1957 cite 18,000 hectares in corn, 3,500 in cotton, 2,000 in tobacco, 1,000 in coffee, and 700 in sugar cane. The latter would appear to be gross underestimates of total crop areas but seem more reasonable at least if interpreted as areas devoted to production for market. In any case an idea of the overall crop distribution is presented by these figures.

Fishing and Hunting

As inhabitants mainly of riverine regions, almost all Lao are fishermen. Yet fishing has never been an important aspect of the natural economy. Certainly few Lao live solely from the profits of fishing, for this activity serves mainly to satisfy family needs. In a village on the Mekong near Vientiane one man said he derived his main income from fishing -- if true, an exceptional case. Should someone happen to make a good catch, it is possible that he would try to sell part provided there were a nearby market town. But in most cases the fish are kept for personal consumption, and therein lies one of the main reasons for the shortage of fish in the towns and for the importation of dried fish.

Most Lao villagers share a passion for fishing. During the dry season several families or even an entire village will organize collective fishing outings. Any surplus above daily needs is preserved in salt to be used in the preparation of the Lao dish padek made of fermented fish and eaten when fresh fish is not available. For this purpose a household needs about forty to eighty kilos a year, and the individual farmer catches just the amount of fish he needs (Serene 1959: 175).

Certain kinds of fishing are traditionally associated with ritual observances. Catching of the pa-bouek, a large sheatfish that sometimes grows to a length of six and a half feet, has been observed at Ban Ang, a small village upstream from Vientiane where the Mekong suddenly widens to almost a mile. Fishing here lasts three days and is always fixed for the fifteenth day of the new moon in the third month of the Lao calendar: it is forbidden to fish for the pa-bouek at any other time. A few days before the fishing is to start, the Lao administration appoints an official to direct operations. The fishermen, arriving early on the morning of the appointed day, wash their pirogues and sink them keel upwards at the river's edge, then attach small bouquets of flowers with white thread as an offering to the phi. Before the fishing starts the phi of the village is invited to come down to the river bank where a shrine has been set up and offerings of fruit and flowers are displayed. The first fisherman to catch a pa-bouek will offer the head to the phi. These ceremonies are the occasion for a village fair, at which traveling merchants set up stalls. A female shaman communicates with the phi of the village and of the local cave where the fish supposedly dwell. At least one occasion is reported on which the shaman found the spirits displeased and the quest for this particular fish was put off to the following year (Serene 1959: 177-82).

Fish also act as repositories for sins. At Luang Prabang small fish are caught to be sold during the Lao New Year's celebration and then released into the Mekong, in the hope that they will carry away the purchaser's sins.

Fishing is done with nets, traps, poles, and dams, some of which are fairly elaborate. Not all Lao fishing is done in streams, for when the rice fields flood during the early part of the rainy season, a good part of the village, particularly the women and children, can be seen casting nets in the fields. The children appear to take this as a game and the adults enjoy themselves also. According to one explanation, the fish are disturbed and often killed by the plowing of the flooded fields; the villagers simply gather fish that have risen to the surface.

Fishing might be regarded as going counter to the Buddhist doctrine forbidding the taking of life but the Lao rationalize their fishing, which is as much for pleasure as food, by saying that they merely take a fish out of the water: "If it dies, that is not my fault, I have not killed it" (Dooley 1958: 25). Some villagers make a slight differentiation between animal and fish life, which permits them to spear and club fish, but Buddhist monks and devout laymen abstain from killing in any form.

Those Khmu who live along streams also do some fishing, and it plays a minor role in the economy of the Lamet (Izikowitz 1951: 174-77). Neither group, however, is able to use pirogues.

Although fishing does not appear to be of great importance to the Meo of Luang Prabang province, it has been observed in other Meo areas (Savina 1930: 230):

> In the evening after dinner, the young people like to go fishing and look half through the night for fish under the rocks. One can see weirs at the foot of all waterfalls . . . Community fishing in the villages usually takes place at the beginning of summer, when they set up dams in the water courses in order to put the rice fields on the mountain slopes under water. The Meo then poison the fish with the help of the bark and leaves of certain trees.

In contrast to fishing, hunting is of negligible importance among most Lao groups. It is not mentioned as an economic activity in studies of Lao and related Thai village economies, nor did any Lao village informant volunteer information on the subject. This may in part be related to Buddhist beliefs, though many of the presumably Buddhist Lao officials possess rifles and shotguns and take great pleasure in hunting as a sport. Buddhist doctrine is reinforced by strong folk beliefs that tend to discourage hunting, but here again an exception must be made for the Westernized elite, who are apparently unafraid of the phi and who may even have animal trophies on display in their homes.

Among the Khmu, Lamet, Akha, Meo, and other mountain peoples in Laos, hunting is a significant supplementary economic activity. An idea of different types of hunting practices can be gained from this Khmu description (Smalley 1952):

> The hunter has a gun and goes wandering shooting animals in the forest. When the fifth month arrives, he goes and waits at the water-hole where different kinds of deer come down to drink. We take our guns, our cross-bows, and shoot them. All kinds of animals come down to drink. We take our cross-bows and shoot birds, chipmunks, [wild] chickens, pigeons, monkeys and gibbons. We take

our guns and shoot big animals -- deer, wild boar -- so that those who live in [up-country] villages have more than enough to eat. When the rainy season comes we wander around hunting deer and elephant.

When we are tired of traveling we return home and dispose of this meat. There are those who buy and there are those who ask for this meat free. The house of the hunter is the one where people want to come and stay. If he is going to go hunt far away in the forest, he takes two or three people with him as bearers. He takes rice to eat, chili and salt. If he stalks and shoots an animal and it doesn't die, then it is necessary to stay in the forest two or three nights. If he shoots and gets game such as a deer, he takes the antlers and sells them. Those who are master hunters do not have houses or rice fields. They hunt all the time which is very hard. Some people have enough to fill their wives' and childrens' mouths this way. People who live in the country have no place to buy, no place to sell. All you can do is to look for food intelligently. Those who do not know how to do this go hungry.

If there are a lot of people and they know there are a number of animals in a certain abandoned field, they say to each other, 'Call the dogs,' and they take them along. Those who have dogs drive, and the others lie in ambush. It is necessary to make a noise, to cry, to shout, and to spread out and surround the field. Shout and move toward the group which is waiting in ambush. The animal tries to slip away and the waiting people take a gun and shoot. When the animals have been killed, they return to the village and divide the meat in equal portions, a portion for each person, each gun and each dog.[36]

If you are going to hunt wild boar, either a herd or a single one, a person or two takes dogs and a gun and traces the track of the animal. When he is close by, the dog finds the boar and barks. The man shoots. Sometimes the animal charges him and vigorously attacks the man and dog. Many people die because of wild boar, and sometimes hunters shoot each other.[37]

The Khmu account continues with a description of the distribution of meat:

> Brothers and sisters of the same parents with the same ancestors and same family love each other. When a person gets some meat -- wild boar, deer, an animal shot with a gun, or an animal caught in a spear trap, whatever it may be, he performs the custom of dividing the meat. The meat is distributed among all the houses, wherever there is an older or younger sibling or a blood brother. Older brothers and father's older brothers eat the shoulder meat. Younger brothers eat the hind quarters. The headman eats the fillet. [Classificatory] brothers and in-laws eat the haunch.[38] When we marry unsuitably we are doing violence to this distribution custom. If anyone does not get meat according to this pattern, then that person is eligible for marriage [within the exogamous group].

Much of the Lamet meat is obtained by hunting, but in comparison with other sources of food, meat plays a minor role in the everyday diet. Lamet hunting techniques contrast in certain ways with those of the Khmu: the Lamet catch most wild game by means of traps and organized hunting does not seem to exist. Neither dogs nor nets are used but hunting with the crossbow, considered a noble sport, is the popular way to bag smaller animals such as birds, squirrels, and rats. The Lamet have used guns bought from the Chinese or Thai.

Like agriculture, hunting is a sacred activity with many associated rites. The crossbow is believed to have a spirit which is propitiated by using blood to fasten a feather on the tip of the nose of the bar. This ensures that the arrow will hit its mark. Sacrifice to the forest spirit is made on the spot where an animal has been trapped; when this has been done the game is carried back to the village. A ten-day feast occurs when a _gaur_ is caught. Bits of meat are sacrificed and the people sing and drink to celebrate (Izikowitz 1951: 178-99).

Meo hunting techniques are distinctive due in part to the more mountainous environment. Traps are used -- chiefly for birds and rodents -- but the Meo strongly prefer to hunt with their own handmade guns and appear to be the only group in northern Laos which uses poisoned arrows. The Meo also seem to do less cooperative hunting than the Khmu, but they do use dogs to assist them.[39] The Xieng Khouang Meo hunt bears and tigers in addition to other game. This is done in part to protect the crops, for bears in particular are destructive during the rice and corn harvests.

In northern Thailand the Meo hunt all year round, particularly after the harvest has been brought in, and are so fond of hunting that they will sometimes abandon work in the fields to pursue a large animal such as an elephant. Game is usually stalked by groups of three men who remain together in order to help each other if an emergency arises. This is an important precaution because the Meo guns are more likely to wound than to kill.

The Akha usually hunt in larger groups and use dogs but do not pursue large game. Beaters drive the game in the direction of hidden hunters armed with rifles and crossbows. The Akha also use nets to catch birds, as well as traps for small animals and rodents (Bernatzik 1947: 339-50).

Livestock Raising

In northern and central Laos there are no groups that can be categorized as hunting and gathering or pastoral peoples, i.e. all groups gain their living primarily from agriculture.[40] However, all possess livestock. Aboriginal groups such as the Khmu and Lamet appear to have the poorest economy in this regard, while livestock raising is much more developed among the Lao and, especially, the Meo.

The Lao have the greatest variety of livestock, including, for example, work and ceremonial elephants. On the other hand the Meo raise horses, which are relatively rare among the Lao, and the quality of their cattle and pigs is also generally considered to be better.

Poultry is kept by all groups. In the Vientiane area eighty per cent of the Lao households own at least four chickens, a few as many as sixty. Around Paksan, however, only fifteen per cent of the households keep chickens. In all cases the chickens are raised as a small cash product and are consumed only on special occasions; the eggs represent most of the income.

Ducks are raised by ten per cent of the households, primarily for eggs. Cholera attacks the ducks nearly every rainy season and as a result most farmers have given up raising them (Kaufman 1961: 8). In one village along the Nam Ou in Luang Prabang province fifty households raise about 600 ducks whose eggs are exported to the royal capital (Duclos 1959a).

Egg production is not at all systematized; the chickens lay their eggs anywhere and the people often have to go search for them. In view of this, it is not surprising that about fifty per cent of the eggs available on the Luang Prabang town market turn out to be rotten, although this may also reflect a Lao dietary preference. As might further be expected, the chickens themselves are undersized when compared to Western varieties, and their meat is very tough. They are also subject to epidemics, e.g. in 1956 most chickens in Khmu villages near Luang Prabang died.

As one way of avoiding these problems, domestic fowl are often raised on pile-coops. In this way they cannot destroy the garden seed beds and are quite dry and warm during the muddy rainy season. Because of their belief in not taking life in any form, some Lao will not kill chickens but will ask a non-Lao such as a Khmu tribesman to do it for them.

Pigs are raised by about forty per cent of the households in Vientiane province. Villagers claim that there is never enough food for these animals and that during the rainy season the muddy ground makes it difficult for the animals to forage for themselves. Half of the households possess one buffalo, twenty per cent have two, and wealthier farmers three or more. The buffalo are used primarily for rice cultivation and occasionally are sold for slaughter in the capital (Kaufman 1961: 1).[41] A household with a wagon also possesses two oxen for pulling it.[42] Since animal milk is traditionally not used by peoples east of India, it is interesting to note the relatively large quantities of canned milk, both evaporated and powdered, purchased by Lao villagers for their small children.[43]

Buffalo are also kept by all groups, although there are appreciably fewer among the Khmu and especially the Meo. In the case of the Khmu, an impoverished economic status and the relatively small extent of their irrigated cultivation make this type of livestock impractical to own though buffalo are highly desirable for Khmu sacrifice. The Meo seem to concentrate more on the keeping of cattle, which are better adapted to the mountainous terrain. As for the Lao in the Luang Prabang area the situation varies from household to household, and even more from village to village. In some villages almost every home has at least one buffalo; in others the percentage is very small, as for example in a particular village near the royal capital where two households out of seventy kept buffalo. The disproportionate numbers of buffalo kept by individual households is illustrated in another village where out of some twenty households four owned buffalo, with a 7-2-1-1 distribution respectively.

Villagers claim that during the Vietminh war soldiers confiscated much of their livestock for food. Lack of adequate pasturage is another reason cited by some villagers for the paucity of buffalo in the Luang Prabang area. Although neighboring Khmu are willing to pasture the Lao villagers' buffalo for 80 to 100 kip a month outside the plowing or harvesting seasons, most people feel this is too high a price to pay.[44] As a result, some villagers around the royal capital purchase a buffalo at plowing time and then sell it to the local Vietnamese slaughterhouse a month or so later after the plowing season.

Among the Lao particularly, but also among the Khmu, the buffalo are kept under the house. Among the Meo, whose dwellings are built directly on the ground, pigs and buffalo are housed in pens which adjoin the house, although a village may construct separate corrals for cattle and horses (see Figure 2).

After pigs, cattle are second in importance among the Meo and are raised primarily for meat. In some areas they are also used as pack animals but their milk is never utilized. Meo cattle are of relatively good quality and are like the corn-fed Meo pigs given great care. Over sixty years ago Reinach (1901: 406) remarked with reference to Meo livestock: "He raises fine poultry, pigs, oxen, goats and horses with particular care and success." Bernatzik emphasizes that pigs are raised by the Meo not only as a food source but also as their most important sacrificial animal. There is evidently some cross breeding with the wild species. Many pigs are fed refuse and cooked corn in the morning and evening, as well as the stems of wild banana, but more commonly pigs serve as scavengers who aid the chickens in keeping the village clean.

Chicken and pigs raised by the family provide all groups with their most important sources of domesticated meat, with only a limited number being sold to supply the needs of the town market. Hunting must also be taken into account as an important source of meat, particularly among the Meo and Khmu. Buffalo meat is sometimes eaten after an animal has died a natural death.

In addition to these common types of livestock, most Meo families keep horses for use as beasts of burden. These horses are usually larger than the typical horse in Southeast Asia and are fed on corn and bamboo shoots as well as grass. The Meo are proud of their animals, care for them fondly, train them well, and produce a creature with the surefootedness and stamina necessary on the rugged trails (Barney 1957a: 32).

The Meo also have a characteristic dog with a woolly coat and no tail. Although regarded as a pet it is also sometimes used for purposes of sacrifice, particularly in connection with the ceremony of the guardian spirit. Cats are also kept. Sometimes goats are raised by the Meo and Khmu and are often used for sacrificial purposes. Elephants are kept by certain Lao, and there is a small herd which is retained in a Khmu village near the royal capital and used on ceremonial occasions. Elephants are brought in from Sayaboury province to Luang Prabang from time to time to haul teak logs up from the river. In the latter province in particular, they are the usual means of transport through the jungle. The Phou Noi of Phong Saly raise bees in hollow logs near their homes (Jumsai 1959: 26), but it is not known how many other groups follow this practice.

Livestock Sacrifice

Having sketched the basic picture of livestock raising in central and northern Laos, it must now be pointed out that except for a few strictly utilitarian functions -- such as the use of buffalo for plowing paddy fields and of horses and elephants for transport -- the various types of livestock appear to be used chiefly for religious and ceremonial purposes.

Among many groups the situation is sometimes reversed; that is, meat is desired, so a sacrifice is made. Obviously these two factors are closely related and it is illusory to seek a primary cause. Belief in the various forms of phi, strong among all groups, makes heavy demands on their economies.[45] Table 19 briefly summarizes some of the occasions when the Lao, Khmu, Lamet, Akha, and Meo sacrifice their livestock and poultry, though this is by no means an exhaustive list.

Poultry are frequently regarded as sacrificial objects:

> The Lamet have no knowledge of breeding of chickens. They set most value on a handsome cock with beautiful tail feathers suitable for sacrifice. The color of the cocks is of importance, and the Lamet do not care to sell them for they are needed for the numerous sacrifices. Hens are only fit for the less important sacrifices (Izikowitz 1951: 204).

The following text deals with the buffalo sacrifice to dedicate a new house and provides an idea of its significance to the Khmu (Smalley 1952):

> The house spirit makes it known that he wants to eat buffalo. There are no buffalo to be killed. We pray to the spirits to delay the ceremony and we go out and look

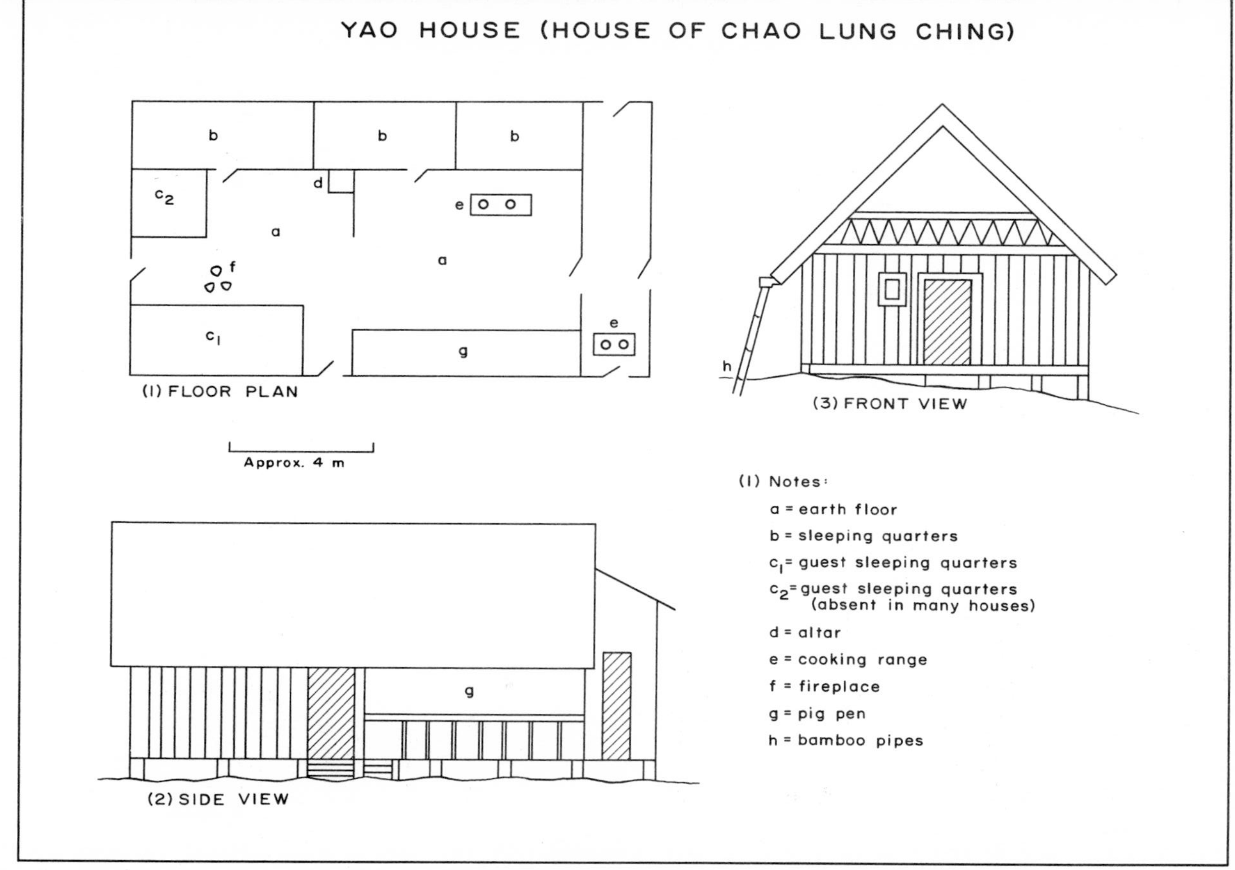

FIGURE 2

From Keiji Iwata, "Minority Groups in Northern Laos, Especially the Yao," Laos Project No. 16.

for money and [more] money. Finally we go and buy a buffalo. We return and gather wood for a house.[46] We build a house. We take the buffalo and fasten it to the post of this house and pray to the spirits. Then somebody takes an axe and cuts the back of the buffalo's neck. Another person takes a knife and cuts the hocks. When the buffalo is dead, the meat is sliced and cooked. After it is cooked the meat is given to the house spirit. Then we eat and drink alcohol at the same time. Then we sleep until morning. In the morning we slice up the hind legs and forelegs of the buffalo and perform the custom of distributing the meat.

Although of primary significance, religious motives cannot be separated from the social significance of feasts or, as indicated, simply the desire to eat meat, for which a supernatural rationalization is usually sought. Religious imperatives are, however, the crucial determinant and often impose harsh obligations on the Khmu. When someone is ill the Khmu sacrifice a chicken. The feast for the spirit of the village, held in the sixth lunar month, calls for offerings of chickens by individual villagers, as well as a pig or an ox or a buffalo, which is bought by taking up a collection. The flesh is offered raw; when the flies begin to buzz around the offerings, the villagers assume the spirit has finished eating and the village feast begins. Any food left over cannot be taken home because it is felt that the spirit will cause illness. There are also forest and field spirits. If a person believes that he has been afflicted by a spirit at any place, an offering of boiled chicken and liquor is made there.

In the case of death, the host provides liquor and food for the three nights that the corpse is kept in the house. All the animals of the deceased are slaughtered; if there are children the animals are first divided among them and then killed to feed the guests. A similar situation exists among the Kha Ko where the largest hog owned by the household is used as an offering to the soul of the aged head of the household on the day after his death. On the day of death the four biggest pigs of the Khmu household are slaughtered as well as a large number of chickens. In richer homes oxen, buffalo, goats, dogs, and pigs are killed. At the death of a woman, child, or young man, either an ox or a pig is killed depending on the importance of the person and the economic status of the head of the family. If the head of the village dies, the largest pig owned by every family is killed, or in some villages a collection will be made to buy oxen, buffalo, goats, pigs, and black dogs to offer to the soul of the deceased (Srisvasdi 1950). The Khmu will even go into debt to obtain money to buy livestock for sacrifice, sometimes turning a son or a daughter over to a creditor to work off the debt. This practice continues although outlawed by the Lao government. Among the Lamet, too, funerals are a great expense, the number of livestock sacrificed depending on the family's wealth (Izikowitz 1951: 106). Upon the death of a poor Meo, only a few pigs and some chickens are offered, but if a rich man dies one or more cows or buffalo are sacrificed. Meo sacrifices include chickens, buffalo, pigs, cattle, and occasionally dogs, but, as far as is known, never horses.

The Lao never sacrifice elephants, but buffalo sacrifice has been practiced by the Lao of both Vientiane and Luang Prabang. This ceremony, which functions both to propitiate the spirits and to control rainfall, is held just before the beginning of the monsoon rains. In certain regions of northern Laos there is active collaboration in sacrificial ceremonies among the Lao, Kha peoples, and tribal Tai, and it is possible that the cultural influence of aboriginal peoples is a factor in Lao buffalo sacrifice.[47]

Sacrifice is also institutionalized among the Black Tai in Nam Tha, who make offerings to the god of the soil and sacrifice a pig and a buffalo to the guardian spirit of the village. In addition, a duck is offered to the spirit of the water, a dog to the spirit of the forest, chickens to the spirit of heaven and the spirit that guards the entrance to the village, and a tray of food to any errant spirits and other phi in general (Hickey 1958: 147).

There is no precise data available for any one group, but one Lao official estimated the annual cost of sacrifices to the village spirit in two Lao villages in Luang Prabang district on the basis of conversations with the people there. In the first village, the forty-four households each sacrificed two chickens which, at the then current market rates, amounted to an expense of about 8,000 kip; in the other village, approximately the same size, two buffalo were sacrificed by the village as a whole, each buffalo valued at 4,000 to 5,000 kip.[48] These sacrifices represent of course only those to the phi of the village, for which the village population shared expenses, and not those to spirits involved in individual matters. Since the Lao and other peoples of northern Laos can hardly be termed wealthy in poultry and livestock, it is not difficult to see that the propitiation of phi constitutes a considerable drain on their economy.

It has been noted for "Kha" villages that "there are hardly any animals. They have killed them all for sacrifices; even if they have to starve afterwards they will have to work to buy some more. There are periods when every chicken in the village must be killed for sacrifice, and they vie with each other because they can thus appease the spirits by selfless denial" (Jumsai 1959: 20).

Some missionaries maintain that Christianized Meo and Khmu villages have become more prosperous since abandoning sacrifices to the phi. The desire to be freed of sacrifices is cited as a common reason for conversion to Christianity. One observer goes so far as to say, in speaking of the Meo, that "one should certainly not say they raise livestock; rather they keep animals chiefly for the purpose of sacrifice." (This would not apply to their horses, used exclusively for transport.) Izikowitz (1951: 269) writes that the owning of buffalo, primarily for the purpose of sacrifice, is the highest aim of the Lamet.

To all of this must be added the element of prestige: buffalo definitely appear to be a wealth symbol among Lao villagers and cattle play the same role among the Meo. Some Lao also keep cattle, particularly in the area of the Vientiane plain and in the capital city itself, where these prestige symbols can be seen grazing in front of the National Assembly building.

Government-induced Change in Agriculture in China and North Vietnam

In concluding this discussion of the traditional rural economies in northern and central Laos, it might be useful to take a brief look at the situation in neighboring China and North Vietnam where government officials have had to deal with certain crucial agricultural problems, particularly the matter of hai cultivation, arising from very similar cultural patterns. A major difficulty in this connection is to obtain reliable data. Generally speaking, Communist states make available only information that reflects to their advantage. Although much of the information is of a bombastic and propagandistic nature, criticism is permitted and often encouraged when it deals with the implementation of programs already decided upon. As a rule, no discussion of broad policies previously determined is permitted. Nevertheless, the importance of developments that have occurred on the borders of Laos cannot be overemphasized, particularly since the area under Communist (Pathet Lao) control has been increasing.

The following is an abbreviated account of the resettlement of a group of Yao villagers (_People's Viet-Nam Pictorial_, _19_ (1959), No. 3, pp. 19-20):

> Looking down from the high hill to the foot of the mountains how envious we were of the green rice fields of the

Tay [Tai] people.[49] How we dreamed of the day when we also could live in the merry hamlets below. We did not want to stay at home, even if it did mean a long day's journey to go to the village below on market days.

More than four years ago, families of the Man [Yao] minority people of Cong Hoa hamlet lived a lonely, isolated life on the steep slopes of the three mountains of Na Nghe, Cam Nam and Can Khao. . . .

Life on the highlands in these parts was very miserable The people toiled hard from morning to night, yet still could not get enough to eat.

Every year the Man people had to move higher still up the mountainsides to open up new land for cultivation.

It happened that the groves would not catch fire due to frequent rains, or that the paddy and maize were scorched by the burning sun. Then they had to feed on tubers or roots dug up in the forests to live through the hard days. Added to all this was the serious damage done to their crops by wild beasts. Hunting is no pastime for the Man minority people, but a necessary measure to protect their crops.

Due to undernourishment, the health of the adults deteriorated constantly, and the children were stunted and pale. Diseases were rife, rendering life still more gloomy.

The way to the village was steep and difficult. All year round, the villagers knew almost no other friend than the wind wailing through the forest, the rustling of the stream down the mountain and the permanent white veil of mist hanging over the majestic mountain ranges.

This is why the Man people in this hamlet have long nurtured the simple but bold desire: to go down the mountain to till the land in order to have a better life.

Yes, the cadre is quite right! Just to hear it said is reassuring! But will there be enough land to till when we go down the mountain?

Who knows how to guide a buffalo in ploughing and harrowing? Are the Tay and Kinh [Vietnamese delta] people really friendly toward the Man people?

Such were the worries of the Man people.

Being well aware of the wretched life of the Man people, the Vietnam Lao Dong [Communist] Party and the Government of the Democratic Republic in 1955 sent cadres to the mountains to persuade the Man to leave for the lowlands to earn a stable livelihood.

Being for many generations accustomed to an isolated life in the highlands, with customs and farming methods entirely different from those of the delta, and strong prejudices against other peoples as a result of the French 'divide and rule' policy, the Man people could not help feeling some anxiety when making a decision which would totally change their life.

But finally they followed the cadres' advice and moved to the delta.

There are 13 families, more than 100 people in all, now living in Cong Hoa hamlet.

Only four years have passed, yet great changes have occurred in the life of the Man people. What surprised us when we visited them was the speed with which they have adjusted to life in the delta. We visited many houses of the two producers' teams Dan Chu and Khe Can. All were clean and well ordered. The hosts served us with boiled water, a thing never seen in the past in the highlands. As a result, the sickness rate has fallen rapidly.

The head of the hamlet guides us to the plots of land newly opened up by the people alongside national route number 3:

'Here in the past there was only wild grass, taller than a buffalo. It took several days of burning to get rid of it. The Tay have taught us how to plough and harrow and in all ways helped us in our work. Before the land was ready for cultivation, we grew maize on the hill. Of course, there were problems in the first days, but

> everything has become better and now famine is a thing of the past, I can assure you of that.'
>
> Besides rice fields, the Man people have also opened up scores of mou of land in the surroundings to grow manioc, groundnut, soya and other bean crops.
>
> To help the people to get sufficient water to expand the tilled area, the Water Conservancy Service of Thai Nguyen Province has built an irrigation canal to bring water from the stream to the fields.
>
> The state trade shops have also undertaken to buy firewood gathered by the people to help them over the pre-harvest days.

In Laos, before larger resettlement problems arose, a number of Meo and Yao voluntarily settled in valleys and undertook irrigated rice farming, often with state subsidies, but there was no integrated government policy. Although the North Vietnamese government appears to have a clear policy, its implementation is another matter.

An indirect admission of the persistence of traditional agricultural and cultural patterns is found in the following statement:

> The Meo people grow much opium. Formerly sold to the French for opium it is now sold to the State store, at a much higher price than in the past. It is now used medically. Many of the older Meo people still smoke it -- it is good for the health, they say (Fox 1958: 129).

In a discussion of political and social changes allegedly brought about by the Communists we read:

> It is typical of the North-West that a large proportion of the population live a long way from the roads; the Meos on the mountaintops usually, then the Man people at a slightly lower level. Many other minorities, though in the valleys, are a long way from the roads (Fox 1958: 126).

These quotations refer to the Tai-Meo autonomous area which abuts the Laos province of Sam Neua. It is possible that the resettled village described above, which happens to border the main road through the area, is a demonstration or model village.

Despite political differences North Vietnam has been strongly influenced by China and we can gain further insights into the problem of agricultural resettlement if we look at the situation in neighboring Yunnan and similar areas of large Tai, Meo, and Yao minority groups. In a popular review article discussing progress of national minorities, we get the following picture for the Lisu ("China's National Minority Areas Prosper," Peking Review, May 26, 1959, p. 10):

> In the southwest, many national minorities have moved from feudal, slave and even primitive clan societies directly to socialism. The Lisu people inhabiting the Nu River valley in Yunnan Province is one of them. For centuries they lived deep in the mountains in a very primitive state of society. They made a living by hunting or by cultivating small patches of land on the mountain slopes. Liberation gave them a direct transition to socialism. In 1954 the Nukiang Lisu People's Autonomous Chou was established. In 1956 the first groups of agricultural cooperatives were set up. In 1958 the people's communes were established.

The next account, "Three Years in Hsishuangpanna Tai Autonomous Chou," goes into more detail: 50

> The 23rd of last January was the third anniversary of the founding of the Hsishuangpanna Tai Autonomous Chou, the first region in the frontier province of Yunnan that was granted autonomous government.
>
> Hsishuangpanna is known as the 'Granary of South Yunnan' but under the long reactionary rule and oppression in the past, the people of various nationalities could only use rough and coarse methods in their tilling, and some mountainous areas still lingered on in the stage of 'sowing without plowing, and by cutting down the old stalks and burning them.' The result was that the people in the 'granary' could not keep themselves from starvation.
>
> After the People's Committee of the autonomous chou was set up, its first central task was to unite the people of various nationalities and to develop agricultural production. In a span of three years, it has led the peasants in building and repairing more than 4,700 small irrigation works, and irrigating some 50,000 mou of fields that had been allowed to lie fallow. In some mountainous regions inhabited by Hani and Yao minorities, paddy fields and draft cattle

appeared for the first time. The People's Committee also loaned to the peasants of various nationalities over 900,000 yuan's worth of draft animals, farm implements, seeds and provisions and issued production subsidy funds and various relief monies amounting to more than 360,000 yuan, enabling the autonomous chou to raise agricultural production gradually. The grain output of the whole chou increased by upwards of 20 per cent in three years; in some places the increase was even greater.

This evangelical approach to propagation of what are considered modern farming methods and the almost magical transformations claimed are not, of course, limited to the abandonment of swidden agriculture in favor of irrigated rice cultivation. Involved in the changes of method of cultivation are a whole complex of social practices and strongly held traditional values, including the division of labor and the basic religious beliefs of the culture. The Communists clearly state the relationship between Marxist philosophy and their development programs.

One important objective is to increase the participation of women in all phases of agricultural work, from the plowing and transplanting of rice to the spreading of manure. A New China News Agency release (August 21, 1958), "Minority Nationalities Dispel Superstition and Break Old Customs," included this account from the Hsishuangpanna Tai Autonomous area:[51]

> . . . a story is going the rounds telling how a girl named Wang Ai-yang dispels the mistaken idea that women cannot plow the land. Wang Ai-yang is an assistant secretary of the Young Communist League. Coming back from a conference of youth representatives, she decided to respond to the Party's call and took the lead in swinging the plow side by side with men. Conservative elements derided her, stating that crops grown on land plowed by a woman 'would not be eaten even by Buddhas' and that if women could handle this work, there would be no point in having men in the first place. She brushed aside their derision and worked on. She plowed deep and obtained 15 'shoulder poles' of grain more than the neighboring land. The CCP _hsien_ committee awarded her a red flag, and asked all other women of the Tai nationality to follow her example. An increasing number of women began this year to learn to plow, and 360 of them in nine _hsiang_ were reported to have mastered the technique.

The Communists favor the participation of women in all agricultural tasks at least in part because it ensures a more complete utilization of the labor resources in the society. These actions, however, may well lower the prestige of certain tasks such as plowing.

The significance of belief in the phi, the complexes of livestock sacrifice associated with this culture trait, ceremonies involved with harvesting rice and the offerings made to the "soul of the rice" -- all discussed earlier in this study -- stem from the cultural pattern the Communist Chinese government is attempting to modify among the Tai and Meo peoples, as the following accounts show:

> In the Menghai district of the Hsishuangpanna Tai Nationality Chou there were farms which could only be cultivated when the rainy season came. During the big leap forward this year [1958], peasants of Tai nationality in the entire district built an irrigation project carrying water to all the farms. When the water channel was built to Mengfu village, it had to pass through the Dragon mountain where the dead were buried. According to traditional custom, even a single piece of grass and wood could not be removed, otherwise disasters would fall on the entire village. The Tai people of the village held a debate on this question. The conservative said: 'The old rule of our nationality forbids anyone from removing anything from Dragon Mountain." The progressive replied: 'For several hundred years we have not removed anything from it, but what good has this brought us? When irrigation channels are built, more grain can be harvested, and our children will enjoy prosperity.' The conservative retorted: 'If we offend the spirits of the mountain, disasters will fall upon us. Who takes the responsibility then?' And the progressive refuted him by saying, 'During the past several hundred years we have not removed anything from the mountain, but did the people not suffer from disease and die of it? Now sick people are treated in the government hospital. What should we be afraid of?' The oppositionists then became dumb. The masses said: 'Water is most important and our lives can be better off only when production is developed.' The irrigation channel was built across the mountain, and thus new ideas triumphed. . . .
>
> Even the most primitive and backward Kawa nationals[52] are now awakened and march forward. When Chia hsiang of the Ts'angyuan Kawa Nationality Autonomous

> Hsien decided to discard the primitive mode of production and open up paddy fields, the people were told that 'to open up paddy fields would involve our being beaten to death by the ghost.' But some of the braver people, with the determination that 'a beating by a ghost is not a thing to fear, because food is more important,' took the lead in opening up the fields. The masses, seeing that they were not beaten by the ghosts, also went one after another to the farms. Since this year, more than 1,000 mou of paddy fields were opened up in the entire hsiang. Once the Kawa people come to recognize their strength, they will not pin their hopes on the gods and spirits. Kawa people in many villages have stopped killing animals for offerings and have learned to use them for farming.[53]

Actual figures on the number of sacrifices and their economic cost were given in a Communist article called, "A Major Victory for Atheism -- Smashing Gods and Spirits: The Struggle of the Aini [Tai group] Nationality in Kelangho Ch'u Menghai Hsien, Yunnan Province":

> The Aini nationality . . . was much given to the worship of gods and spirits in the past. For family it had a 'family god' and for fields a 'field god' or 'land god.' These gods were regarded as the protectors of men. Pigs and chickens were killed as offerings to them on festivals twelve times a year and at 'ritual performances.' The hills, streams, meadows and trees; natural phenomena such as wind, rain, thunder and lightning; wild beasts such as tigers and leopards and domesticated animals such as oxen and horses; men's illness and death were linked with the work of spirits. To ward off devils, a 'lung-pa' gate was erected in front and at the rear of each stockade. The structure was believed to have the usefulness of keeping off evil spirits. Whenever some untoward event happened such as a storm, hail, fire, death, an insect plague . . . the inhabitants believed that the spirits were causing trouble. To escape the devils, the inhabitants inside would not venture out of the 'lung-pa' gate. These were called 'lung days'. On these days they also killed chickens, pigs or oxen to offer as sacrifices. . . .
>
> The working people each year handed out a large sum of money to offer sacrifices to the gods and spirits, which rendered it more difficult for them to extricate

themselves from the quagmire of poverty. They resorted to loans and worked as domestic laborers, enduring the exploitation of the landlord class. According to the estimate of a poor peasant named Jih Yu, his outlay for superstition in 1949 amounted to one-fourth of his total income, which was a very common case. Some people spent more than half of their income for the sake of superstition. Statistics show that over 300,000 working days were wasted in the whole ch'u last year on account of 'festivals,' 'lung days,' and 'ritual performances.' Over 5,000 pigs, 7,000 chickens, 500 dogs and 100 sheep were killed each year as offerings, and over 10,000 yen spent.[54]

The class basis of superstitious beliefs was gradually eliminated in 1958, and the prestige and influence of the Party rose to a great height in this year. A troop of anti-superstition activists emerged in the course of the class struggle, the production struggle and various anti-superstition campaigns over the past several years. They related their personal experience of breaching the superstitious traditions handed down from their ancestors without incurring any calamity, and bolstered the awakening masses in the campaign to stamp out beliefs in gods and spirits.

During the free criticism and debate, the masses exposed not a few cases of the landlord class exploiting the working people, sabotaging production and wrecking the Party line through the utilization of superstition. The superstitious customs and practices of the Aini people in Kelangho ch'u have been completely obliterated following the campaign. The people have dismantled the 'lung-pa' gate, tossed away family gods, reclaimed the wasteland on the Lung Hill, the earth of which they never dared touch before, collected manure, launched production in a big way and reaped the most bountiful harvest in their history.

The people remarked, 'For several thousand years, generation after generation, we believed in gods and spirits and offered sacrifices without ever being able to rear our head. Last year we listened to Chairman Mao and no longer believed in gods and spirits. Now we rely on the Communist Party, the people's commune and ourselves for our livelihood.' This is the folk song popular with the Aini people:

Pull down the Lung-pa gate
Believe not in gods or fate.
Hills become a paradise,
Production shows a big rise.[55]

The propagandist fervor of these accounts is, of course, obvious. But the dubious accuracy of certain statements and statistics is in a sense a minor matter: the important thing here is the ultimate intention of remaking, according to a preconceived pattern, the lives of the people concerned. The Communist attitude toward the cultures of the minority peoples seems to parallel that of old-fashioned Christian missionaries at many points although the former used coercive force which the latter did not.

Lao Government Planning

One of the tragedies of the Laos situation has been that the government has never defined, even in theory, any long-range program of resettlement of the tribal peoples. The Department of Water and Forests has evidenced concern, proposing several limited resettlement schemes, but their interest has been mainly in the preservation of the forests. A speech by the Lao Commissioner for Rural Affairs at a UNESCO International Conference on "Social Research and Problems of Rural Life in Southeast Asia" (1960) does not even mention this problem. The closest approximations to a policy statement are the comments of the former Lao Director of Social Welfare (quoted in Kaufman 1963: 17) who defined "resettlement" as a long-term program consisting of six steps: (1) psychological preparation for valley life and wet-rice cultivation, (2) temporary subsidization during the transitional period, (3) technical advice and assistance, (4) schools with instruction in Lao, (5) medical aid in the form of dispensaries, and (6) conversion to Buddhism.

The first step was intermittent propaganda dispensed by various government rural aid programs, in some cases closely associated with the military and in all cases almost completely financed by foreign aid, largely American. With regard to the other points, performance has been spotty, with lack of coordination by the various government agencies concerned. A few cases of direct subsidies for resettlement exist, some technical advice has been given, a few schools have been built, but health facilities remain nonexistent in most areas. Sporadic attempts have been made over the past few centuries, by Lao monks, to convert tribal peoples to Buddhism; in no sense can these efforts be considered part of a government program in the way that Communism as a secular faith relates to Chinese and North Vietnamese efforts. What is implied here is a not-so-subtle Laotianization to be linked up with a change in agricultural practices. This position appears unintentionally designed to increase opposition among the mountain peoples even if the subsidies and health services might be welcomed. The Communist authorities also aim for assimilation and the destruction of religious practices which they consider to interfere with the process. In their mode of operation they do, however, make explicit concessions to cultural distinctiveness in terms of using the local language and implementing these programs through trained officials of local origin.

An example of difficulties involved in Lao government attempts at resettlement is given in the case of a comparatively small group of two thousand Black Tai refugees from North Vietnam who originally settled in Xieng Khouang in 1955 on the advice of the Vientiane government. Promised funds for an irrigation dam never materialized, and the headman petitioned the government to transfer the group. Subsequently the group was moved to an area north of Vientiane town. The government began clearing some land for houses; the American aid mission, acting through the government, made available forty tons of rice; and the French government contributed money for agricultural tools. But before the job was completed the government withdrew its bulldozing equipment, in order, rumor had it, to work on a road leading to the home of a high government official. In any case the Black Tai were unable to make their traditional wet-rice fields and so utilized swidden techniques. A number of men became small-scale merchants and some of the women went to work as domestics in Vientiane.

Presenting a sharp contrast was the quick resettlement of about two hundred Lao who had returned to their ancestral homes in 1957. These Lao had originally migrated in the eighteenth century, due to warfare, to the area of the Burma-Laos-Thailand border, and current conflicts among the Karen forced them to retrace their steps. Undoubtedly ethnic factors were involved in their quick resettlement in Laos and in the friendly help extended by the government. In the case of the Black Tai the government claimed that the Black Tai were unwilling to contribute to the cost of their own resettlement. Perhaps more significant was a lack of confidence and understanding between the two groups which, combined with the lack of a clear program, would be more than sufficient to defeat half-hearted efforts.

The traditional agricultural techniques described in these pages for the Lao, Khmu, Tai, and Meo are now subject to increasing external and internal pressures for change. The relationship between agriculture, livestock raising, and religion on one hand and politics on the other seems destined to become much closer in Laos.

The government's Five Year Plan (Laos 1959), implemented with foreign technical and financial assistance, listed major objectives in agriculture and livestock raising.[56] Stress was also placed on increasing the number of trained personnel.[57]

Lacking sufficient trained personnel and financial resources to implement its programs, the government of Laos has had to look abroad for aid, which has come in the past from a variety of sources -- the United States, the Colombo Plan, France, and the United Nations. For example, experts from the Food and Agricultural Organization made surveys and recommendations; French technicians have been working directly with officials in the Ministry of Agriculture; and the United States Operations Mission to Laos, major source of financial support, has for several years maintained a separate agriculture division with experts in irrigation engineering, rice production, poultry breeding, and veterinary medicine.

In the private sphere, two nongovernmental organizations -- International Voluntary Services (American) and Operation Brotherhood (Filipino) -- have done extensive work in the provinces. The American group is composed mostly of young men with rural backgrounds who work for a nominal salary under the direction of a professional agronomist. Their activities, mainly among the Meo in Xieng Khouang, have ranged from the introduction of improved varieties of sweet potatoes and the importation of block mineral salt for livestock use to practical education in the use of fertilizer on rice and other crops, insect and rodent control, the raising of rabbits, ducks, and pigeons, and the importance of castrating scrub bulls. In addition, IVS groups have been studying the possibilities of improved marketing and storage procedures.

Some of the operational problems involved in such technical assistance programs are illustrated by IVS resettlement efforts. The headmen of two villages in the Phongsavanh area of Xieng Khouang took the lead in advocating a shift to irrigated rice cultivation despite the strong doubts of many of the Meo that their survival was possible in the lowlands, where the temperature was higher and the cultivation of rice necessitated working long hours wading in water. Further assurance came from Touby Lyfong, the nominal leader of the Meo people, who publicly endorsed the proposed change.

In 1958 the district officer planted several hectares of paddy rice on the plains. This first attempt coincided with a year of below-average rainfall and a resultant drop in the yield of upland rice. The higher yield in the paddy fields convinced some people that it would be wise to consider a change in agricultural methods. But there were several drawbacks, notably that most of the easily irrigated lowlands were already being used by the Lao and that, in order to provide water for the new, higher areas, canals would have to be dug for several kilometers along the contours of the mountainside to provide a gravity flow of water to the rice fields. An irrigation ditch one and a half kilometers long was built but, partly because Lao farmers diverted a large part of the water and partly because the ditch was damaged by buffalo in several places, adequate water never reached the Meo area. Attempts continued for a while to work out the difficulties, but those Meo who stayed had to purchase na fields from the Lao.

Basic to the continued implementation of these and similar programs is the education of Lao technicians. France has, of course, been the most important country in this regard, providing scholarships for study in France and in the schools established in Vietnam and Cambodia. The American aid mission has sent many more students and administrative personnel abroad, chiefly to Thailand but also to the Philippines and the United States. The training periods have ranged from a few weeks for a conference or tour for Lao administrative personnel to up to a year for intensive courses for more junior employees.

How significant are these programs in coming to grips with the basic agricultural problems of Laos? It is certainly easy to criticize them as being scattered, superficial, and lacking in continuity. For example, a major factor in the improved seed and livestock program has been the distribution of both the materials and techniques on a broad scale. There are also many small technical problems, some of which are not always anticipated; an imported boar or chicken often has too hearty or fussy an appetite to scavenge.

Western veterinary medicine is not always easy to practice in areas which have long relied almost completely on traditional cures. Minor officials, sometimes overimpressed with their importance, may substitute coercion for patient explanation, and frequently a new program dies as soon as the foreign technician departs. On another level, communication is a problem for the foreign technician and his Lao counterpart. More often than not Americans have lacked knowledge of either French or Lao. For the Lao educated abroad there is the problem of adapting complex foreign techniques to specific situations in Laos, often without the tools he has been taught to use.

None of these difficulties, however, is insurmountable. Groups like International Voluntary Services and Operation Brotherhood, based in the provinces and staffed by personnel usually concerned to learn the local languages (Lao or Meo in these cases), frequently are much more effective than American technicians in Vientiane who get out only on field trips. Many projects of the American aid program have been of a long-term nature with no immediate or dramatic results (and, more significantly, the major part of aid funds has been spent for military purposes).

The key problem here appears to be the training of Laotian personnel from all ethnic groups and at all levels to assume a greater portion of the responsibility for programs of innovation and extension. But for such developments political stability is essential. The overall outlook is not bright. On the other hand the Communists, in destroying the traditions associated with agricultural production, may also find that the tribal peoples will become increasingly dissatisfied with village life and less interested in being farmers.

ELEPHANT HAULING TEAK LOGS

WATER BUFFALO GRAZING IN PADDY FIELDS DURING DRY SEASON

VEGETABLE GARDENS ON THE MEKONG AT LUANG PRABANG

SWIDDEN LANDSCAPE IN NORTHERN LAOS

LAO WOMAN STEAMING GLUTINOUS RICE

MEO TRADERS AT LAO ROADSIDE VILLAGE

WASHING CLOTHES IN THE RIVER AT LUANG PRABANG

KHMU VILLAGERS DRINKING RICE WINE

III

THE RURAL AND URBAN ECONOMIES

Just as great differences exist in the economic productivity of different societies, so too are there variations in the amount of expenditure on basic necessities. Certain minimum expenditures or allocations of resources are determined by biological imperatives, but beyond these irreducible minimums cultural traditions play a most important role. The degree of economic productivity and resulting surplus provides a limiting but not determining factor for the rural population.[1]"

Food

In the Laotian context a minimum with regard to food involves getting enough rice to avoid hunger and to carry on one's daily activities. In peacetime, actual starvation is rare or nonexistent in Laos and people do not have to struggle to survive in an inhospitable environment. Still hunger is not uncommon, particularly in the period before the rice harvest when the previous year's stocks near depletion. Malnutrition is also prevalent, often in extreme forms, a significant factor being the preponderance of rice in the diet. Crudely milled glutinous rice is the food staple and to a certain extent is actually more nourishing than the Laotians would desire: the foot- and hand-pounders which mill most of the villagers' rice are far less efficient in destroying the outer hulls than the power-operated machine mills used extensively in Thailand. This would lead to a conclusion that town dwellers suffer from malnutrition more than villagers, but a compensating factor in the towns is the relatively greater access to a larger variety of foods (see Table 20).

Rice forms the basis of every meal and is reflected linguistically in the verb "to eat" (kin khao) which, literally translated, means "to eat rice."[2] The Lao often mentions his preference for glutinous rice as a means of asserting cultural identity, differentiating himself from the Chinese and Vietnamese.

It is difficult to categorize any group as regularly underproducing or overproducing rice since there is a good deal of variation among ethnic groups, villages, and even households, in addition to yearly differences due to fluctuating climatic conditions. But some general patterns are discernible. The Khmu and the Lamet often have surpluses to sell to the valley Lao, though the very opposite is sometimes the case, e.g. in the area surrounding the royal capital where the impoverished Khmu frequently must purchase rice from the Lao. The Meo appear for the most part to be self-sufficient. Poor crops due to lack of adequate rainfall in recent years have compelled Khmu and Lao to buy rice to a greater degree than was previously the case.

In order to get an idea of rice consumption among the Lao, aspects of "consumption" other than as food for the family have to be differentiated. These include losses in the process of milling, seed for the next year's crop, the daily contribution to the bonzes (regarded as an obligation by all Lao), daily special offerings to the phi, food for guests, the making of rice wine, and the sometimes considerable losses due to rats.[3] Another important but variable form of rice consumption is as payment in kind in the case of land rental.

The largest individual uses of rice are of course for food, for seed, and for making alcohol, the latter showing considerable variation. Rice for seed ranges from about ten per cent to less than two per cent; estimates of daily rice consumption per person from .2 kilos cited for the Lamet (Izikowitz 1951: 287) to from .5 to .8 kilos in the Vientiane and Luang Prabang areas.[4] In terms of yearly individual consumption, rural figures from the Vientiane area and the Bangkok plain are almost the same, roughly 250 kilos. Since there are significant differences in crop yields in these two areas, this approximation implies that although production increases personal consumption tends to remain the same.

What happens in those cases where there is not enough rice and the villagers cannot secure an additional supply? The Meo of the Luang Prabang area turn to corn, which is pulverized on grindstones turned by hand. To a much lesser extent some Khmu and Lao also eat corn. Among both the Khmu and the Lamet the gathering of forest plants, particularly bamboo shoots and tubers, is of considerable importance. Forest products such as various roots, greens, and flowers, as well as frogs and insects, figure in the diet of the Lao. For all groups these other sources are particularly significant in the month or so before the harvest.

But would it be possible for any of the people to survive without rice, living only on gathering, fishing, and hunting? Izikowitz (1951: 174) posed this question to some Lamet, who replied that they could get along for most of the year but that many people would surely starve during the difficult spring months. The women would have to seek wild plants in the forest constantly, and the men would be obliged to fish and hunt day and night. Living would not be tolerable again until the rainy season.

The Lao eating pattern of three meals a day consists of glutinous rice served with chilis and padek, a spicy fish paste, sometimes accompanied by curries or other vegetable dishes. Fish is served occasionally; meat is rarely consumed (see Table 21). Often fruit is eaten between meals. The morning and evening meals are served warm and the noon meal is usually cold leftovers from breakfast. Variations in the supply of certain fruits, vegetables, and fish account for minor regional differences in diet but other differences arise from the economic status of the household, particularly with regard to store-bought foods such as beverages, bread, and canned goods.

As noted earlier, the consumption of meat among all groups is usually associated with ceremonial and ritual occasions. Products of the hunt, although significant, are fortuitous and in any case can be considered a possibility only when there is a slackening in the primary tasks involved with agricultural work. Dishes utilizing small amounts of meat or fish combined with other ingredients are traditional Lao delicacies and as such are often on sale in the town markets. (Table 22 describes some of these specialties and their method of preparation.)

Like the Lao, the Meo practice certain preserving techniques: pork is smoked and beef is sometimes salted and dried. These simple methods are easier for them than for lowland peoples because of the cooler, drier air on the mountaintops.

The Lao, Meo, and Khmu reflect Chinese rather than Indian civilization in making no use of fresh milk or milk products.[5] Canned evaporated milk is sometimes added as a luxurious touch to coffee, tea, or cocoa by prosperous villagers but is not part of the diet of children or of pregnant women.

A survey in the Ubol area provides some interesting data on protein sources of the Lao in Northeast Thailand which with minor modifications hold for the Lao in Laos. It was found that the average villager eats meat only about twice a week, and even the more prosperous villagers but three or four times a week. Approximately ninety per cent of the time meat is purchased for these occasions (Bertholet 1958: 76-91). This supports the view that buffalo and cattle in particular are raised largely for prestige and ritual purposes. As noted, no use is made of their milk, limited slaughtering occurs, and cattle are not used as draft animals.

By contrast, chicken is eaten as frequently as once a week by practically every family in the rural area around Ubol. Most of the poultry is raised at home and about seventy-five per cent of the villagers consider chicken eggs a normal part of their diet. For the Khmu it is felt that game and poultry are more important than buffalo and pigs as sources of meat (Smalley 1952).

Fish constitutes a very important part of the villager's diet in Ubol, being the only high-quality protein food eaten at least once a day, sometimes more often. Especially popular are the small fish (less than two inches long) which abound in the rivers, ditches, lakes, and rice fields during the rainy season. Their availability and therefore their consumption gradually decrease during the dry season although fish can still be caught in the rivers. Fish figures less prominently in the diet of the Lao in Laos and, of course, still less among the mountain peoples.

After fish, the most frequently used protein food in the Ubol district is the frog, which can be caught throughout the year but becomes particularly easy to find during the rainy season. As in Laos, the villagers eat several kinds of insects, some of which are available only seasonally. Snails, shrimp, and small crabs are also consumed during the rainy season. Sometimes silkworms are eaten.

There appears to be a strong cultural preference by pregnant women for certain foods such as citrus fruits and larger amounts of glutinous rice are consumed. During the weeks immediately before and after delivery, women are restricted to a diet of rice and salt. Infants are breast-fed for about twenty months or until another baby is born. A few weeks after birth, the child is introduced to small amounts of pre-chewed glutinous rice and banana and by about one has approximately the same diet as the average villager.

Although it cannot properly be called an item of diet, betel nut is regarded as a necessity by many rural Lao and Khmu. At one time the blackened teeth and stained gums which result from continued betel chewing were considered a sign of beauty. Now it is largely older Lao who chew betel, most of the younger, educated Lao regarding the habit with disdain. Many Khmu, of all ages, still use betel. The juice is spat out rather than swallowed and the presence of a spittoon in most urban Lao homes attests to the persistence of betel chewing. Tobacco, both home-grown and processed, is also widely used, particularly by males. It is chewed as well as smoked.

To sum up, rice is the basic food of the peoples of Laos, supplemented by vegetables and meat, fish, and forest products. Fish is of varying importance among the Lao and meat is consumed sparingly or on special occasions by all groups. With the exceptions of rice, salt, certain vegetables, forest products, and possibly crude sugar and tobacco, all other items of food for personal consumption are considered luxuries to be enjoyed only on special occasions.

Housing

There are a number of features common to all Lao village dwellings: a rectangular plan, location near paths and rivers, and orientation away from the west, the direction said to be traveled by the dead (see Figures 3 and 4). Their typical construction on wooden piles about six feet off the ground offers many advantages, namely, the living quarters are raised above the rainy season mud and are protected from the village dogs and chickens. The space underneath provides storage place for a loom, firewood, livestock, and sometimes the rice bin. In cases of minimum standards the house itself has a split bamboo floor and woven bamboo walls, with one main room. The thatch roof slopes over a bamboo veranda running along one length of the house, and at the rear of this porch is usually a wooden frame filled with sand, the base for the charcoal or wood fire over which cooking is done. Here too is the place where food, utensils, and sometimes people get washed, with waste water poured off through cracks in the bamboo flooring. Garbage is disposed of in a similar manner, to the pigs and chickens below. On a post next to the entrance ladder there is often a moss-covered clay pot for drinking water.

An average dwelling can be constructed rapidly with a minimum of expense when a group of villagers pool their labor in customary fashion. A 1957 estimate put the cost of materials for an all-wood house with thatch roof at approximately 16,000 kip and for an average bamboo house at about 10,000 kip. The builder supplies food and rice wine for the workers, who usually contribute their labor on the same reciprocal basis used in transplanting and harvesting rice. Often the construction and dedication of a new dwelling are marked by a celebration in which the women of the neighborhood share the cooking; in the evening the village youth participate in a traditional love court.

The following is a description of the ceremonies connected with house construction in the Luang Prabang region (Srisvasdi 1950):

> In building a new house they ask each other's help, calling it 'taking a meal to build a new house.' There is no hiring at all. The principal pillar has bananas, dried areca, and

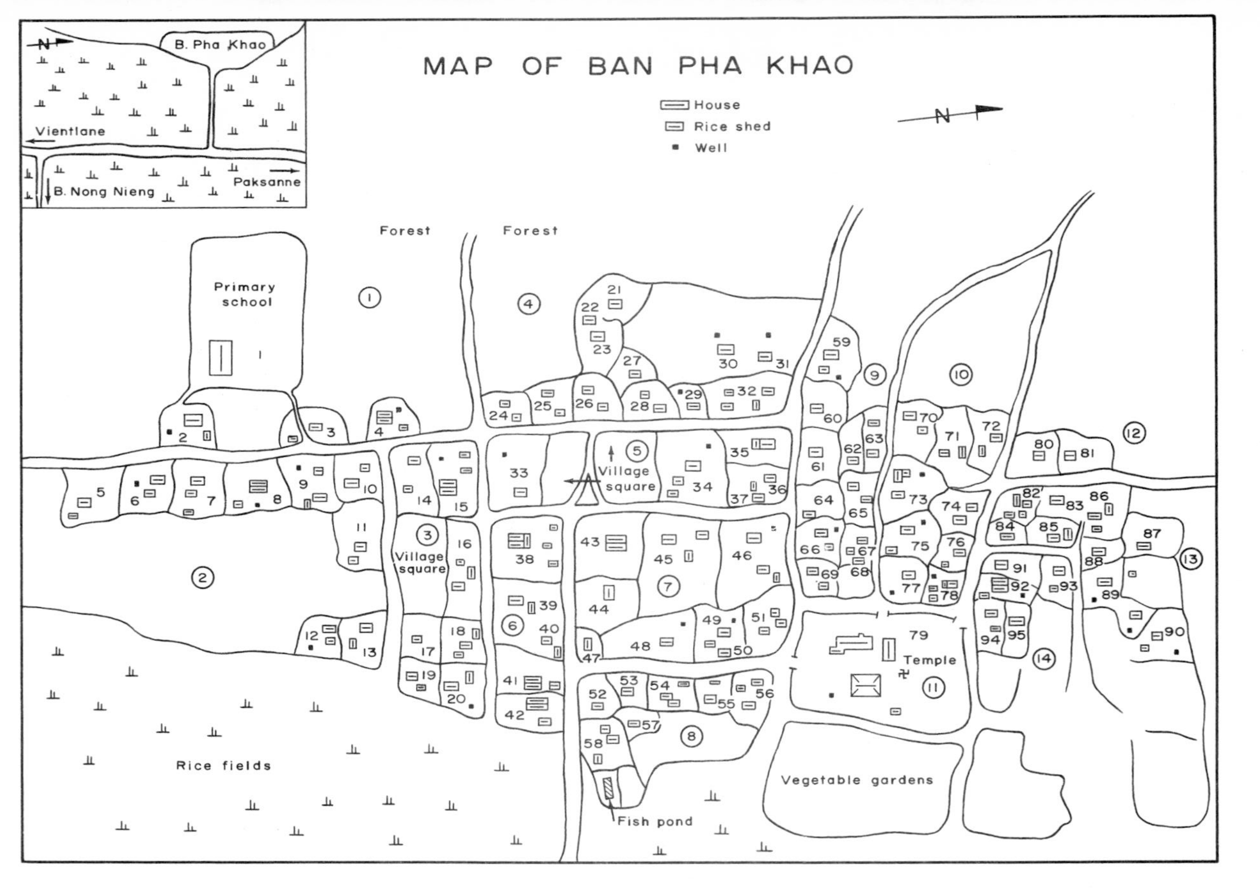

FIGURE 3

From Tsuneo Ayabe, "The Village of Ban Pha Khao, Vientiane Province," Laos Project No. 14.

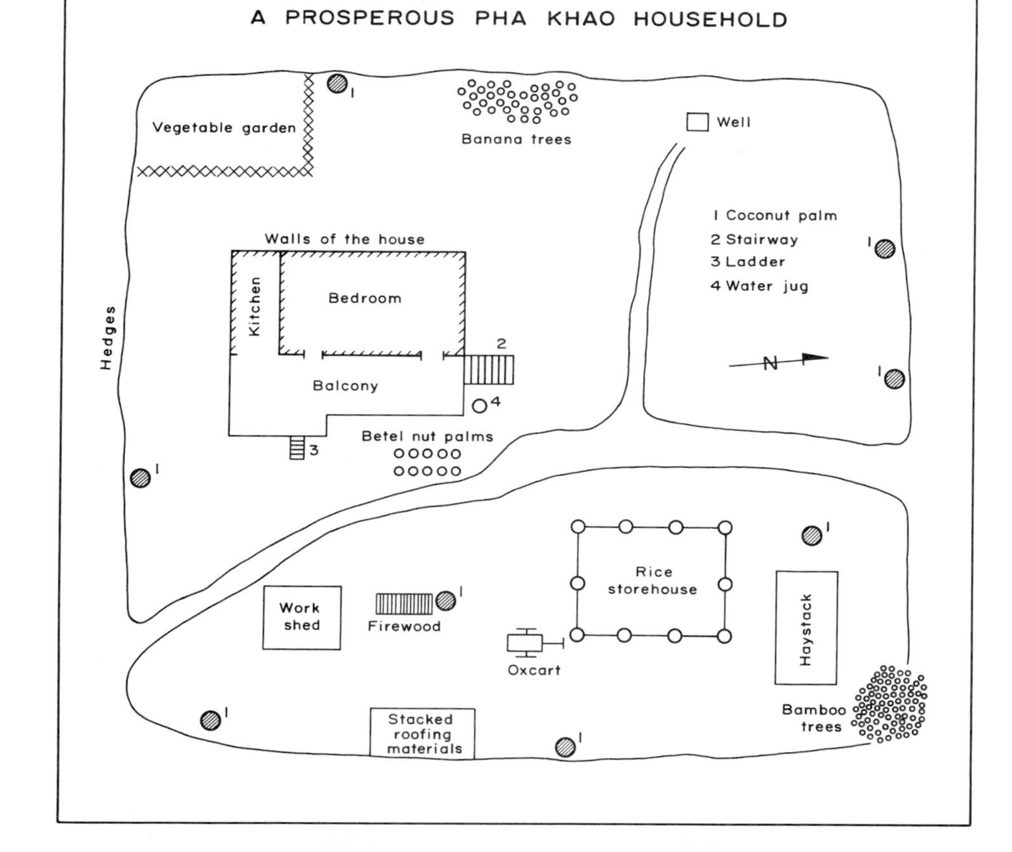

FIGURE 4

From Tsuneo Ayabe, "The Village of Ban Pha Khao, Vientiane Province," Laos Project No. 14.

white thread tied to it, together with a fishtrap. This is called lag chai, literally 'stake of victory.' When this is finished, they find a prop for it and then invite monks to come and chant in the evening. Next morning at the time of the 'silver and gold light' they bury it, because they believe that if they set the principal pillar when the silver and gold light is shining in the sky this is tantamount to putting these precious metals into the new house. When they have finished setting up the principal pillar, they set to work until the house is finished. When it is finished the monks are invited to come and pray for the second time. Then the old people are invited to enter the house after which the possessions are moved in and a feast is held.

Bamboo is usually available locally, as is hardwood (usually teak) for the house posts. The woven bamboo walls allow for relatively free circulation of air, and a bamboo floor has enough give to make sleeping on it on mats comfortable. Windows are found only in the more prosperous homes.

A bamboo house is neither very prestigious nor adequate for a large household, so that bigger and better houses are built whenever possible. More space is usually the first requirement and among certain groups such as the tribal Tai, where extended family groups live together, becomes a necessity, with the main room subdivided into a number of sleeping compartments.

A larger house is constructed of wooden planks but with thatch probably retained as the roofing material. In some more developed areas, such as the Lao villages around Vientiane, wooden plank floors are a regular feature in house construction. These floors per se imply a higher standard of living, because of the accompanying use of kapok-stuffed sleeping pads instead of woven fiber mats. In more prosperous homes the walls are also of wood and the traditional roof may be replaced with corrugated tin or, more customarily, tile. A further development is the use of a sort of wattle-and-daub cementing over a bamboo framework.

Sometimes there are separate sheds for cooking and storage, a small granary on piles adjacent to the house, and, occasionally, seed beds on platforms out of reach of the animals. Larger compounds include a vegetable garden. Clumps of bamboo and banana trees commonly serve as boundary markers.

Although wooden houses doubtless offer more protection during chilly winter nights, many lack sufficient ventilation --

windows, if constructed, are frequently small and ineffective -- and for most of the year are actually less comfortable than the simpler bamboo houses.[6]

Only the major towns of Laos are electrified. Some rural homes use crude kerosene lamps made from tin cans, and a very few have pressure lamps with incandescent mantles. In others there may be a resin torch or a flashlight. Because of the constant drafts, candles are impractical as a source of light. The villagers retire when it gets dark.

Rural Lao consider their homes sacred places presided over by a resident spirit (phi huan). An altar is built near one of the posts for this spirit, who is consulted frequently and offered balls of rice, flowers, and candles. Several small images of Buddha may also be kept here.

Since the Lao live and eat on the floor, home furnishings are minimal, typically consisting of a few low, round stools and tables made of plaited bamboo on a rattan frame, some wall pegs for clothing, and perhaps a bamboo cradle hung from the rafters. Sleeping mats are rolled up along the wall during the day. The home of a village headman might have in addition a table and chair for conducting official business,[7] a few cheap suitcases for storing clothes, and some enamel dishes and other utensils (including a spittoon).

The use of mosquito nets is a conspicuous status symbol in the homes of teachers, headmen, and some of the wealthier farmers, but for most villagers netting is not only too expensive but not really a felt need.

Khmu houses are basically similar to those of the Lao but more modest. This description of the setting up of a household as described by a Khmu can also be taken as indicative of the fundamental requirements of the Lao in the Luang Prabang area (excerpted from Smalley 1952):

> Husband and wife wish to put up a house and live apart from their parents.[8] They go and cut saplings and trees and carry them back. Then they go and cut thatch and when it is carried back to the house site the wife makes thatch panels. When the panels are ready they build the house.[9] When the house has been built they go and look for furnishings, clothing and tools. They buy a machete then a weeding tool, a digging stick with an iron tip, an ax and a small pointed knife. Then the husband goes and

> brings in vines from which he makes a large basket for storing seed rice for the next year. Then he weaves a basket for cooked rice and a flat tray for winnowing rice.[10] When these things have been woven he goes and looks for money and buys earthenware pots, dish, spoon, cup, blanket, pillow, sleeping mat and clothing. Then he goes and buys chickens, pig, dog, duck, buffalo and goat.

The only absolutely essential purchased items are the iron tools used for building the house, cultivating the fields, and cutting the vines. The clothing and livestock mentioned represent more of an aspiration than an easily achievable reality.

Meo houses are, like most other aspects of their culture, quite distinct from those of the Lao and, as the material culture of the Meo has changed relatively little in recent years, Reinach's observations of over sixty years ago (1901: 407) still apply:

> A Meo house is built at ground level. Walls are made of puddled clay or ill-fitting boards, and the house is roofed with thatch or crudely squared wooden shingles. The doors are made of wood shaped with an ax, and there are no windows. Often several [nuclear] families live in the same house, and each family has a fireplace and a compartment which serves as a bedroom. In the common room there is an oven and a fireplace above which objects are placed to dry on a bamboo framework. . . . In front there is a narrow veranda where the horses are kept when not housed in a stable built on piles and overhanging the mountainside, as are the animal barn, pig sty, the rice granary and the goat pen. This protects the animals from dampness. Inside the house there are few furnishings . . . benches, tables, crude beds, dishes, iron and copper utensils and opium smoking accessories, all very dirty.

It takes several minutes for a person entering a Meo home during the daytime to get accustomed to the darkness inside. This darkness of the windowless Meo house is intensified by the accumulation of black soot on most of the interior, caused by the fact that the Meo house has no chimney. This dark, closed atmosphere is in dramatic contrast to the airiness of the Lao house. Since the Meo move their villages every few decades, house construction tends to be casual. The boards, beams, supporting posts, intersecting walls, and all parts of the roof are roughly hewn, the wooden parts lashed together with rattan; nailing or notching is rare.

The size of the house is directly related to the size of the family and reflects the household wealth, which is roughly proportionate to the number of able-bodied males. Every house has two entrances and, along one side, a series of elevated compartments in which the individual nuclear families sleep.

Against the wall facing the main entrance is a fireplace for cooking, with tables and shelves for utensils nearby. On the same wall is the altar to the house spirit, a rice mortar, and a place where guests can rest. The Meo, more than the Lao, live off the floor, which is earth rather than wood or bamboo. Each house has a separate storage loft for saddles, carrying bags, nets, smoked meat, corn, and grain. The loft, in contrast to the house, is built on piles as protection against dampness and the intrusion of mice, rats, pigs, or other animals.

The site of a new home is chosen with care. The ancestor spirits are asked whether the choice for the site is an auspicious one, and omens or unfavorable dreams may affect the choice. When the corner posts are driven in, the future owner proclaims loudly, "May the evil spirits stay away from this place in the future, for now I am going to live here." Once the house is completed, a temporary altar is erected and the owner sacrifices two chickens, inviting the ancestors and spirits to move into their new residence (Bernatzik 1947: 298-318).

Lamet houses are built on piles but are not as far off the ground as those of the Lao. A distinctive feature of housing among the Lower Lamet is that every sleeping place has its own hearth -- the fires providing illumination as well as warmth during the damp, cold nights of the winter months and the smoke helping to ward off gnats and mosquitoes. The row of hearths forms a line of demarcation dividing the rest of the room from the private area into which a stranger is not supposed to intrude. It is possible that these fires are also regarded as protection against evil spirits for fire is used ritually in driving out the spirit of death and as a safeguard from it.

Every Lamet village has a community house which functions as the gathering place for the men and as sleeping quarters for bachelors and strangers. This house, constructed of bamboo, is distinguished by double doors adorned with a carving of a buffalo head and typically contains the large village drum, partitions and shelves for implements and hunting equipment, sacrificial poles anchored by stones smeared with the blood of a sacrificial pig, and, often, the forge of the village smithy (Izikowitz 1951: 65-79).

Knowledge of the traditions associated with house building can be of great importance to government administrators in charge of resettlement programs, as numerous recent examples attest. The failure of government planners to consider cultural patterns has resulted in certain cases in villagers' refusal to occupy new housing built by the Lao government. The sanctity of the home is also significant in any program of resettlement of mountain peoples and, furthermore, their attitudes with regard to village and household spirits must be taken into account. This is not to say that these customs are immutable but that a successful program cannot ignore them. The Communist governments in neighboring North Vietnam and Yunnan have deliberately set out to destroy similar beliefs with intense propaganda campaigns. How successful these campaigns will be remains to be seen. But, even if successful, the Communists will not have solved the whole problem for the decline in the sacredness of the home and the village may heighten dissatisfaction with rural life. Selective destruction does not appear to be possible.

Clothing

Just what constitutes the basic clothing requirement would be rather difficult to define, since during most of the year it is possible to survive quite well with only a negligible amount.[11] Among the Lao, infants and small children frequently go naked. More important than clothing, particularly for children, is silver -- or preferably gold -- jewelry in the form of anklets, bracelets, or small Buddha medals suspended on chains or cords around the neck. Jewelry is believed to protect the wearer from harm and prevent the khwan (soul) from leaving his body and so causing illness. Village people believe the khwan has an affinity for gold. In terms of Lao culture, this jewelry can, because of its supposed protective and therapeutic value, be considered an essential item.

Most Lao villagers have at least one set of clothes for work in the fields and another for bouns or holidays. The former is usually woven at home, while the good clothes, a Western-style pair of trousers and shirt, are bought in town. Men regard homespun clothing as inferior to and less attractive than Western-style clothing. A handwoven indigo-dyed cotton shirt and short pants are the most common male outfit for work in the fields, with perhaps a few men wearing Western-style shirts. A man will sometimes work in, and usually bathes in, a pakhoma or short cotton sarong wrapped around the waist. In addition, he may have a longer plaid silk sarong for informal use around the house.

The traditional male garment, still worn on ceremonial occasions, is the sampot, which is usually woven of bright silk in shades of pink, purple, blue, or emerald green. The sampot is wrapped around the waist like a sarong, drawn up loosely between the legs, and tucked into the rear waistband. Some older men wear the sampot all the time, and it is official Lao dress for formal occasions when worn with a high-necked white jacket. Shoes and socks are uncommon in rural areas but are often worn in towns.

The basic dress of the rural Lao woman is the sin, a handloomed sarong-like skirt embellished with a characteristic Lao border at the hemline. It may vary from a simple striped cotton skirt to one of dark red, wine, or brown iridescent silk trimmed with an elaborate silver or gold woven border. This skirt is made exclusively within Laos by the Lao women themselves. Urban Lao women too, even those who go abroad, continue to wear this distinctive garment, which is something of a national trademark.

Formerly no upper garment was worn and there are still today towns as well as villages where small girls and old women wear only a skirt, but Western notions of style and modesty have penetrated into many rural areas. Girls and younger women wear blouses imported from Hong Kong, and older women wear a simple white cotton halter. On ceremonial occasions the traditional draped scarf is always worn. In urban areas it is of shimmering silk, with finely woven elaborate designs in bright metallic thread. Older women wear an unadorned white scarf.

Gold jewelry is worn by both men and women, though women wear the greater amount. This is said to be because the khwan of a woman is weaker than that of a man and so requires more protection. Among wealthier Lao, investments are quite significant, amounting to several thousand kip just for hair ornaments, This ornament, a characteristic feature of Lao female dress, consists of strands of small gold beads arranged around the traditional chignon and surmounted by an ornate gold hairpin. Other popular items of jewelry are bracelets, necklaces, rings, earrings, and silver or gold belts. The Lao say: "A chicken is pretty because of its feathers, and a women is beautiful because of her dress." The villager considers jewelry a sound investment and sometimes uses it as security for a loan when in need of cash. The wristwatches worn by some men can also be included in the category of jewelry, since the need for accurate time-telling cannot be called necessary or even desirable in rural Laos.

The clothing of the Khmu is quite similar to that of the Lao (see Table 23). In fact, much of it is obtained from the Lao since the Khmu do no weaving themselves.[12] Very often their clothing has been bought second-hand or come as a gift from the Lao and is in poor condition. Some Khmu have but one set of clothing which will be worn until it literally falls apart. The men wear mostly homespun pants and shirts, and the women have striped cotton Lao skirts. One characteristic feature of their dress is a red or yellow draped headband or manufactured towel worn as a turban. Where possible, hairpins ornamented with old silver coins are added to the costume and, in some areas, necklaces of red and white beads. A Khmu woman may save the one blouse she owns to wear on a trade excursion to town.

Like the Khmu, the Lamet neither spin nor weave, obtaining their clothing from the neighboring Tai Lu. It is claimed that their wearing of clothes is of a relatively recent date (Izikowitz 1951: 111). The Khmu and Lamet who can afford to purchase blankets, which often are shared at night by two or three people huddled together. In cases where there is no money for blankets, a fire is kept burning on cold nights.

To a certain extent because of their sale of opium the Meo and Yao are generally the most prosperous tribal groups. Here there exists a very definite cash surplus which is invested in silver jewelry. Most adult men and women have at least one silver neck-ring (usually a hollow collar among the Meo and a slender solid ring among the Yao) and many have two or three, as well as solid silver bracelets.[13] This heavy jewelry is decorative but also has religious significance, and sometimes neck-rings are consecrated by a shaman. The flat rectangular plaque that hangs down the back and links the chains by which the neck-ring may be removed is intricately incised with symbols to ward off evil spirits.[14]

Meo neck-rings cannot be considered luxuries, like coffee or canned milk, but are essential items of social prestige. One couple in a Meo household of very modest means, where only salt and some fabric were purchased during the course of an entire year, complained of being chilly during the cold months from lack of adequate clothing and blankets. But when asked if their photograph could be taken, husband and wife disappeared into their house for a moment and reappeared with three large neck-rings apiece. These silver neck-rings represent a complex of values -- a convenient bank account, an item of social prestige, and a protection against evil forces.

Meo subgroups are distinguished by the dress of their women.

The Meo Kao (White Meo) wear short handwoven pleated skirts of flax with a batik imprint, painstakingly made by Meo Kao women in what time can be spared from household duties. Meo Lei (Striped Meo) women wear loose-fitting trousers and shirts of manufactured black fabric, with horizontal strips of red appliqued on the sleeves and large square collars embroidered in geometric designs. All Meo women wear distinctive black turbans. The front part of the head is usually shorn.

Male dress consists of loose-fitting black trousers secured around the waist with a large red sash. Instead of a shirt, the men wear brief bolero-type black jackets. A small black skull cap is frequently worn, and many men retain the pigtail. Evidently Meo dress, like housing, has changed little during the past few decades, as this description indicates (Franck 1926: 270-71):

> . . . the men wear a shirt or jacket that covers everything except what a shirt is most expected to cover, leaving bare a foot or more of the waist, with the navel as its central point of departure. But to every race its own ideas. The girls are not prudish, yet not at all forward, for their jackets, open almost to the navel and giving frequent half-glimpses of the breasts, were plainly designed for comfort rather than coquetry, as were their plaid skirts reaching hardly to their bare knees . . . a few men wore Chinese skull caps, red sashes, and dressed their hair in old Chinese fashion and the majority still had queues, while sometimes those of both sexes have as many as half a dozen silver collars on a single neck.

Meo dress has evidently proved more stable than that of either the Lao or Khmu, both of whom have adopted many items of European dress, e.g. the halters of the Lao village women, the short pants of village men, and the high heels and business suits of their urban counterparts. The Lao skirts have also become shorter under the Western influence. Those Meo who go to live in towns, however, adopt the dress of urban Lao. This is sometimes true of prosperous rural villagers and students as well. There appears to be a parochial stigma attached to tribal dress, which is as a result worn only in the rural areas today. These attitudes reflect acculturation to the dominant Lao culture as well as Westernization. One Meo village headman living near Luang Prabang, asked why he no longer wore the dress of his people, replied flatly that he wished to be modern and live like the Lao.

Within Laos, groups such as the Tai Dam, Yao, Kha Ko,

and Vietnamese have sharply defined forms of dress. In all cases it is the women's costumes which are most distinctive, perhaps because the women tend to be more conservative or tradition-oriented in matters of dress. As manufactured fabrics become more easily available and cheaper, these distinctive modes of dress will gradually be abandoned, although rising national consciousness could slow or even reverse the process. A case in point is the proud wearing of the characteristic Lao skirt in Bangkok or Saigon and its adaptation as the Air Laos hostess uniform."

In directing the acculturation of tribal peoples, the Communist countries of China and Vietnam favor the retention of such innocuous manifestations of cultural variation as dress. In fact, museums have been set up to preserve traditional costumes, and publications for foreign consumption frequently carry articles describing tribal dress.

Ceremonial and Religious Needs

As noted earlier, the use of livestock for sacrifice to the cult of the phi constitutes a great expense in Lao, Khmu, and Meo economies. Additional religious and ceremonial expenses are incurred by the Lao in their support of Buddhism.

Almost every Lao village has a wat with a few bonzes and several novices; larger villages have two or three pagodas. In accord with Buddhist doctrine it is considered a privilege as well as an obligation of the village population to fill the bonzes' begging bowls with rice as they make their rounds of the village every morning (or sometimes the villagers go to the wat, where the bonzes wait in line for their food). On holidays special meals are brought to the wat, and on ceremonial days gifts are made to the bonzes. These may be in the form of money, sacred manuscripts, or personal needs such as sandals, fans, and the traditional yellow robes, or more modern items such as cigarettes, pillows, mosquito nets, pencils, notebooks, kerosene lamps, teakettles, brooms, umbrellas, and cuspidors. In fact, since the bonzes have no independent source of income, everything they use must be supplied by the laity.

A villager does not regard these contributions as an onerous burden; rather it is one of the ways in which he may gain merit for his future life. Thus expenditures for religious gifts are extremely important to emotional security. Nor are the monks strangers to the villagers: fathers, sons, and brothers of the villagers predominate in the bonzehood, for in the Buddhist faith as practiced in Laos and Thailand it is the accepted pattern for a man to become a bonze for a few months or years and then, except for the few who choose to be monks for life, freely revert to his secular way of living. Often a villager can give support directly to the relative who is a monk.

In addition to maintaining the personnel of the pagoda, villagers are responsible for the upkeep of the wat itself. The bonzes may do some repair work in the pagoda, but it is the laity who provide whatever tools and materials are needed and often the labor as well. The wood or sometimes concrete-and-stone pagoda is invariably the largest and best-kept structure in the village. Significant sums are spent on decorating the interior, a particularly important item being gold leaf for the statues of Buddha. Villagers bring candles and elaborate floral offerings on their frequent visits to the pagoda. In a modest village of fifty houses near Vientiane the nai ban estimated that over 30,000 kip had been raised for a new wat. Government aid was also solicited for this construction, although the road was poor and there was neither a school nor a first aid station in the village.

A further example of the value system with regard to the allocation of resources is provided by a program undertaken by the Bureau of Rural Affairs in 1959. Of 992 projects, 238 were for the repair of pagodas throughout Laos. (This was exceeded only by the school projects, 249 constructed and 59 repaired; nevertheless in some provinces pagoda projects outnumbered school projects.)

Marriage, death, and ordination into the priesthood are for the Lao major ceremonial occasions, demanding considerable expenditure and providing a crucial means for validating social prestige. Examples of the cost of these ceremonies among both rural and urban Lao are given in Table 24. The many religious and ceremonial expenses which the Lao regard as essential represent a major allocation of resources, and no understanding of Lao economy is possible without taking these factors into account.

Barter Trade and Lam

The transition to a cash economy is evident all over Laos, but barter continues to be of great significance, often supplementing cash transactions (see Table 25). Moreover, barter remains the preferred medium of trade for both the Meo and the Khmu, who have a lingering suspicion of Lao paper currency.

Language and transportation difficulties, once major obstacles to contact between the Lao and the other ethnic groups, gave rise in northern Laos to the institution of lam.[15] The lam was a person who acted as an intermediary between traders(occasionally the government) and the tribal peoples (primarily the Khmu but also the Meo). Himself a Lao, the lam more often than not was the local nai ban or tasseng, whose home was in a village with relatively easy access to markets.[16]

Traditionally the Khmu came to their lam whenever they had some forest products to sell or wanted to buy salt or clothing. He provided their food on these visits and would arrange the trade with a merchant. Sometimes the lam himself engaged in commerce directly with the tribal peoples.

The institution of lam rested on a distinctly reciprocal relationship: head taxes levied by the French were often paid by the lam; the Khmu in return worked in the fields of their lam when necessary and supplied him with game and forest products. In those cases where the lam was also a merchant, he enjoyed a complete monopoly, with all the tribal trade funneled through his hands. The relationship between a lam and his client was not formalized and depended largely on individual personalities. A man might act as lam for a few tribal families or for entire villages. He might be their lam by virtue of inheriting the position from his father. If the Khmu found him to be dishonest in his dealings, they could seek another.[17]

Smalley (1961a: 13) feels this is too idealized an interpretation, claiming that the Khmu have traditionally feared to cross the Lao. Smalley goes on to cite cases where Khmu en route to market were detained in Lao villages while the Lao searched their produce and removed items at will with little or no payment. The Khmu, he says, have no effective means of redress.

The lam appears never to have been of importance among the Meo, since much of their opium trade was carried on directly with the Hô, the Yunnanese who traveled in horse caravans throughout northern Laos.[18]

Reinach (1901: 312) describes the importation of goods in this manner at the turn of the century, listing as exchanged for opium such trade items as iron and copper pots, small utensils, articles for opium smokers, swords, machetes, rifles, silk, cotton, light woolen goods, tea, and horses -- all originating in Yunnan, Tibet, China, India, or Europe. This caravan traffic was of great importance in the Luang Prabang area. An official customs report of 1917 estimates 1,200 "Chinese" (Hô?) with 2,000 horses entering Luang Prabang province in caravans composed of about thirty horses and nine well-armed men each.

By the mid-1920's caravan traffic appears to have declined and Bangkok became the source of much of Luang Prabang's imports. Luang Prabang functioned mainly as a center for the exchange of goods, since little in the way of trade items appears to have been consumed within the town itself. This would indicate that the blacksmith villages in the vicinity of the town are of recent origin.[19] In fact, since the Khmu produce part of the surplus rice bought to feed Luang Prabang and Meo opium cultivation has attracted a good portion of the commerce in the area, it would not seem an exaggeration to say that without the tribal peoples Luang Prabang would lose much of its commercial significance, bearing in mind that historically it has functioned primarily as a religious and governmental center.

The Yunnanese traders and the institution of lam appear to have existed simultaneously in northern Laos. Undoubtedly their functions overlapped, but it appears that the lam, being mostly Lao, specialized chiefly in trading with the Khmu and to a lesser extent with the Tai peoples, while the Yunnanese engaged in trade with the Meo and Yao, the major factor being opium. In both cases there was a substantial foreign market for the items being traded (see Table 26). The Khmu forest products such as benzoin and lac were channeled by the Lao to European exporters, and the Yunnanese passed the opium to other Chinese merchants in the towns.[20]

At one time many Meo could speak Yunnanese, but the situation has been changing and younger men today are more likely to learn Lao, particularly in those Meo settlements some distance from the Chinese border. Trade with the Yunnanese is by no means extinct, and according to many sources remnants of Chinese Nationalist troops in northern Laos, Thailand, and Burma have recently played a prominent role. A trip through northern Laos in 1959 turned up several cases in which "Chinese" from Yunnan were carrying on opium trade, having in some instances stolen the raw opium from the Meo. The Meo are hardly a docile people, however, and one Meo proudly related how the villagers with their flintlock muskets pursue, and sometimes vanquish, the robbers.

Some Khmu, too, are learning to speak Lao and to transport their own market goods. A difficulty in this regard is that the Khmu do not know how to make or use pirogues, despite the great importance of the waterways for transport, nor do they have horses like the Meo. But a few Khmu groups make bamboo rafts and float down to Luang Prabang to make their annual purchases of salt. There they break up the rafts, sell the bamboo, and then trek back through the mountains on foot with their purchases.

Transportation

Hand-poled pirogues, by far the most numerous river craft in northern Laos, are owned by a significant number of Lao villagers along the Mekong and its tributaries and are used for transporting goods, for traveling, and for fishing. The less common pirogues with outboard motors generally belong to traveling Lao merchants.[21] Chinese operate, often with Thai crews, the antiquated river barges whose main business is large-scale freight, e.g. sacks of rice and garlic, wood, machinery, and heavy crocks of fish oil (passengers are incidental). Finally there are the bamboo rafts of the Khmu.

The wooden barges are the most significant in terms of commercial river traffic though there are no regular schedules, departure taking place after a full cargo has been obtained and provided the day is auspicious. A little shrine is set up on the prow, with flowers and rice as offerings to the spirit of the river. The vessels have a maximum carrying capacity of forty to fifty-odd tons and may be seventy feet long. Barges capable of carrying as much as 200 metric tons were put into service on the Savannakhet-Vientiane run following World War II, but there has been a notable decline in all river traffic since the early 1950's due to the very significant increase in air traffic. Augmented ferry traffic between Thadeua (below Vientiane) and Nong Khai in Thailand has, however, multiplied twelve times since the beginning of 1958.[22]

An important function of the barge and pirogue traffic is to connect the many small villages along the Mekong which are inaccessible by either road or airplane. Travel by river is most favorable during the rainy season when transport by air and road are often impossible, but navigation is difficult for big barges during the dry season (see Table 27).[23]

A good example of the significance of transportation costs is the difference in the prices of two vital commodities, rice and salt, at their place of origin and at the town market. In Ban Puong in Nam Tha province, about eighteen miles from the Mekong, there is a valley where a relatively large surplus of rice is produced. Here the price of rice was 20 kip per kalon in 1959. By the time the rice had been transported on mountain trails overland to the Mekong the price to Lao merchants at a river trading center such as Ban Houei Sai or Pak Tha was 30 kip or more (see Table 28).

If a large enough amount had been received, the rice above the needs of the local Lao was shipped by barge to Luang Prabang town, several days downstream, to sell for 60 kip a kalon. Finding themselves some years with more surplus rice than can be profitably sold, Ban Puong cultivators either feed the rice to their animals or destroy it. At the same time, fairly large quantities of rice must be imported from Thailand to feed the population of Luang Prabang. There are also surplus rice producing areas near the Thai border in Sayaboury where the price of glutinous rice is approximately half that in the royal capital.

A similar situation exists with regard to salt. One of the most important sources of salt is the mines at Bo Tene, about four days' journey by foot east of Muong Sing near the Chinese border. These mines are worked by the Tai Lu, whose major income derives from the sale of salt. In 1957 a kilo of salt sold for about 5 kip at Bo Tene. After being transported by horseback for two days, it brought double the price in Nam Tha town and on reaching Luang Prabang sold for 15 to 20 kip per kilo. At a Mekong river village north of Luang Prabang town, Khmu coolies labor an entire day for three kilos of salt, while Meo villagers south of Luang Prabang barter a part of their opium crop for it.

This relationship between price and transportation is by no means unique to relatively isolated areas of northern Laos. An official citing the need for roads in southern Laos gave as an example the fact that pineapples cost (in 1959) 5 kip for three in Pakse and 30 to 35 kip apiece in Vientiane.

In the above examples overland transportation was by foot and horseback. Horse caravans are still used in northern Laos for transport from areas inaccessible by truck, boat, or plane, Meo ponies being famous for this purpose.

As far as automobiles are concerned, negotiable roads are nonexistent in northern Laos except for the one connecting Luang Prabang and Vientiane, with a branch going to Xieng Khouang.[24] This was originally built by the French colonial government before World War II and was at that time of great importance since the Xieng Khouang branch led to North Vietnam, the shortest route from Laos to the sea. This branch road was closed when that part of Vietnam came under Communist control but appears to have been reopened in 1961 as a supply route for the Pathet Lao forces in Xieng Khouang. The section between Vientiane and Luang Prabang, never an all-weather road, was badly damaged during the Vietminh war and has been rebuilt with modern machinery supplied by the

American aid program. But its usefulness is still confined to the dry season. During the rains the crude plank bridges wash out and the roadbed is undermined by erosion, necessitating expensive repairs each season.[25] Nevertheless, this road plays an important role in local trade and has been the scene of much fighting in recent years.

In a way it can be compared to a major river such as the Mekong, with the qualification that the river be navigable for only half the year. There are a number of Lao villages situated along the road which function as trading centers, and in some cases administrative centers as well, in the pattern of Mekong river villages. Some of these roadside villages are recent, established specifically for the purpose of trade. For example, in a small village north of Muong Kassy several dozen Lao families moved their homesites about a thousand feet from their valley up to the level of the road to set up a small trading center. Both Meo and Khmu villagers come here to trade, and even after the road is no longer passable this village and others like it remain active since enough goods are stocked to last through the rainy season.

The Vientiane-Luang Prabang road has also enabled town merchants to buy items from villages located near the road. This is particularly important in the case of bulky items such as the charcoal needed in large quantities as fuel for Luang Prabang's electric plant. Vegetables and occasional livestock are also transported by road from the villages to Luang Prabang. Vang Vieng, Muong Kassy, and Xieng Ngeun, typical examples of the administrative and trade centers that have expanded as a result of the road, have grown from small district seats to large villages of a thousand or so people, with stores, government offices, and even army detachments housed in bamboo huts or wood shacks strung along the single-lane dirt highway.

In what seems to be a developing trend, cultivators now sometimes take their produce to town themselves instead of acting through an intermediary. An exceptional illustration but one perhaps indicative of the future is provided by a group of Meo who, dissatisfied with the prices the Vietnamese middleman from Luang Prabang was paying for their potatoes in the village, arranged for about a ton of potatoes to be transported by jeep from their village down to Luang Prabang town. At Luang Prabang the potatoes were loaded on a river barge for the trip downstream to Vientiane where the Meo, still accompanying their produce, sold the potatoes for several times more than the normal price in their village. The transaction completed, the elated Meo returned to the north by plane.[26]

Although some goods are carried by jeep or truck the entire length of the Vientiane-Luang Prabang road (approximately 250 miles) during the dry season, this type of commerce is at a decided disadvantage: the charge for road transport from Luang Prabang to Vientiane has been about double that by motorized river barge.

With regard to air transportation, there are thirty-two airstrips in Laos, three of which -- at Vientiane, at Seno, and at Pakse -- serve international flights.[27] A few strips aside from these three can handle four-engine planes, but the majority accommodate small craft only. While major towns have regularly scheduled air service, in the smaller provincial capitals this represents an ideal which is achieved only when sufficient passengers and cargo make it profitable. Frequently the passenger has had to wait for days before a small craft arrives to pick him up. In isolated areas the airstrips are simply rough clearings cut from the jungle, and the town or village may be some distance away. In northern Laos there are bungalows for transients only at Luang Prabang and Xieng Khouang, with no hotel facilities at smaller places. Someone traveling on official business can usually stay with the chao khoueng or chao muong. Within Laos much bulk cargo, e.g. vegetables from Pakse to Vientiane and rice, salt, and petroleum products to various towns in the north, is carried by air. Most imports, however, come from Bangkok, although in many instances the trip through Thailand costs more than the ocean freight from Europe or America to Bangkok.

When asked to name the major economic problems facing their country and the priorities in an aid program, government officials invariably mention the lack of transportation facilities and roads. The American and French governments have responded with programs of road construction in Laos and the North Vietnamese, albeit for different reasons, appear to have improved their road links with the provinces of Phong Saly, Sam Neua, and Xieng Khouang.[28] Two other aspects of the transportation problem in Laos deserve attention too. First, there is the problem of the integration of water, land, and air transport systems to complement each other. Second, maintenance of these systems have presented varying degrees of difficulty for the Lao. In the case of the river barges and port facilities, with the exception of the ferry terminals at Thadeua, the local Lao-Thai-Chinese crews appear quite capable of running them without foreign assistance. The Lao are also capable of repairing jeeps and maintaining stretches of road with local labor but cannot yet operate complicated road machinery. As for aircraft, all the pilots outside the military were

French as of 1959, although the Lao did run the ground installations.

Changes in transportation facilities in the recent past have been dramatic: in 1952 there were but a few hundred vehicles in all of Laos; by 1959 there were 1,350 trucks and 3,580 cars. A disconcerting proportion of the new cars are the Mercedes-Benz and other luxury automobiles bought by high officials and wealthy merchants in Vientiane and justifiably criticized as abuses under the American aid program, which provided the currency for their importation. But the large numbers of jeeps which are used as taxis in rural areas and help villagers market their produce have undeniably played a positive role in raising living standards.

Generally speaking the greatest amount of individual travel is undertaken by the tribal peoples who come down from the mountains, usually on foot, to the Lao or tribal Tai settlements in the valleys, often traveling along trails for several days to reach their destination. Most of these journeys are made by men, but women of the Meo, Khmu, Yao, Kha Ko, and other tribal groups can frequently be seen in the towns. By contrast Lao village women and most men seldom venture far from their homes, leaving only to visit relatives or go to the market. Long pilgrimages do not appear to be important. In villages located near major towns some of the villagers may come to market almost every day; men from tribal villages a week's walk away may appear in town but once or twice a year.

There is also a relationship between trade, transportation, and politics. According to an official in the Ministry of Social Welfare, during a salt shortage in Sam Neua in the first half of 1959, the Vietminh established depots at the border where the tribal peoples could come and receive up to 5 kilos each -- and at the same time be indoctrinated with Communist propaganda. To counter this the Lao government began to fly salt to the remote province, a method that proved very expensive.[29]

Land Tenure

Traditionally the state has been the ultimate proprietor of all land.[30] But it has been estimated for Vientiane province that over eighty per cent of the rural households own their own rice fields. The remaining families rent land from wealthier farmers in the community. In most parts of Laos the approval of the traditional leader of a district may be required for land transfers: the sole surviving member of the hereditary princely family performed this function in Muong Sing. In many areas the government is now trying to establish exactly which land belongs to whom, an undertaking which has created many problems. For example, where the government has taken action to reclaim land there has been much bitterness on the part of uprooted farmers. Also the resettlement of peoples such as the Meo in Xieng Khouang has created conflicts about land ownership and water rights as well. Little reliable statistical information is available concerning the size of landholdings in the Vientiane area. An official in the Lao Ministry of Agriculture estimated that there is a one to five hectare variation in the size of peasant land holdings, with the largest holding he could recall being one of 30 hectares.[31]

In Luang Prabang province the royal family, others of noble rank, and some merchants are absentee landlords. In a number of villages in the immediate vicinity of the royal capital only a small minority of the villagers own land; in others about half the villagers possess land. As far as can be determined, this situation is not general throughout the province but is limited to Lao villages in Luang Prabang district. In addition to this absentee landownership there exists, as in Vientiane province, the rental of land by more prosperous villagers. A villager may also own one piece of land and rent another. A chief advantage of renting land is that the parcel is probably well irrigated by systems maintained by the royal family or other owner. Rental for land use alone amounts to from fifteen to thirty-five per cent of the crop. If the landlord supplies buffalo, provides the seed, and maintains the irrigation system the tenant must turn over fifty per cent of his crop as rent.

These figures approximate those for the Vientiane area, where rental fees commonly vary from one-quarter to one-third of the crop, or half the crop if the landlord supplies seed and tools (Gaudillot and Condominas 1959: 1, 70). With regard to inheritance among the Lao, usually the youngest daughter receives the major share of the land and household, a practice stemming from the basic matrilocal nature of Lao culture. It is also possible for parents to make a will. In either case, Lao ethos shuns any contention among the heirs over their inheritance (Gaudillot and Condominas 1959: 1, 67; Kaufman 1961: 21).

According to the traditional practices of the Tai Dam in Nam Tha and neighboring areas, the district land belonged to the chao muong, a hereditary political and social position held by a member of one of the noble clans of the community. The individual farmer had no title to the land he worked and was also compelled to contribute labor to the chao muong's fields in return for military protection. The peasant was free to leave the area, but if he did so his fields reverted to the village and were distributed to the other villagers (Hickey 1958: 138).

No clearly defined patterns of individual land holdings have been discerned as far as the Lamet are concerned. A man is free to make his swiddens where he wishes, even in the neighborhood of another village if, as is generally the case, the preferred locations nearest his own village already belong to the most prosperous members of the Lamet community (Izikowitz 1951).

Among the Meo the village headman is regarded as the owner of uncultivated land; cultivated land belongs to the cultivator or to the person who inherited it. The head of every family has the right, without special permission, to cultivate untilled land in the proximity of the village, the land that in theory belongs to the village headman. Ownership then accrues through the labor performed on the land to the cultivator (i.e. the head of the household group). There is no distribution of land among the nuclear family groups. The members of an extended family often cultivate several fields at the same time or several extended families may join forces in order to cultivate a large field. In the latter case the land is divided into sections, each tilled by a single extended family (Bernatzik 1947: 239).

Uncultivated land in Akha areas is at the disposal of the community, as are the forest and streams. Accordingly, anyone may occupy land by simply clearing it. There is apparently no concept of selling or leasing land, nor are the Akha familiar with the Meo practice of joint land ownership or at least usufruct of several extended family groups (Bernatzik 1947: 242).

Land tenure practices are certain to change with the inevitable transfer of effective authority from local hereditary and traditional officials to a central government. But it remains to be seen whether land tenure for the hill peoples will evolve in terms of individual nuclear family landownership, as practiced by Lao villagers, or of government-sponsored groupings, the likely prospect for any areas subject to Communist control.

In the absence of such an impetus, there is little reason to expect changes in land tenure practices for the time being. No real pressure on the land in Laos means no incentive for assembling large land holdings and therefore no landowning class in the historic sense. As pointed out earlier, Laos remains underpopulated despite recent population increases and even in the river valleys (particularly in northern Laos) extra rice land is usually available to those who will take the trouble to clear it. Of course, clearing is not always an easy task and takes considerable time as well as labor: a poorer Lao farmer with a small family cannot always clear land by himself and to invite others to help would necessitate incurring the expenses of a feast. Still, as we have seen, most Lao do work primarily on their own land.

Extent of Participation in a Cash Economy

Our examination of the economy of Laos has so far been mostly in the context of what has been called a natural or subsistence economy, that is, a non-cash economy. But every group in northern Laos, no matter how "simple" their economic or cultural state, participates to some degree in a cash economy.

The most common way for a Lao villager to acquire cash for his purchases is the sale of rice, fruits and vegetables, forest products, domestic animals, and home-prepared foods. As to the latter, some villages distant from Luang Prabang provide special food products for market. Another specialty comes from Dane Lom, in the valley of the Nam Ou, where it has been estimated that the fifty households each year produce 85,000 pineapples as well as raise 1,500 to 2,000 coffee plants. These villagers, though lacking sufficient rice and without buffalo or cattle, also have approximately 600 ducks producing between 5,000 and 6,000 eggs per year. The Nam Bac area sends large quantities of oranges to Luang Prabang by pirogue, though transportation difficulties and improper care of the trees drastically cuts the income that might be realized. The trip by pirogue to Luang Prabang takes about four days, but poor packing and waterlogging ruin about two-thirds of the shipment and the pirogue owner makes a net profit of only a little over 600 kip. It has been estimated that the oranges from this region could yield a million kip per year, or 373 kip per inhabitant of the Nam Bac valley (Duclos 1959a: 5, 8).

In recent years many towns and villages in Laos have been sites of military camps, and soldiers and their families provide an important market for nearby villagers. Near Luang Prabang, farmers have been abandoning their fields to set up stores and to build houses in response to the needs of the military and their families. Similarly, Khmu coolies come to military sites in great numbers to work for brief periods. Both Khmu and Meo trade at the town markets, in much greater numbers than was the case earlier. According to a Lao agronomist, there was a noticeable rise in the Vientiane area during the period 1956 to 1959 in the production of vegetables such as cucumbers, eggplant, pumpkins, and beans, partly the result of new bus lines linking Vientiane and surrounding villages. Previously these products were either raised by local Vietnamese truck farmers or imported from Thailand.

The line between village and town dweller is not always sharply drawn in this respect (see Table 29). Many of the inhabitants of Luang Prabang town raise vegetables in riverside gardens and others do considerable fishing. Similarly, there is in Vientiane a woman living next door to a brand new air-conditioned movie theater who grazes her cattle and water buffalo on the grassy area in front of the National Assembly building. Roaming animals are such a nuisance in Vientiane that many of the Lao elite erect fences to keep them out. Not a few embassies and villas in Vientiane are encircled by rice fields.

Three other supplementary, and in certain areas primary, sources of cash are: village crafts, self-employment, and wage labor.

Special Crafts

An apparently unique situation in Laos is presented by the craft villages in the Luang Prabang area whose specialities such as blacksmithing, pottery-making, and weaving are thought by some to have developed for the purpose of serving the king. In southern Laos the techniques of boat building, healing, goldsmithing, and the making of musical instruments and agricultural tools seem to be passed on within families rather than villages. Family traditions in these crafts do exist in the north but appear to be less rigidly confined to particular families. But everywhere in Laos today craftsmanship is for the most part not well developed as compared to surviving examples of past Lao art, and craft products generally are derived from and usually inferior to Thai products.

Silver and goldsmithing have a long history in Laos.[32] The king of Laos has a collection of gold and silver boxes, bowls, and betel services made in Luang Prabang reputedly over five hundred years ago. All are intricately incised with fanciful arabesques and, in many cases, scenes from the Ramayana. A private collector long resident in the area has a somewhat similar collection of pieces from the nineteenth century. In contrast to the graceful beauty of these earlier objects, most of the work done today makes use of geometric designs. While the once popular, ornate betel services have all but lost their practical value among the Westernized elite, large silver bowls and vessels for floral offerings and ceremonial foods for a wedding or baci are important urban furnishings. Traditional articles include silver knife handles and all forms of gold jewelry, hairpins, and buttons. A new item is the ashtray.

Blacksmithing is an exclusively male village craft, the chief products being metal tips for digging sticks, machetes, hoes, and axes. Charcoal is bought from the mountain people, and the iron bars, imported from Europe, are purchased in town.[33] The very simple forge consists of a hand-operated piston bellows and a small round anvil. Sometimes as many as seven or eight men work together. In addition, in some villages women and children help by fashioning the wood and bamboo handles for the machetes, though digging stick tips and hoe blades are also sold separately without handles. Net income varies with the demand and may range from 100 to 300 kip a day for the average blacksmith. Unlike the gold and silver smiths in Luang Prabang town, blacksmiths in nearby villages practice their craft as a part-time specialty, devoting the rest of their efforts to farm work.

It is essential to note that the Lao do not value permanence in their art work -- with a few such obvious exceptions as works of silver and gold or the artistic aspects of their wat structures. A special art form practiced today is that of decorating coffins with elaborate geometric designs fashioned from gold-colored paper. This takes long hours of work by groups of men, yet the product will go up in flames the following day in the funeral pyre. Equally transitory is the painstakingly arranged floral offering. Minute concentric rings of varicolored buds and blossoms assembled by the women are skewered by bamboo splints to a core of banana stalk, surmounted by a crown of frangipani, and set in a silver bowl for presentation to the village wat.

What all Lao art forms share, however, is religious motivation. Even a cursory examination of the many wats in Luang Prabang or Vientiane cannot help but impress the visitor with the high degree of skill that went into their making, from the graceful lines of the architecture itself to the painting of wall frescoes, carving of the Naga balustrades, and casting of the bronze Buddhas. Unfortunately many of the wats are in a state of disrepair, and, worse, those that have been renovated lack some of the sweeping grace and aesthetic sense of the originals.

One is tempted to draw a rigid line and state that certain crafts are urban or were connected with former royal courts and that others are exclusively rural. But this happens not to be the case. Such highly developed arts as gold and silversmithing are found in small Lao towns outside of Luang Prabang as well as Meo villages. Even such items as fireworks and rifles are made both in towns and villages.

Usually a craft is practiced by a single artisan with perhaps the help of a relative or neighbor. There are no organized factories or marketing cooperatives, nor have there been any training schools until very recently, the crafts being acquired wholly within a traditional context. Generally the items are produced in limited quantities for local sale. To date, in Laos' programs of economic development the crafts appear to have been ignored by planning authorities.

The only exceptions seem to be the annual New Year's fair held in Luang Prabang in April and the Tat Luang fair in Vientiane in the fall. At these exhibitions are examples of silverwork, weaving, basketry, and other local arts collected for display by governors and district chiefs. Here is one of the few areas in the world where authentic folk handicraft products predominate over tourist-inspired items, and many of the displays can truly make a museum collector's mouth water. Most of the items are for sale and foreigners as well as some urban Lao do a fair amount of buying. When the fairs are over the crafts sink back into their former obscurity. Laos has not yet reached that stage in psycho-economic development where local products and museums are developed not only for local business reasons but also as an accompaniment of assertive nationalism. In fact, the Lao are notably lacking in the latter characteristic.

It is ironic, but the most eagerly sought souvenirs in Laos are the "Kha" ceremonial bronze drums, no longer used. These are reputed to have been fashioned after traditional designs by European firms and imported into Southeast Asia about half a century ago.

Possibly separation of part-time and full-time specialists offers a way of distinguishing between urban and rural craftsmen. Some Meo villages have blacksmiths who are also part-time specialists, and the Lamet and Khmu also have forges for repairing tools. The Lamet have used as raw material special ingots imported from Sweden, which is particularly significant as evidence that even before World War II groups as seemingly isolated as the Lamet were involved in world trade, the price they paid for their iron depending on the trade value of their rice (Izikowitz 1951: 312-13).

Among the Khmu the making of a new forge, done annually, involves special rituals with sacrifices offered to the spirit of the pump. A chicken and rice are offered on the bellows, hammer, and anvil, these surfaces having first been smeared with chicken blood. Although smithing has in part been made a sacred activity, it would be interesting to know the approximate date of the introduction of iron tools to the mountain peoples. Presumably groups such as the Meo have had them for a long time because of their contact with the Chinese, while the Khmu and Lamet have probably obtained them through trade with the Thai and Lao.

In the pottery villages work is now done by both men and women though this was formerly a male occupation. Only in recent years has pottery-making come to be considered a dirty and undesirable task, at least to some young men in the area of Luang Prabang. Made from local clay, turned on a wheel, and crudely fired, the pots are available in several sizes for cooking, storing, and preserving food and as water receptacles. All are of poor quality and most have no decoration or glaze. Some items are given a shiny black finish by a second firing in paddy husks. The craftsmanship of contemporary Luang Prabang pottery compares unfavorably with that of Chiengmai pottery, for example. Whether this marginality has any historic depth is an intriguing question, and detailed comparisons of pottery types from both areas might provide a clue to broader cultural features. Unfortunately not enough archaeological research has yet been done in either area. The ready availability of pots and pans and enamelware from Hong Kong suggests the possibility that pottery-making has degenerated only in recent years, as a result of foreign competition.

Weaving is practiced exclusively by women among the Lao. Despite the availability of a wide range of imported fabrics and the growing popularity of manufactured clothing, about sixty-five per cent of the village households in the Vientiane area still have looms. There is a village on the outskirts of Luang Prabang where the women specialize in weaving the traditional scarves and skirt borders but there is no organized sales outlet there.[34] A former government minister established a small weaving industry in Savannakhet, and the wife of a prominent Lao businessman has set up a twenty-loom factory in Vientiane with a retail outlet. Since it takes two or three days to weave an ordinary skirt length, and over a week for a more elaborate one, production is on a small scale.

Weaving is also done by some Meo and Yao, but only the more Laotianized Khmu are skilled in this craft. Meo women make elaborate pleated skirts and headcloths; the Yao women's hand-loomed indigo trousers with front panels embroidered in intricate multi-colored cross-stitch designs are perhaps the most colorful of the many magnificent costumes of northern Laos. The Tai groups do their own weaving. Among all these groups, Lao included, it is in the manufacture of women's clothing that traditional techniques have persisted.

The best basketmakers in Laos are the Kha, although all the inhabitants of Laos practice basketry to some extent. Lao and Khmu men work bamboo in many other forms as well. In more modest houses the walls are panels of woven bamboo and the floor consists of thin split strips worked between the main supports. Animal and fish traps are also made of this material. As we have seen, woven bamboo and rattan materials are indispensable in fashioning household furnishings, which provide one of the most important trade items for the Khmu. An additional craft is the making of string bags by the Khmu and Lamet women. The Lamet women are also experts in making cord and fine rope.

Carpentry, particularly the building of pirogues, has been a traditional Lao craft. Except for some ceremonial racing, the larger pirogues are no longer used, but smaller ones are still hollowed out of single logs for local use. In Luang Prabang, Vietnamese carpenters have taken over at least some of the jobs of the Lao boat builders.

Common village industries not requiring specialists are those which produce lime, rice alcohol, and charcoal. The first is made from local limestone, using charcoal as fuel, and is an essential item in the betel masticatories still consumed by a large proportion of the population. Rice alcohol is made by both the Lao and the Khmu. The latter always offer the guest a crock from which alcohol is sipped through a long reed straw. Charcoal is also produced by these two peoples.

An interesting minor industry practiced by the Meo and Lao is the manufacture of gunpowder and homemade rifles. The Meo make rather elaborate flintlocks with a smooth-bore barrel around which their smiths often place bands of silver to link the barrel to the wooden stock. Despite the fact that these rifles do not always fire and that the bullets are often little more than hunks of metal, they are used with considerable success in both hunting and warfare.[35]

Homemade rockets, often made by monks, are used for

religious celebrations and sometimes funerals, and Boun Bang-fai, the rocket festival, is a highlight of the Lao cycle of holidays in Vientiane. The Lao also construct elaborate paper lanterns in cylindrical shapes with candles inside for illumination. A series of cut-out images are pasted to the inside of the cylinder and as the candle's heat makes the lantern revolve there is an illusion of movement. Subjects for these cut-outs range from boatmen paddling a pirogue to couples making love. In Luang Prabang town during the festival associated with the end of Buddhist Lent, these lanterns are made by individuals as well as by groups such as the police.

The occupations of craft specialist and trader are by no means mutually exclusive. In fact both the potters and the weavers usually merchandise their own products in stalls at the town market, e.g. the silk weavers of Ban Panhom are well known in Luang Prabang town. Blacksmiths may travel into the countryside to market their wares but do not sell directly to the town market and often make materials on consignment to local Chinese shopkeepers.

Self-employment and Wage Labor

In discussing the lam we have seen that some rural Lao run small shops or peddle goods to mountain villages. There is no division of labor, although women do most of the petty trading in village shops. In the larger settlements the shops and commercial activities are run almost exclusively by the Chinese, only in a few cases by Pakistanis. Lao women in both town and village indulge in small-scale business, such as the operation of a roadside food stand. This is simply a cleared space spread with clean banana leaves, where rice cakes, noodles, sugar cane, roasted peanuts, and other tidbits are offered for sale. Bigger businesses for Lao women are the fresh fruit and vegetable or prepared-food stands in the town market. The women may both raise and sell the produce or only act as middlemen. As a rule there are no stores in smaller villages, but a family may set up a booth, operated by the women, to sell such items as cigarettes, beer, soap flakes, dried fish, rice whiskey, powder, matches, cotton thread, and candles. In part because of the impact of the American aid program, which has promoted large-scale imports of consumer goods, there are a growing number of village shops, particularly in easily accessible areas on the Vientiane plain. All over rural Laos at the various wat festivals, young marriageable girls of the village set up small tables within the wat compound where they sell fruit, candy, soft drinks, cigarettes, and beer to the young men.

Larger villages in Vientiane province often have one or two tailors, male or female, who earn their livelihood making pants, shirts, mosquito nets, and sheets. One or two members of a community may supplement their income by being herb doctors or midwives. There is usually a barber in each village, plus a few carpenters.

Farmers owning buffalo add to their income by renting out their animals during the plowing and harrowing season. Payment is in rice, the amount being determined by the number of days the animal is used and by the consanguineal relationship of the two individuals. In larger villages there is usually one villager who owns and operates a rice mill.

Logger guilds also exist in some Vientiane villages and are usually composed of several members who cut the trees, share the cost of transporting the logs to town, and divide the profits. In the vicinity of Vientiane, there are a number of logging truck companies owned in many cases by Chinese but operated by Lao crews (Kaufman 1961).

In a village near Vientiane (Ban Pha Kao) there is a professional curer. There are also villagers who make pottery and charcoal as secondary occupations during the dry season. Two families have rice mills, one of which is a full-time business. In the case of other occupations such as road laborer, chauffeur, and soldier listed in Ayabe's survey (1961), the wives in almost all instances do some agricultural field work.

But to the average villager real wealth is determined not by these secondary sources of income, or even by size and number of fields under cultivation, but by the amount of rice harvested. In Vientiane province a man harvesting under 200 myn or 5,300 pounds (one myn equals 26.5 pounds) is poor, while a comfortably situated farmer harvests over 300 myn. A man obtaining 400 (10,600 lbs.) or more is considered wealthy.[36]

As to wage labor, some Lao may work for others in the village and receive payment in cash or kind, while others will go to work as laborers in town. They dislike being designated by the term coolie, which they feel is properly applied only to various Kha groups. These Lao work for local merchants, the army, and the various government offices, doing menial chores. Sometimes they work for only a month or so and then return to their villages. Recently an increasing number of people from villages near Luang Prabang have tended to give up agriculture for permanent jobs, a trend accelerated by poor rains and army confiscation of some rice lands.

In Vientiane there are a large number of samlaw (pedicab) drivers from the villages of Northeast Thailand who were originally attracted to the city during the period of artificial prosperity created by the favorable dollar exchange rate. By 1959 their incomes had fallen due to the increased competition and the larger numbers of taxis, whose prices were in many cases competitive. In addition to the licensed drivers, there are many unlicensed ones, and the turnover rate appears to be high. In Luang Prabang all the samlaw drivers are local Lao, many of them farmers from nearby villages who do this work part-time.

Neither in Luang Prabang nor Vientiane do the local Lao perform most of the common labor, these tasks falling to Khmu in the royal capital and to immigrants from Northeast Thailand in the administrative capital. In Luang Prabang women and occasionally even children participate in heavy labor such as road building and construction, sharing these jobs with the men.

As part of this new urban group, there are now in Vientiane itinerant young shoeshine boys, mostly from impoverished regions in Northeast Thailand, whose parents came to Vientiane to work as coolies, as samlaw drivers, and in other unskilled jobs. In some cases the boys appear to have lost contact with their parents and now associate in groups, sleeping in abandoned buildings or those under construction. Their earnings range from 50 to 100 kip a day and, in contrast to general Lao behavior patterns, there is often noticeable aggressiveness in their solicitation of customers.[37]

Another occupation making its appearance among the Lao, and a further indication of the growth of Vientiane, is prostitution. Although the overwhelming majority of prostitutes in Laos have been Vietnamese or Northeast Thai, in recent years some have originated from villages in the Vientiane area. A few have made their appearance in Luang Prabang where their contacts are mostly soldiers and younger civil servants. These girls work in brothels owned by Lao; the Hong Kong and Vietnamese girls operate from Vientiane's foreign-managed night clubs patronized by the elite.

There is often a largely traditional relationship with household servants. A Lao employer almost always provides his domestic with room, board, and clothing. The actual cash salary is quite small. In some cases a village girl will be taken in and the money sent to her parents. The strength of these mutual obligations is evidenced by the fact that Europeans rarely if ever employ Lao as servants, preferring Vietnamese or Thai on a cash basis.

A Lao urban proletariat composed of migrants from rural areas may emerge, but at present the population of the two major towns is mainly composed of Lao officials, and other government employees, Chinese and Vietnamese merchants, and craftsmen, with most of the common labor supplied either by migrant tribal Khmu in Luang Prabang or Northeast Thai in Vientiane. In both cases the immigrant labor groups appear to be the least stable elements in the population. An important factor here, of course, has been the absence of industry, with the towns functioning mainly as commercial, administrative, and religious centers. A Lao proletariat based on emigration from rural areas may be some time in developing because of this lack. Another important factor seems to be a labor deficit in rural areas, at least in the vicinity of Vientiane. Although some Lao move to the city, a significant number come from Northeast Thailand at planting and harvesting time to work in the countryside. They receive from 30 to 50 kip per day with food, depending on the number of days worked (Kaufman 1961).

There are also many farmers in the villages around Vientiane who would prefer off-season work in Vientiane. It is possible that the labor deficit in rural areas is due to the explosive growth of Vientiane and with it the spread of "modern" ideas, particularly the concept that rural life is backward.

Most, or at least many, of the jobs created by Vientiane's expansion, outside of official positions, appear to have been taken over by groups with more training than the rural Lao, undoubtedly increasing the frustration of the latter, who would like to move to town.

Expenditures

It has been estimated that a typical rural Lao family in central Laos spends about $150 a year, or approximately $35 per family member. Of this sum, about half goes for supplementary food and perhaps as much as twenty per cent goes for clothing. The remainder is divided among expenses for tools, entertainment in the form of gambling at bouns, and gifts to the wat and bonzes. Although the Lao villager is not poor, in that he has ample food to avoid starvation and frequently small luxuries as well, this figure is not very high even by Asian standards. The most prosperous villager in Vientiane province may have $250 a year to spend in contrast to a prosperous Bang Chan farmer on the Bangkok plains who spends about $500 a year (Sharp 1953: 218).

A rural household budget for the Luang Prabang area would be approximately the same, the fact that fewer commodities are purchased being offset by a somewhat higher cost of living due to transportation costs. In most cases cash income would be proportionately less in areas away from the vicinity of the town.

Prices on manufactured goods tend to be consistently higher in Luang Prabang than in Vientiane. Certain items, notably skirts and scarves woven in the Luang Prabang area, are cheaper there, as are regional fruits and vegetables. More detailed statements are difficult to make because of seasonal variations as well as price fluctuations due to variation in quality and in the relationship between buyer and seller (Europeans as well as tribal peoples are frequently charged higher prices). Table 30 provides an idea of these variations.

The size and importance of religious and ceremonial expenses have already been discussed, but mention might be made here of the numerous bouns to raise money for the wat. Throughout Laos the most common type of village boun is one featuring the reading of scriptures at the local pagoda by prominent bonzes from a town or other villages. Villagers pay for the privilege of hearing these recitations, often presenting the payment in the form of "money trees," i.e. branches adorned with small banknotes decoratively folded in the shape of leaves. At bouns in larger villages, and especially nearer towns, there is almost always dancing. Money for the wat comes from payments to selected young village women who have volunteered their services as dancing partners during the boun. The dance is the lam vong; Western dancing is unknown.[38] Although the monks themselves do not encourage it, gambling is sanctioned as an amusement at bouns and it is logical to suppose that a proportion of gambling profits are ultimately used for religious purposes. Proceeds also go to benefit the local schools.

Gambling expenses are closely related to the opportunities available and consequently to the extent that an individual participates in urban culture. In Vientiane many samlaw drivers and coolies claim to be unable to save money, although some earn as much as 10,000 kip a month, because of the lure of gambling. Some Lao women gamble, at least among more prosperous urban groups, and occasionally go into debt.[39]

Considerable sums are sometimes spent on lottery tickets. The outcome is felt to be of sufficient importance to call upon monks to predict the lucky number. It has also been reported that, in the Luang Prabang area, buffalo have been sacrificed to predict lottery results.

Religious expenditures in Luang Prabang province are at least equal to those in Vientiane -- probably greater. The villager of northern Laos does not have opportunity for many secular pleasures available to his countrymen in the south. The town of Vientiane is much larger than Luang Prabang and as the secular capital of Laos offers a variety of movies, gambling, drinking places, and prostitution. Easy access to towns across the river and regular bus service from nearby rural areas makes these entertainments readily available. Luang Prabang, as the royal capital and residence of both the king and the highest ranking bonze of the country, is a conservative town. Diversions exist, but on a considerably more restricted scale.

Taxation does not constitute an important item in the villager's budget. The head tax which existed under the French was abolished with independence and, as far as the writer is aware, no effective land tax exists. The government derives its chief revenues from custom duties, levies on urban merchants, and foreign aid. Theoretically certain types of taxes are levied on farmers, on goods shipped from one village to another, on store sales, and on forest products, but exemptions are liberal. A farmer who breaks an arm or leg is exempt for one year. Even more to the point is the fact that for all practical purposes the government, largely for political reasons, makes almost no effort to collect taxes. In recent years the government has begun to think about reinstating the colonial head tax.

Throughout Southeast Asia there is considerable indebtedness by the local population to the Chinese merchants. (According to one Lao official, many Chinese are indebted to Lao in the urban areas. This may be a reflection of the channeling of foreign economic aid through the Lao government.) Someone wishing to borrow money ordinarily makes a contract before three witnesses, listing his house, garden, livestock, or gold as security. The interest rates in urban areas vary from 4 to 10 per cent per month. The larger the amount borrowed, the smaller the interest rate. Generally speaking, there is more indebtedness among the urban, as opposed to the rural, Lao who may want to build a house (hired labor is usually used in town), start a business, or buy a car. There is a tendency for Lao farmers to go into debt when there is a failure of the rice crop but rural debt does not appear to be a major problem. This may be a reflection of the generally undeveloped state of the total rural economy as far as cash exchanges are concerned. By contrast, indebtedness is a major problem among urban Vietnamese and Lao-Thai coolies and samlaw drivers, due in part to their enthusiasm for gambling. On a small scale, however, a great deal of borrowing is done by Lao villagers, with sums of 500 kip or less borrowed from relatives. Larger amounts are borrowed from merchants.

Tribal Economies

The key factor in the Meo economy, as we have seen, is the cash value of their opium crop. The history of this crop is rather interesting, with important political as well as economic implications. Evidently in the early years of their colonial control the French, aware of the revenue potential, encouraged this crop and even experimented with improved forms of cultivation.[40]

The opium crop varies with the size of the family, that is, the amount of land a household can clear and cultivate, though the weather is an important factor too. In some cases there are two crops a year, one planted in the eighth month of the Lao calendar, the other between the ninth and tenth months. The Meo cultivate three different types of opium, easily distinguished by the white, red, or purple color of the poppies. The soil is loosened with digging sticks and the seeds are sunk into the earth. Six months after planting, the opium is ready to be gathered. Scratching the poppy heads with a knife causes the opium, a milky fluid, to ooze out for collection. Opium poppies can be grown in old corn fields and will yield harvests for ten to twenty years from the same field, depending on the fertility of the soil (Bernatzik 1947: 358).

Most estimates of production per household range from a minimum of two or three kilos to a maximum of nine or ten, with an average of about four. Prices range from about 2,000 to 6,000 kip a kilo for raw opium, occasionally more, depending on supply and demand. In general, prices are higher in central Laos than in the north, e.g. in the Luang Prabang area prices are as low as 1,200 kip per kilo for raw opium and 5,000 kip for the cooked variety; comparative prices in the Vientiane area, where there are relatively few Meo, are 3,000 and 9,000. It has been estimated that about sixty-five tons of crude opium are produced in Laos annually -- all of relatively poor quality.

Incomes range from a possible minimum of 4,000 kip to a conceivable maximum of 60,000 kip per Meo family per year. These incomes are from opium alone and presuppose no marketing of other products though the Meo living nearer Luang Prabang also sell charcoal, firewood, potatoes, and other vegetables. One village headman's income was estimated at 70,000 kip from potatoes and cabbages and 40,000 from opium; another received 50,000 from opium and 10,000 from vegetables and pigs. The first instance is atypical in both magnitude and relative importance of vegetables and opium. In another Meo village it was estimated, on the basis of maximum and minimum yields cited, that cash income varied from about 14,000 to 40,000 from opium.

All these figures are based on the questionable supposition that the Meo do not consume any of the opium they produce. Although they use but a small portion of the crop, a number of older men and women appear to be addicts, often to dull the pains of various ills. Most of the younger people seem to be healthy, vigorous, and hard-working and Meo cultural values do not appear to encourage their smoking.

Some investigators have stated that the Christianized Meo tend to abandon opium growing in favor of vegetable crops, especially potatoes. There is some evidence to support this claim both in the Luang Prabang and Xieng Khouang areas, although a number continue opium cultivation. There does seem to be a growing self-consciousness about opium among some younger more urbanized Meo, and it has been suggested that their continued opium cultivation reflects parental pressure (Barney 1961).

The considerable cash surpluses of the Meo are readily illustrated by their accumulations of silver jewelry. In addition to jewelry, many Meo have hoards of silver bars buried in the ground. Naturally it is difficult if not impossible to get reliable figures on the extent of such holdings, but confirmation of this custom is provided by a workshop in Luang Prabang town which specializes in melting down old French, Chinese, Indian, and Burmese silver coins to fashion into bars to be used in trade with the Meo. In most cases the Meo will not willingly accept paper money. To illiterate people the value of silver is more readily ascertained, and silver cannot be easily destroyed as is the case with paper currency. The Meo reckon both income and purchases in terms of silver bars.[41]

The chief purchases of the Meo are salt, clothing, and iron bars for making tools; less frequent purchases might include kerosene for lamps or such luxury items as powdered coffee and condensed milk, which are reserved chiefly for guests. One prosperous family estimated that expenses for purchases came to about 10,000 kip a year. Presumably the surplus income goes into silver. An example of the potential use of surplus income is provided in the case of Kiouketcham, a large village on the Luang Prabang road with a resident Catholic priest. Here the villagers turned over to the priest sufficient funds for the purchase of a power-operated rice mill for the community.[42] Although this particular project never materialized, the availability of funds for it is highly significant. In any case, there is little doubt that because of opium the cash income of the Meo is much higher than that of the Lao.

This situation may be subject to change in the near future as both Vietnam and Thailand have officially banned the use of opium. Enforcement is another matter of course. While the trade has not been previously conducted in legal channels, it has often had a certain amount of unofficial cooperation. Thailand has recently embarked on an anti-opium smoking campaign, and although it might be incorrect to assume that opium trade with neighboring countries will cease entirely, the future of the Meo's chief cash crop remains in doubt.[43] One of the leaders of the Meo community in Xieng Khouang gave as an excuse for the persistence of the trade the fact that there were still smokers.

The international implications cannot be ignored. In Laos one hears rumors on this subject and of the machinations of rival export dealers who wreck each other's planes in Xieng Khouang. A recent magazine article cited Laos as one of the sources of narcotics reaching the West Coast of the United States. Transportation across the Pacific is probably controlled by Chinese secret societies presiding over a series of Asian networks which get most of their opium from growers in Red China, Burma, and Laos.

Oriental opium is converted illegally into morphine base in Rangoon and several other cities and is then usually shipped to Hong Kong and Singapore to the heroin laboratories located there. Thereafter it is smuggled to the United States, Canada, Japan, the Philippines, and South America at profits similar to those in Europe, roughly calculated at a hundred times the price of raw opium.[44]

Another source detailed the operations of some of the opium exporters in Laos, who buy raw opium from the Meo in Xieng Khouang through Chinese agents acting for a group of Frenchmen of "Mediterranean" and North African origin. Beavers and Piper Cubs with extra gas tanks take off from Pong Savanh and parachute the opium into valleys near Saigon, where it is transshipped to Hong Kong. Some is consumed there, the rest is sent on to the United States.[45] With the Communist conquest of Xieng Khouang it can be assumed that this trade has been interrupted or redirected.

The existence of this traffic should not be construed as advocacy of opium cultivation. One high Lao official said the government ban on opium traffic is not strictly enforced because of the dislocation it would cause in the Meo economy. It cannot be denied that profits derived by merchants and some unscrupulous officials also play a part. In cases of more flagrant violations, however, there have been arrests resulting in imprisonment. This is in Luang Prabang province; in neighboring Xieng Khouang, where a majority of the Meo are concentrated, opium is sold on the open market.[46]

Factors significant to the economic and social status of the Meo in northern Laos can be summarized as follows: the size of the family and the number of able-bodied workers; amount of opium production; amount of vegetable and rice production; amount of silver owned in both bars and jewelry; numbers of livestock (particularly horses and cattle); ability of the men as hunters; and capacity of the men to speak Lao. Convincing evidence of relative Meo prosperity is found in the fact that although Meo tribesmen are often seen shopping in Luang Prabang, they are almost never seen working as coolies.

Just as the absence of Meo laborers provides some insight into Meo economy, so the prevalence of Khmu coolies is indicative of their economic patterns (see Table 31). The walk to town from their villages may take less than a day or as much as a week. Luang Prabang, although a small town in many respects, is nevertheless the major center of cash labor in northern Laos. The Khmu come mostly during the dry season when there is not much work in their own fields, appearing to be most numerous in Luang Prabang from December to March.

Although some stay as permanent workers, most remain only for a few days to several months, engaged chiefly as road gang laborers, construction workers, or sometimes as domestics for private households. For the most part the Khmu wage laborers are men. Usually their purpose is simply to earn enough money to buy some salt and clothing before returning home, and the number and length of such excursions are dictated by their needs. Sometimes certain Khmu work as coolies for the Meo and are paid in opium. Like the poor Lao who work for other Lao farmers some Khmu will hire themselves out as agricultural laborers to more prosperous Khmu and are paid in rice.

A Thai investigator, writing of the period just before World War II, describes in some detail how Khmu were recruited for work in the logging forests of northern Thailand. Young Khmu were brought in from Laos by men called "captains" (in the northern Thai dialect) who had promised the parents to escort their son to the place of employment and guarantee his return at the end of a year or pay 50 Indochinese piasters. When about twenty individuals had been recruited -- and after the rice fields had been cleared and planted -- the group departed, usually at the end of May. A short knife and sword served as weapons of defense and the captain provided tobacco and food, the latter usually consisting of rice, peppers, and salt. The trip to the Mekong, where they made sure to avoid the French officials, took about two weeks. The employer paid the captain one month's wages for each of his recruits and this payment was in effect deducted from their earnings. After the contract year was over the captain led the workers back to their homes in Laos. The captain had to pay the parents of any worker who failed to return, even if this was because their son had himself chosen to remain in Thailand (Srisvasdi 1950).

Nor is this a new pattern. A European traveling in the area eighty years ago makes the following observations (Bock 1884: 363):

> The labourers [in the teak forests] mostly employed are men belonging to a hill tribe called Komaws [Khmu], living to the eastward beyond the Mekong River. They are darker in colour than the Laosians, short of stature, but very muscular . . . . These men are hired as a rule for three years, and receive as wages the munificent sum of about eighty rupees a year in return for their arduous labor. Even so, I am sorry to say that they are often cheated by the lower class of employers. For every Komaw hired on the three-years system the employer has to get a permit from the Chow Radjasampan, for which he has to pay twelve rupees, and as a setoff against this, the unfortunate labourer is mulct in a portion of his hard earned money. These primitive mountaineers do not take away their money, when returning to their hill-retreats, but invest in one of the much-prized gongs made by the red Karians. 'If,' they philosophically argue, 'we take the money back to our country it gets less every day till at last it is all gone; whereas the gong we can keep, and hear its beautiful sound daily.'

These gongs as well as jars, both once of tremendous value to the Khmu as symbols of prestige and wealth and still characteristic of many tribal peoples in Southeast Asia, have virtually disappeared from Khmu culture (Smalley 1956: 50). Although the gongs were doubtless acquired through trade long before they were purchased with wages, the historic importance of wage income in the Khmu economy cannot be ignored. It is possible that the relatively large number of Khmu laborers in Luang Prabang is a comparatively new development, but their tradition as part-time coolies is definitely not. Certainly neither they nor the Lamet, nor the Meo, can be regarded as isolated tribal peoples living exclusively in a natural economy.

Some Khmu, particularly in the Luang Prabang area, act as merchants for their fellow villagers. A few manage to build up a modest prosperity through this trade, but the process is also reversible, as related in this Khmu text (excerpted from Smalley 1952):

> Some people have no money saved up to go and buy things. They go and borrow and obtain money from other people. Then they go and buy clothing, animals, a buffalo, a pig. They come back and sell these things and make a profit. They pay back where they have borrowed the money. With their small profit they go and buy a chicken, a duck. They do this again and again. They buy and they sell. This continues and they make a lot of money. They hire people to work in their rice fields and to build a house for them. This continues and they become great merchants. They are people who have money, they are rich, they are very well off, very lucky.
>
> Then there are people who have a lot of money as an inheritance [47] from their parents, which they think they are going to keep. They go and buy clothing, animals. They take a loss. This continues two or three times. Finally they change and become thieves. They steal from people. Sometimes they take money. The inheritance which they thought they could keep is all gone. They gamble money. People like this are very bad and very unlucky.

We have seen that the Khmu and Lamet sometimes sell rice to the valley Lao. Why then, it may be asked, if some Khmu produce a surplus of rice, is it necessary for them to work as coolies for the Lao? There are several reasons for this seeming paradox.

First, their rice crop varies with districts, households, and years. Second, the traditional relationship between Khmu and Lao has been similar to that of slave and master. Formerly the Khmu were forced to do corvée at the pleasure of the Lao without compensation (see also page 94). A provision in the constitution of Laos now makes this illegal, although word has either not reached many Lao tassengs or nai bans or else they choose to ignore it, while the Khmu are usually unaware of their new rights or afraid to resist.[48] Many Lao merchants do not hesitate to take advantage of the situation, driving hard bargains with the Khmu and in some cases cheating them. The Lao also have been known to do this to the Meo who come to town to trade but, unlike the Meo, the Khmu passively accept their inferior status and do not protest.

It would be most unfair to the Lao to attribute the poor economic position of the Khmu solely to Lao exploitation, for in an economic and political sense they are inferior -- that is, less developed. The Khmu lack the crops that might bring a high cash return and, even counting their superior basketry, seem to be unable to find a compensating source of income in their crafts. The making of baskets and mats is not an exclusively Khmu activity, nor does the limited demand for basketry products constitute a sufficient basis for further development of this craft. Permanent political organization above the village level does not exist.

Their position of cultural and social inferiority has given rise to a messianic cult not dissimilar to those found among suppressed peoples in other parts of the world. In 1956 word spread among the Khmu of Luang Prabang province that their "king" was about to come and save them. A popular tale regarding this king claimed that when he was born he would be able to help all his people and establish a kingdom for them. One Khmu tribesman is supposed to have visited his cave "in the north"[49] and reported that it was very large, that people there spoke a language similar to Khmu, and that it was very civilized, containing all sorts of things -- automobiles, airplanes, pirogues, plenty of gold and silver, clothing, buffalo, and even chickens. The king was supposed to leave the cave and go out among the Khmu to distribute his bounty. To show their respect for him, the Khmu stopped work and did not plant any rice. They feasted on what little livestock they had and awaited his coming. Upon learning of the situation, the government arrested some Khmu and supposedly broke up the movement -- though not in time for the Khmu to be able to plant a rice crop. As a result an even greater number of Khmu than usual were forced to seek work as coolies.

This belief has evidently been widespread in Laos and seems

to have been connected with previous revolts of the Khmu. In addition a recent appearance has also been reported among the Meo. An interesting point made in some of the versions is that the "king" is supposed to be white-skinned.

Suppression of these movements does not, of course, eliminate them, since they are symptoms of deep cultural conflicts. As we have seen, the Khmu engage in extensive trade with the Lao, not infrequently receiving the worst of the bargain -- particularly in market transactions which require the handling of unfamiliar paper currency. And despite the fact that many Khmu work as coolies in such tasks as road building and construction, their financial and other material returns are modest and enable them to participate only to a very limited extent in the obviously superior culture they encounter in the towns. With their desires simultaneously stimulated and frustrated, it is not surprising that they resort to magical ends to attain that which is denied to them by rational means.[50]

Lao-tribal Interdependence

In both barter and cash economies the relationships among the Lao, Khmu, and Meo are very close. Conceivably these groups could survive independently, but it would be at considerable sacrifice to all concerned. The dealings between the Lao and Meo are roughly on a basis of equality while those between either the Lao or the Meo on one hand and the Khmu on the other imply a superiority-inferiority relationship.

Economic interdependence has deep roots within the region, with all the groups inhabiting northern Indochina and neighboring areas dependent to some extent on trade. The hypothesis has been advanced that for certain basic economic items plains villages may in many respects be more self-sufficient than hill areas.[51] In the Luang Prabang area economic and craft specialization among the Lao functions mainly to serve the royal capital, while among the hill peoples it has the more basic function of maintaining the cultural inventory. Thus the Luang Prabang crafts villages contribute to a luxury subculture, enhance the position of the elite, and help perpetuate the state; the rural village does not participate in this special economy. In contrast, the mythologies and prayer texts of the Khmu and other peoples refer at length to the material culture of the lowland peoples, not merely with envy but with an assumption of their own past involvement. Their myths are complete with legends of how they once had similar cultural trappings, and the Khmu cult cited above may well have historical antecedents. Ritual linkage between hill and valley peoples is also important. Lao and Khmu participate jointly in buffalo sacrifices, the Lao considering the Khmu better acquainted with the phi, since the latter were the indigenous inhabitants before the coming of the Lao. In addition the Khmu participate in certain rituals for propitiating the spirits.

In marked distinction from the Lao, the Thai, dwelling in a homogeneous ethnic environment, have their villages united more by formal political ties and less by regional trade and specialization although these factors are doubtless interrelated -- for example, by the institution of lam.

It is possible to suggest that some of the unique features of the various Southeast Asian cultures may revolve around the type of economic and cultural symbioses existing between the valley people and the hill tribes. The long-term stability of such relationships would be questionable, however, in view of the constant migration of new groups from China.

Thus economic specialization is a continuing factor in the economy of the lowland Lao, with several kinds of specialization observable: full- versus part-time crafts; those designed primarily to serve the Lao elite; agricultural versus nonagricultural specialization; and, finally, special occupations of a group of villagers versus an individual. In many cases there is an overlap of one or more kinds of specialization. The silver and goldsmiths in Luang Prabang town are examples of full-time specialists whose original clientele of a select social and political elite has widened to include prosperous town dwellers as well. Certainly few villagers in the past (or even today) were able to indulge in silver or gold bowls or betel sets. On the other hand, part-time specialists serving the king of Luang Prabang still exist, e.g. the elephant riders, elephant keepers, and royal dancers who live in nearby villages as farmers and perform only on ceremonial occasions or special holidays.

There is definite agricultural specialization on the part of Lao villages, as illustrated by Dane Lom with its pineapples and ducks or Nam Bac with its orange cultivation. The reasons for this, beyond simple ecological factors, are not entirely clear.

Unlike the situation of smiths, weavers, and potters in crafts villages, traders do not appear to be specialized by villages in areas where there are mountain peoples (and in northern Laos this includes virtually all areas); some households act as traders whether as part of the formalized lam pattern or otherwise.

Although economic integration and interdependence, formal or informal, is an established fact, political integration does not seem to have really occurred up to the present day. Neither the Lao kingdoms nor the French colonial government ever really integrated the upland peoples into their government structures. The French had to cope with a series of Meo and Kha uprisings up to the time of World War II. To be able to combine political and economic integration would appear a major challenge facing the government of Laos. Significantly, crucial trade items have become part of political and military warfare, as in the example of the establishment of salt depots by the North Vietnamese to lure some of the mountain peoples across the border. Regardless of the outcome of the present fighting in Laos, the closer integration of the Lao and tribal peoples seems assured, either in the formal Communist pattern of the so-called autonomous regions or an improvised structure such as the Thai border police (Halpern 1964b).

Urban Economy

In the period between the two world wars there were very few Lao who could be classified as urban in any sense of the term, and these few were mostly titled officials plus a few merchants and craftsmen who were very much outnumbered in the towns by the Chinese and Vietnamese brought in under the French to perform many of the skilled jobs in the colonial administration. The so-called urban Lao purchased few imported goods. According to one long-time European resident, twenty-five years ago any Lao woman who wore shoes was considered a harlot. Concrete houses, except for those of the French administrators, were rare; differences in levels of status were indicated by homes with plaster (over bamboo) wall, plank floors, and tile roofs, by the variety of foods consumed, and by the amount of jewelry and other items of craftsmanship possessed by families. An additional factor was the possession of servants, who, in Luang Prabang, were often Khmu in hereditary positions. The small elite also had wealth in the form of land and buffalo. Automobiles were practically unknown: as recently as twenty-five years ago, the only cars in Luang Prabang town belonged to the king, the French commissioner, and the director of public works. Ironically perhaps, although the material differences between groups was less, the power position of the elite was more secure and the prestige that went with rank more widely accepted.

The significance of the term "urban" in relation to the present economy of Laos can be summarized by comparing the facilities of the administrative capital of Vientiane with those of Luang Prabang and the provincial town of Nam Tha (see Table 32). Luang Prabang is roughly equivalent in facilities to Savannakhet, Thakhek, and

Pakse, while Nam Tha approximates the other provincial capitals such as Sayaboury, Phong Saly, Sam Neua, and Attopeu; Xieng Khouang occupies something of an intermediate position.

Growth of Vientiane

The metropolitan area of Vientiane is the center of what little industry exists in Laos, with 146 of the total 194 companies officially incorporated under Lao law as of 1959. A majority of these companies were in the hands of the Chinese (Halpern, ed. 1961: No. 1). In addition, there were reportedly over 300 small industries and businesses scattered about the city or its environs, most being operated by an individual or family with a limited number of poorly trained employees. The principal businesses were charcoal plants, brick kilns, sawmills, carpentry shops, and rice mills (see Table 33). Enterprises above the level of cottage industries included a few of the rice mills, several construction firms, two carbonated drink plants, an alcoholic beverages plant, a match factory, a soap factory, and a cigarette factory. Established in 1959 on the outskirts of Vientiane with French and Lao capital amounting to 25 million kip, the cigarette factory was managed by a Frenchman with much of the labor supplied by young Lao girls. Tobacco grown in the provinces of Champassak, Nam Tha, and Vientiane was blended with imported leaf from Thailand, South Vietnam, and the United States. The daily production of 25,000 packs was sold within Laos, aided by a local advertising campaign appealing to Lao national consciousness.[52]

With regard to services, there were two hotels (equivalent to what might be found in a provincial town in Thailand), a few movie theaters (one of them air-conditioned), several restaurants and nightclubs, five or six garages, trucking lines, and two domestic aviation companies. Two main open air markets, one operating in the morning and the other in the afternoon, should also be mentioned, as well as a slaughterhouse staffed mainly by Vietnamese.

The largest category in terms of number of installations, although not of kip value, was that of charcoal production, which is largely a small-scale rural industry based on local resources. The sawmills, the rice mills, and the raw sugar processing plant also use local products, although the first two require considerable capital investment and were controlled by Chinese merchants, with a number of prosperous Lao, including government officials, holding shares. At the time, seventeen foreign companies were licensed to do business in Laos, all but one (a French tin mine near Thakhek) located in Vientiane. These included insurance companies, two banks, an oil company (Shell Oil Company and Stanvac have subsidiaries incorporated in Laos), an airline, and import firms.

Many "industries" have grown up only in recent years as a concomitant of the American aid program, which makes their future development problematical since they are largely, if not completely, dependent on foreign imports and exchange for their continued maintenance. A large number represent luxury aspects of the economy, with utilization limited to the urban population and, in some cases, to a very small proportion of even this group. Garages provide an example: certainly there is a need for jeeps, buses, and government vehicles, particularly in maintaining contact with rural areas, but it is hard to justify the excessive use of automobiles within the town of Vientiane -- more so as all vehicles in Laos rely entirely on imported gasoline paid for with foreign assistance funds.

A key day in the development of the Lao economy was October 10, 1958, the effective date of the monetary reform. Previously, with the aid of American subsidies, a 35 kip to $1 U.S. rate had been maintained with licenses issued to importers. This provided tremendous opportunities for graft and corruption since the free market rate in Bangkok and Hong Kong ranged between 80 and 100 to 1. When the kip was stabilized at 80 to the U.S. dollar, with free convertibility, there was no longer an incentive to smuggle goods out of Laos to Thailand, and Thai prices exercised their influence by stabilizing some prices and causing others to fall. For several months after this change, local economic activity slowed considerably.

Vientiane's urban growth problems are manifold. A diesel power plant was installed in 1958 with American aid but by 1959 already appeared inadequate to the needs of the expanding city. Only about twenty per cent of all houses in Vientiane have even limited electricity and very few have electrical appliances of any sort. Kerosene is imported in large quantities for lighting homes and shops. There is only a limited central water distribution system, most of the town's water being supplied by truck or by coolies. About a tenth of the homes (mostly those rented to foreigners) have limited and uncertain indoor plumbing. Open sewage is a major problem.

In addition to these considerations the development of Vientiane in recent years raises serious questions with regard to class structure, the efficacy of foreign aid, and the total problem of culture change in Laos.[53]

Traditional Urban Commerce

The typical range of small businesses found in the provincial towns is illustrated by the following inventory of businesses in Luang Prabang town in 1957. Most important in terms of the local economy were the three rice mills, one located in town and the other two in nearby villages. A brick kiln run by a local Chinese employed seven laborers, each operating a separate kiln, and about half a dozen coolies worked at a sawmill, also owned by a Chinese. At times extra workers were hired to saw wood by hand when the sawmill machinery could not handle the load, which fluctuated because of the erratic supply of lumber. There were also several local building contractors, both Vietnamese and Lao. The number of their employees varied with the amount of work at hand but seemed never to be more than a dozen or so. At the time the building contractors had been busy erecting government buildings, shops, and private residences. This construction bore an at least indirect relation to the foreign aid program and, as in Vientiane, seems to have been a popular way for merchants and government officials to invest surplus profits. For example, during the 1957-59 period a movie house, numerous shops, a military warehouse and headquarters, and private residences for the governor and military commander were built. These were all two-story concrete structures which, although modest by the standards of any Asian city, were quite impressive for this small town.

Luang Prabang in 1957 also had two dye shops, owned and operated by Chinese, where cotton imported from Bangkok was dyed and the skeins hung to dry on the roof of an old barge in the Mekong. The six coolies employed were given a free place to sleep on the dye shop premises. The town's two ice plants were owned by a Chinese merchant and by a Lao who was at the time a local representative in the National Assembly. Each employed three to four workers and turned out about 200 kilos of ice per day. Ices using sugar and sometimes grenadine syrup provided a sideline, for which the busiest season was during the holidays, particularly the New Year's season in April which coincides with the hottest time of the year. At New Year's the ice plants operated "day and night" and produced 15 tons of ice per day.[54] Two bakeries producing French bread, one run by a Chinese, the other by Vietnamese, turned out about a thousand small loaves a day. Aside from the usual Chinese retail shops, other Luang Prabang businesses were a soda bottling works, the silver smelting shop already mentioned, and a small slaughterhouse on the outskirts of town. The daily open market ended by mid-morning.

Some perspective can be gained by briefly surveying the situation in the towns of southern Laos: Pakse, with a population of about eight thousand, is located on the Mekong near the frontiers of Thailand, Cambodia, and Vietnam. It is in the heart of the Bolovens plateau and can be reached in about two hours by plane from Vientiane. By Laos standards the economic position of Pakse is relatively good. The main roads within the town are fairly well paved, though outgoing arteries into the province are in need of repair and extension. Improvement of the outlying road system in order to facilitate the movement of goods and people to and from markets is particularly important here, since Pakse is the center through which rice is regularly supplied to provincial areas in Vientiane, Savannakhet, and Thakhek. Pakse is also the market through which some livestock is exported to Cambodia and Vietnam. It has two ports of entry on the Mekong, Vang Tao from Thailand and Kinak from Cambodia and Vietnam. Prior to the monetary reform, the value of imported goods was quite high and the customs offices collected an estimated four million kip per month. Since devaluation, however, there has been a decline in imports and in 1959 only about one million kip per month was collected. Principal imports at Pakse are gasoline, oil, cement, salt, flour, milk, spare parts for cars, sheet iron, and household articles. The limited exports in addition to cattle include unginned cotton, chilis, coffee, soybeans, and dried hides, the overall value of imports being about twenty times that of the exports. The difference has been in effect subsidized by American aid.

Savannakhet has a slightly greater population and is also located on the Mekong. There are several small lumber mills and a tannery for cow and buffalo hides. The central market appears too small to serve the population, with the result that most of the merchants have now opened small places of business just outside the market area. Savannakhet province, of which Savannakhet is the capital, has long been an exporter of cattle to Vietnam and Thailand. The area does not produce enough rice to feed itself and about one-third the necessary rice must be imported from Thailand or obtained from other parts of Laos.

Thakhek is located opposite the Thai town of Nakhorn Panom on the Mekong. A tannery for cow and buffalo hides, a small power plant, an ice plant, and two lumber mills constitute Thakhek's industry. There are several movie houses, a hotel, a few small textile shops which produce for local consumption, and the usual small retail stores. Like Savannakhet, Thakhek must import about a third of its rice. Other imports include textiles, canned foods, salt, and bicycles. Exports include buffalo, beef cattle, hogs, and cow and buffalo hides. As in Pakse, the volume of imports exceeds exports by about twenty to one.

Problems of the Urban Populations

All the major towns in Laos appear to have deficits in both their balance of trade and their public budget. None derive enough food from the surrounding countryside to feed themselves, all depending to varying degrees on rice imports from Thailand. This is, of course, a reflection of the fact that the whole economy of Laos operates at a deficit and that the provinces are unable to produce, or at least transport to market, enough rice to maintain the relatively low level of living in the towns.

Except for some administrative services and a police force, public facilities are almost completely absent in these towns. There are no sewer systems or reliable piped water supplies. Hospitals exist but lack trained personnel. In some of the towns there are fire engines, supplied by the American aid program, but these are not always kept in operating condition. Electric power is sporadic and insufficient.

Although the towns are all located on the Mekong, transportation of goods to market is a major problem because of inadequate roads. The Mekong is not navigable throughout its length due to rapids below Savannakhet and during the dry season there is sometimes too little water even to reach Luang Prabang.

Housing has become a problem as more and more rural relatives come to join their families in town. One Lao source estimated that nearly twenty per cent of urban families live in household units of seven or more members. In Vientiane and Luang Prabang the housing situation is aggravated by the influx of refugees from North Vietnam.

In Pakse, Savannakhet, and Thakhek it is estimated that some eighty per cent of the population living within the town limits are engaged in agriculture, at least on a part-time basis, another ten per cent in small industry and handicrafts, and the remaining ten per cent in administration, transport, and religious activities.

In the Vientiane area approximately sixty-five per cent of the population is engaged in agriculture, twenty per cent in industry, business and handicrafts, and fifteen per cent in administration, commerce, transport, domestic services, and religion.

It is estimated that in 1959 about 250,000 persons or roughly one-eighth of the population of Laos were directly involved in a cash economy. This figure was arrived at by, first, adding together the about 9,500 civil servants in Laos (2,800 of whom are in the administrative capital),[55] about 3,300 police, and about 25,000 soldiers for a total of approximately 37,800 individuals directly employed by the government. Taking the conservative estimate of a little over four as family size, the figure of 160,000 was reached for those living on government salaries. Added to this were some 60,000 Chinese, Vietnamese, Europeans, and Indians, the overwhelming majority of whom were engaged in business, plus approximately 30,000 Lao and their dependents active in business, industry, and crafts of all types.

In a country such as Laos where demographic information is so limited this kind of calculation necessarily involves arbitrary distinctions. How, for example, does one classify the farmer who works as a coolie during the dry season, the rural craftsman, the village family supported in part by a son who is a soldier, the monk living in a town wat? All these obviously borderline cases certainly differ from the farmer who occasionally markets part of his rice crop and purchases a few thousand kip's worth of goods.

In any case, twelve or thirteen per cent of the total population primarily dependent on a cash income is a relatively small proportion. Nevertheless, it can be said with some justification that there are virtually no people in Laos who do not have vital economic contacts outside their village, even if only to acquire salt or iron by barter.

Some index of emerging economic class differences can be gained by comparing the rural standard of living with that of urban officials.[56] For a number of years the government's Bureau of Statistics has been carrying on surveys on the cost of living of Lao officials in Vientiane. This cost of living index (see Table 34) reflects to some degree, one can fairly assume, the standard of living of the urban officials. Certainly if an item appears on the list, one can assume that it figures in urban consumption patterns, and the emphasis may give us some rough idea of its felt importance by the Lao conducting the survey. By perusing this list we can easily see that items such as canned goods, aperitifs, and <u>Paris Match</u> are confined to the elite, but such items amount to only approximately three per cent of the weighted coefficient on which this standard of living is based. If, however, we examine those items infrequently used by villagers we find that more than one-third of the cost of living (by weighted items) is composed of goods or services rarely if ever available to villagers.

Foodstuffs such as bread, canned food of all kinds, certain bottled beverages, and many types of clothing are not found in villages away from the main roads, a situation encompassing the overwhelming majority of the rural population. Also, services such as electricity, Western-style doctors, and urban entertainment are not accessible to villagers. To the rural people of Laos the unavailability of a commodity like bread probably could not matter less. Nor are the lack of toilet articles, bottled beverages, or movies per se, often mentioned by Lao farmers as a reason for envy of townspeople. But these and many similar items, combined with the paucity of education, health, and communications facilities, do combine to form a material and psychological barrier making for friction. It is no coincidence that a good proportion of the commodities are imported, for, with the exception of rice mills and sawmills, the few existing industries are devoted to serving the consumption needs of the urban population. Aside from a few weaving enterprises, cottage industries have not been developed. A Vientiane household buys a teak table made in Thailand although Laos has many teak forests, or Hong Kong clothing although Laos produces both silk and cotton, or canned sardines although the Mekong offers a variety of fish. All this suggests potential small-scale industry which might serve the rural as well as the urban population.

Assuming daily rice consumption of .6 kilos per person, the cost of rice alone amounts to one-seventh of the salary of an average clerk. When an approximately equal amount for meat and vegetables (a minimum estimate) is added, plus outlays for housing, clothing, supplies, and other expenses, it is apparent that the government clerk has difficulty making his budget balance.

The period from 1956 to 1958 was one of intense commercial activity engendered by the increasing American aid program, which made dollar credits available mainly to finance the army and the police. Many small businesses mushroomed and foreign businessmen arrived en masse from Hong Kong, Bangkok, Saigon, and other areas. During 1956 and 1957 the demand for certain services such as domestic help and artisan labor resulted in an approximately 130 per cent increase in these wage scales. The general rise in the cost of living then slowed with the devaluation of the kip in October 1958.

Standards have changed significantly in the past decade. In Vientiane an increasing number of homes have become electrified, improved types of living quarters have been constructed, and forms of recreation have become more diversified. It is true that most of the better housing has been monopolized by the elite, as have many of the imported foods and luxuries, but rural people too have benefited, e.g. in the introduction of evaporated milk and mosquito netting and in the wider availability of certain types of clothing and other items. A number of items on which the current price index is based did not even figure in the expenditure patterns of "Lao middle class families" in 1948 or even 1950. So, although the salaries of these government workers have remained almost unchanged and there has been considerable dissatisfaction, still the developments during the past decade have not been wholly negative.

This steady inflation has also been the concern of the rural population. Prices increase sharply as one goes farther north or south of the Vientiane area. While the price of some articles trebled and quadrupled during the first years of the American aid program, the price of rice little more than doubled. Therefore, a farmer who owned no land paid three to five times as much for essential items in 1959 as he did prior to 1955, whereas those with rice to sell at the new prices found themselves paying two and one-half to three times as much as previously. For example, in 1955 a farmer could take a small pig to market and return with a shirt for himself, a shirt for his son, and a simple cotton skirt for his wife. In 1957 he could return with only a shirt for himself (Kaufman 1961).

As has been emphasized, while the disparity between urban and rural standards of living has been a cause of social conflict, at the same time the picture here is not entirely negative. It appears that the standard of living of people in rural areas has improved somewhat over the past decade and that they now have access to many more types of goods. Here too the change has been disproportionate, with those who live along the main road benefiting most, and the mountain peoples affected to a much lesser degree. These developments are hardly surprising in view of the abundant external aid Laos has received during the past five years.

Problems in Lao Development

Laos is an example par excellence of an underdeveloped country, lacking as it does a stable political climate or structure, a sound fiscal policy, or the basic infrastructure required for economic growth (education and health facilities, housing, a reliable transport and communications network, adequate electric power). In addition there is an inadequacy in trained labor, marketing and distribution systems, indigenous savings, legal and administrative frameworks, management and technical proficiency, and institutional relationships with other countries.

Most of the Lao economy and government has been based on foreign aid. Actually, under its aid program the United States has supported almost all the pay and allowances in the Lao military budget. Also covered has been the major part of the budget of the national police. In addition, the civil budget (which does not include the military) has never been balanced. Of importance here is the extent to which the population can be taxed so local revenues can be raised to meet expenses.

Under the present system the amount of taxes from rural areas is not significant, while two of the most numerous and highly paid categories of government employees -- the police and the army -- are exempt from taxation. In effect the American government has also been paying a major part of the salaries of such government employees as teachers, amounting in recent years to approximately forty per cent of the current operating expenses of the civil government. Customs duties are the most significant source of income and have amounted to some seventy per cent of the tax revenues. Ironically even this source of taxation has been indirectly a result of the American aid program since, of course, the import program is underwritten with dollar aid and not with local exports.

The base of the income tax in Laos is very narrow; actually less than two thousand persons and corporations have paid taxes in recent years, most revenue coming from a few large corporations. This is the consequence of tax exemption and generous credits for dependents, so that the initial tax rate on personal income is only 1.5 per cent. In view of the pressure of inflation on stable government salaries, it is doubtful that much more could be raised from this source without seriously damaging morale. In 1959 approximately 3,250 business firms paid a turnover tax amounting to four per cent on most items, with a fifteen per cent tax on luxuries. Although Laos is a poor country, still with tax revenues under ten per cent of her annual national income there seems to be proportionately lesser taxation effort than is currently being put forth by other countries in Southeast Asia.

It is difficult to foresee any simple solution to the economic problems of Laos. The development of transportation facilities is obviously vital, but this represents an instrumentality only, although an essential one, and not a basic source of income. Of primary importance is the development of agricultural, mineral, and other natural resources. Certainly the country must first produce enough food to feed her small urban centers. A major difficulty has been an almost total disregard of the traditional economies of the diverse ethnic groups. Surveys have been undertaken of airport and harbor development, electric power plant operation, and road construction, and some preliminary work has been done on mineral resources. Yet, with a few exceptions (see e.g. Duclos,

Gaudillot and Condominas), almost no research has been undertaken on the economic patterns of the villagers of Laos, their utilization of forest resources, and the extent to which they engage in trade and are involved in a money economy.

Postscript

This monograph has been presented as a background study of economic and social patterns in Laos, with no attempt to provide an analysis of the contemporary (1964) situation in its political and economic aspects. Despite intensive political maneuverings and some fighting, the basic social and economic configuration remains unaltered. Under the best of circumstances the Laotian government would be faced with very difficult problems in a situation of coup and counter-coup; it is unrealistic to imagine much being done about economic development. On the Communist side it would appear that little comprehensive planning will be done in the areas now controlled until the Pathet Lao have consolidated their power among the scattered tribal groups.[57] Further, there is a large commitment to the war in South Vietnam. The DRV and CPR both have serious internal problems, and it does not appear likely that the Pathet Lao would be getting extensive nonmilitary assistance. The role of North Vietnam in the Sino-Soviet dispute can also directly affect the situation in Laos.

Behind all the international implications and internecine fighting one fact is starkly clear -- the peoples of Laos are being subjected to suffering and privation. According to United States government estimates approximately 150,000 people have become refugees. Most strongly affected have been the Meo in Xieng Khouang and to an only slightly lesser extent the Meo in Sam Neua, Sayaboury, and Luang Prabang. The aboriginal peoples have also suffered, refugees of various groups having been estimated at 50,000 in both northern and southern areas. Added to the total number of refugees are up to 15,000 Lao in northern areas, particularly Luang Prabang, as well as some Tai and Yao. Small resettlement activities have been undertaken but some 80,000 people, mostly Meo, are said to be relying primarily on relief supplies provided by the American government.

According to available figures, it would appear that almost ten per cent of the total population of Laos has been affected. The amount of relocation has been even greater. Historically the Lao as well as the tribal peoples have tended to move into more inaccessible areas in times of conflict, with increasing reliance on hai agriculture. Simultaneously both sides appear to be trying to encourage na cultivation, making the various groups more amenable to central control. Under the American aid program approximately ten thousand acres have been brought under irrigation with the construction of a number of small dams. There are reports that the Chinese have brought some tractors into the areas under their control in Nam Tha.

Details are presently lacking but the trend is obvious. Major resettlement programs are either being undertaken or are planned by both sides. When the major population dislocations resulting directly from the fighting are added to this, the tremendous state of flux in which the peoples of Laos find themselves becomes apparent. Regardless of the outcome of the present struggle, most of the patterns and practices described in this monograph will be altered or severely modified in the next few years. A better life is not assured, but attempts at change, using this theme as a rationalization, are certain.[58]

Americans, Chinese, French, Japanese, Thai, and Vietnamese have all participated in trying to control and change the lives of the peoples of Laos and, in this endeavor, have received help or "supervision" from Canadians, English, Indians, Poles, and Russians. It would seem that seldom in world history has such a large and varied company meddled in the lives of so few.

NOTES TO PART I

1. A Lao report states that there has in the past been an underestimation of some 15 per cent for the provinces of Phong Saly, Vientiane, Savannakhet, and Khammouane; of 20 per cent for Saravane and Champassak; and of 40 per cent for Luang Prabang, Sayaboury, Nam Tha, and Sam Neua. Taking the census of 1936, one then obtains a figure of 1,247,000 instead of 1,018,000 for that year; 1,562,000 instead of 1,309,400 for 1951; and 1,708,000 instead of 1,575,450 for 1957. If one takes the electoral lists, composed of approximately 840,000 persons, an even higher figure for the total population appears reasonable -- perhaps 1,700,000 inhabitants. The report concludes that a population of 2,000,000 is a reasonable estimate on which to base the 1958-63 plan. This assumes an annual increase rate of 1.5 per cent, which is considerably less than the 2.03 estimated for 1951-57. Ministère des Finances de l'Economie Nationale et du Plan, Plan du développement économique et social, Royaume du Laos (Vientiane, 1959), pp. 9-11.

2. Some observers prefer to divide the year into three seasons: summer from March through June, the rainy season from July through October, and winter from November through February.

3. The Lao do not place any great emphasis on exact records. The chaotic condition of official Lao records is in part a result of a lack of technical facilities and in part a lack of interest in precise detail. An aspect of this attitude is that most Lao officials are extremely generous in making available those records they do possess. Referring to the Kha, one investigator states, "There is no system of counting. If you want to know how many men there are in the village, the headman goes around with a bamboo stick, breaking one knot for each person met, and gives you the knots to count. There is no record of births. Their children were born 'when there was prosperity that year,' 'when the tree was planted' and so on. A schoolteacher, when asked for the birthdates of his children, simply named dates in a series, made up in order to have something for the school record" (Jumsai 1959: 20).

4. The distinction in spelling is arbitrarily established here.

5. It should be emphasized that these groupings are approximate. A difficulty in attempting to identify the various ethnic groups in Laos lies in the fact that they are known by a great variety of names in the literature -- different ones being customary in French, English, and Chinese sources -- while there are

additional Siamese and Lao names for these people as well as names by which these groups refer to themselves. "Meo" is used by the Lao and the French, "Miao" is usually found in Chinese and English sources, and some Meo groups refer to themselves as "Mung" or "Mong." In the case of a major tribal Tai group we have Black Tai, Tai Noir, or Tai Dam -- English, French, and Lao versions of the same name. It cannot be too strongly emphasized that Laos, despite the work of French scholars, remains one of the most poorly known areas of the world from the point of view of ethnography.

This system of classification also appears to reflect the desire of the Lao government to spread Lao culture and civilization (principally as reflected in language and religion), which seems to have been encouraged by certain French colonial administrators who used Lao officials to oversee Kha groups. An excellent example is provided by the Kingdom of Luang Prabang which was a semiautonomous area during the French period. However, one French writer remarked, "When the Commissioner assumes his office [in Luang Prabang], he quickly learns that he has to administer not only the Lao but also the Lu, Tai Neua, Tai Dam, Tai Houn, Mu, Lamet, Kho, Lantene, Hoc, Meo, Yao, Ho, Phoutai, Chinese, Vietnamese, and Indians."

6. Although this is true of Laos, these divisions are not irreversible. In parts of China the Meo live in valleys and cultivate irrigated rice (Mickey 1947).

7. Iwata speaks of twelve subdivisions including the Tai Souei, Tai Poua, Tai Pouan, Tai Dai, Tai Nouan, Tai Porong, Tai Et, Tai Soun, Tai O, Tai Sot Bau, Tai Neua, and Tai Deng. These subdivisions are mainly indicative of minor dialect variations and also tend to indicate the place of origin such as Xieng Khouang or Sam Neua. There also appear to be some minor differences in customs. Generally speaking there does not seem to be any restriction on intermarriage and in many cases the Lao are not even sure from which group they have originated. As they come more into contact with the towns these minor variations among the Thai-Lao become less significant.

8. Dam, Kao, and Deng are black, white, and red, respectively, referring in Lao to variations in women's dress.

9. Chen (1949: 1) places the Tai Lu in three different groups.

10. Roux (1954: 301-02). The Khmu are the largest "Kha" group in northern Laos and the only numerically important one in Luang Prabang and Xieng Khouang provinces. They number about 100,000 and are divided into several subgroups (Smalley 1961b).

11. Phou Khao Quai, about forty miles north of Vientiane and also known by its French name of Ritaville, appears to be the southernmost extension of the Meo. It is only a few decades old.

12. According to the French scholar Andre Fraisse there have been Yao in northern Laos for three or four centuries while the Meo began arriving less than a century ago.

13. This is true in Thailand where the Lao represent a minority of inferior social status and the above statement clearly shows the government's policy of emphasizing theoretical unity and equality. In Laos the term Lao has prestige associations.

14. Many of the older men in the Luang Prabang area today are tattooed in this fashion, and in the villages even some of the younger men, but in general the custom appears to be dying out. Khmu of this area are also tattooed in a similar manner.

15. They are descendants of Lao from Vientiane who were taken to Thailand after the destruction of the Lao capital by an invading Thai army early in the nineteenth century.

16. Regarding the linguistic problems of a Bangkok Thai in Laos, Jumsai (1959: 15) writes: "It is not difficult for a Lao from the capital to understand the talking and writing of these [Tai] tribes. The language is also akin to the Thai of Bangkok, so that after a few days' stay with each tribe getting my ears used to a different kind of pronunciation and certain distinctive words locally used, it offers me no difficulty to understand them. The writing of each special tribe needs special study, but after some time one can decipher them, since the system of alphabets is everywhere the same, although different styles of writing have developed over the centuries. With the Lao language one can go almost everywhere because although other groups do not speak Lao, their leaders have learned the language through continual contacts with the Lao people of the plains."

17. The official Thai government handbook previously quoted (Thailand 1957: 23) contains the following description of the Khmu:

> This race has its headquarters to the east of the Mae Khong [Mekong] in the Luang Prabang Province. Numbers of them come over every year to work in the teak forests and some of them settle in the country.
>
> In the north of Kanchanaburi Province there are a few Kamuk [Khmu] villages. These people say they originally came from Luang Prabang, but it is not unlikely they were brought as prisoners-of-war. Some of them still speak their own language, but in dress and customs they conform to their neighbours.
>
> The Kamuk are also found in Northeastern Thailand . . . . They are not indigenous there but were originally brought to these places by Burmese slave traders about half a century ago.

This is also true of many Kha groups in southern Laos, such as the Sô in the region of Thakhek, who were moved across the Mekong by the Thai for political reasons in a forced migration. The Black Tai provide a modern example of the fact that even today the peoples of Laos are still on the move for reasons similar to those that have caused their migrations in the past -- economics and warfare. Just as the Lao from the Vientiane area were deported to Thailand a little over a century ago so Black Tai refugees originating in Dien Bien Phu from the Indochina War have settled on the outskirts of Luang Prabang and Vientiane. Lu from Yunnan have sought refuge in Nam Tha province just as a century or so before some of their forefathers migrated south to Luang Prabang province. Young reports a similar recent migration and notes that they are becoming assimilated into Thai culture faster (1961: 76-79). A further example is provided by the flight of Meo from the current fighting in Xieng Khouang to refuge in Vientiane and other areas of the south.

18. The Communists have stressed education of these groups, and in 1960 it was estimated that 8.2 per cent of all students in the Democratic Republic of Vietnam (North Vietnam) were of minority nationalities. Although this figure is smaller than their proportion in the total population (14.3) it is still very significant and appears to represent a great increase. Traditional trade patterns are also important. In 1960 during the Souvanna Phouma neutralist government's tenure an agreement was negotiated with the DRV on border exchanges, a development of some importance since the same ethnic groups live on

both sides of the political boundary and such items as Vietnamese salt are important in trade. Road connections have existed between these countries since the colonial period.

19. Here the Lao were only 8 per cent of the total population in 1930 -- the majority (56 per cent) were Kha.

20. In 1956 one Lao government source estimated that Vientiane province contained about 600 Yao, 4,000 Meo, and 2,500 Kha. This would make the ethnic Lao about 96 per cent.

21. An article in the New York Times quoting the Yunnan Jihpao states that Chinese settlers have begun a large-scale migration into Yunnanese areas bordering on North Vietnam, Laos, and Burma. Approximately 18,000 migrants from Hunan are included in this move with additional tens of thousands expected to follow during the next few years. According to present plans the total may reach 100,000. The first arrivals were sent to state farms in the Tai autonomous area on the Lao border and to the Red river valley near Vietnam. New villages are said to have been established and roads built. Tillman Durdin, New York Times, January 21, 1960.

22. Xieng Khouang might perhaps be included. That is, these provincial capitals are distinguished from the others by the Lao government in that they each contain certain government facilities not present in the other administrative centers, e.g. a hospital and collège (junior high school). For a summary of provincial services see Halpern 1964b: Table 3.

23. Pietrantoni 1957. Other factors being equal it appears reasonable to assume that the figures for the urban populations and their composition are more accurate than the statistics for rural areas.

24. Obviously this situation has changed with the continuing unrest, although to what extent it is difficult to know.

25. There has doubtless been some attrition of these communities over the years as some of the offspring of mixed Lao-Chinese or Lao-Vietnamese marriages have merged into the general urban Lao population. Schooling seems a key factor here; those who study in the Chinese schools remain in the Chinese community. In 1957 almost 600 Chinese left Laos (Annuaire Statistique du Laos, 1953-1957: 60). Based on an estimate of 15,000, there are 1.1 per cent ethnic Chinese in Laos, as

compared with 1.8 per cent in Burma, 4.1 per cent in Cambodia, and 15 per cent in Thailand (Fisher 1964: 181).

26. In 1957 it was estimated that about 2,700 Thai a month were entering Laos and an almost equal number departing (Laos 1958: 80).

NOTES TO PART II

1. A smaller second crop is cultivated by the Lao of northern Thailand in the region of Chiengmai. Since many of the climatic and traditional cultural factors are approximately similar, the single cropping in Laos is probably related to the generally more marginal economic character of the latter area rather than any inherent cultural or geographic factors. (Kingshill 1960: 39-40). In 1959 a small irrigation system consisting of a low dam and six kilometers of canals was completed near Luang Prabang town under the auspices of the American aid program.

2. This account was recorded and translated by Smalley in 1952-54.

3. The sixth Lao month is the usual time but there may be considerable variation due to weather.

4. Sometimes, in the belief that the more seeds planted the greater the harvest, seedlings are planted so close together that the rice plants do not get sufficient sunlight or soil nutrients.

5. The Lao use these stalks as buffalo fodder, but among many Khmu -- and a number of Lao as well -- there are often no buffalo to feed.

6. The Vietnamese term _rai_ or _ray_ is also frequently used in literature on this area. This is also a Thai word; in Lao speech the _r_ has apparently been shifted to _h_ (Anuman 1958). See Bartlett 1957: 693 for a discussion of this and similar terms used in other parts of the tropics. Volume 20 of the _Proceedings of the Ninth Pacific Science Congress_ (Bangkok, 1958) also contains information on this subject.

7. The men make holes with a metal-tipped digging stick and the women follow them dropping in the seeds.

8. There are usually three different weeding periods, although only two are mentioned here.

9. This custom has wide distribution and was practiced by the Thai peoples of Thailand and Laos, northern Vietnam, Burma, and southern Yunnan. Within Laos the ceremonies were carried out by the royal families of Luang Prabang, Champassak, and Muong Sing. In certain areas, even though royalty has disappeared or no longer performs the rites, villagers have substituted the _nai ban_ or _tasseng_ or have used the Kha, who

have different phi (Sinavong 1963: 105-06). According to Wales (1931: 256-64) this custom is of Indian origin although it was also practiced in China and may have been influenced from this source in its earlier forms.

10. Gongs are a symbol of value; kam is a measure of diameter.

11. Phya Anuman Rajadhon (1956: 19) relates for the similar Thai culture: "The matter of making offerings to rice and to the Rice Goddess no doubt comes from the belief that various things have life; whether human being or animal or plant, everything has something abiding in it which is called the khwan. If the khwan is not constantly present, the living thing dies. Rice is regarded as having life and a khwan, and so the khwan of the rice must be treated in such a way as to cause it to remain present and not slip away, for this might cause the rice not to flourish or cause it to die."

12. Wiens (1954: 318) says the Meo move about once every eight years due to soil exhaustion; Seidenfaden (1958: 131) notes twelve to fifteen years between moves; Bernatzik (1947: 644) says from four to ten years; Young (1961: 114) cites ten to fifteen for the Meo and for the Yao. The latter three sources refer primarily to Thailand.

    An example of Meo migrations is the case of a Meo nai ban of a village some fifteen miles from Luang Prabang town who was born in Xieng Khouang, then moved to an area near Vientiane, and from there returned to his original home before moving again to Luang Prabang province. The Meo village of Kiouketcham about sixty miles from Luang Prabang town was originally settled twenty years ago by immigrants from Xieng Khouang, some of whom within the past few years have moved on to other villages, although some later returned.

13. The process of moving is described in great detail by Bernatzik. The decision to change the village site rests with the assembly of all men who are able to bear arms. Here the opinions of the village headman and the shaman carry great weight. The move is never made by single individuals or even nuclear families but by extended families and usually villages as a whole, a logical expectation in this patriarchally structured society.

14. Another point of view was given by a Meo informant near Luang Prabang who said he was planning to move but felt he should first accumulate a rice surplus.

15. Abadie (1924: 159-60) writes of the Meo of Tonkin: "Maize is the basic food of the Meo. It is boiled, steamed, dried, or reduced to meal in order to be eaten in the form of cakes. The Meo also cultivate mountain rice, but like the Man [Yao] they are coming more and more to cultivate permanent irrigated rice fields, the working of which is easier and more remunerative. To this end they have taken over as much as possible of the favorable terrain, valley bottoms or sides of hillocks on which water may be brought by a simple canalization, and have laid out these areas into terraced rice fields where they often successfully cultivate rice and opium." See also Barney (1957a) on the Meo of Xieng Khouang.

16. Boutin (1937: 105) claims that the Meo of Sam Teu and Houa Muong are obliged to concentrate on corn because rice does poorly at the altitudes at which they live.

17. See also Embree and Thomas (1950: 146-47) and Mickey (1947).

18. See Iwata (1960b); Srisvasdi (1950); and, for additional data on the Meo in Vietnam and China, Abadie (1924: 159-60); Gourou (1951: 33); and Roux and Tran (1954: 391).

19. Savina (1930: 174) notes that if one asks the Meo why they live in the mountains and abhor the plains, they give various answers:

    "The mountains are less hot, humid and unsanitary." [In Laos they frequently cited the menace of malaria.]

    "We do not descend into the plains because we are afraid of the water, the leeches and the buffalo."

    "We cannot live in the plains because we were born in the mountains. Transplanted trees will never thrive."

    "We cannot leave the mountains behind, because in the mountains are the graves of our ancestors."

    "The inhabitants of the plains understand how to work in and how to cultivate the plains, just as we Meo know the work and the cultivation of the mountains."

    "The people on the plains do not speak our language. How could we be able to understand them?" [Today in Laos many adult Meo speak at least a little Lao while older men often know Yunnanese.]

> "If we descend into the plains, our girls would marry people who do not belong to our race."
>
> "In the plains there are too many wars, duties, soldiers, and mandarins."
>
> "If we would settle down among the people on the plains, they would steal our herds."
>
> "We do not want to go down into the plains because there we would not be allowed to plant opium, maize or fruit trees."
>
> "The soil of the mountains belongs to the Meo; the soil of the plains does not belong to them."

20. Water shortages are common in Northeast Thailand as well. Villagers are very conscious of this and of its effects on the rice crops. A usual reply to a question concerning one's rice is, "Not enough -- scarcity of water" (Klausner 1956: 2).

21. Smalley 1952. In Kentung in northern Burma a change from swidden to irrigated rice fields is being encouraged by the missionaries as a means for bettering economic status: ". . . the literate Christians have been approached through books, magazines, and word of mouth to show them the need of finding more satisfactory methods of agriculture. The method to which they are turning is that of the irrigated rice fields in the narrow valleys and lowlands" (Lewis 1957: 225).

22. The late Viceroy of Laos, Prince Phetsarath, in his frequent trips through the countryside personally encouraged the re-settlement of the Khmu and in some cases provided them with implements.

23. The following is quoted from a broadcast of the Hanoi Radio on November 28, 1959:

> In spite of serious and repeated natural calamities which occurred during cultivation, four large fields in the Tai-Meo Autonomous Region have yielded an autumn rice crop which far exceeds expectations. The average yield is expected to exceed 3 tons per hectare while that for the whole of North Vietnam is estimated at 2.5 tons. These fields cover more than 8,000 hectares, that is, about one-third of the rice-growing area in the region. In the Dien Bien Phu area, where the famous battle took place, the average exceeded 3.6 tons per hectare, the highest average yield in the region. Most of the region's 3,000 hectares

of crop land this year suffered serious waterlogging during cultivation. But the local population put in thousands of workdays scooping water out of the fields and doing timely manuring work, preventing crop losses. The local cooperatives, which had practiced close planting, obtained twice as much rice per hectare as did individual peasants who kept to their old habit of sparse planting . . . . In addition, dozens of small fields in the area have also reaped a bumper crop. For instance, on the Tong Lanh and Thom Mou fields, close to Thaun Chau, capital of the Tai-Meo Autonomous Region, the yield ranged from 3.7 to 4.6 tons per hectare.

In Phu Tho Province more than 500 plots were established which recorded an average yield of five or six tons. In Nghe An Province, the experimental plot of young members of the Tran Phu cooperative brought in 9.3 tons per hectare.

On these experimental plots, the peasants have applied in a creative manner the advanced experiences of Chinese peasants to the practical soil and climatic conditions of Vietnam. These fields were plowed more deeply, planted with denser rows of rice plants, spread with more manure and received more care than the other fields. It has positively confirmed the superiority of the new farming methods which have proved very successful in China.

24. Yields from Ku Daeng in northern Thailand indicate that the Vietnamese figures are certainly within the realm of possibility. In this connection Kingshill's remarks about declining yields are interesting (1960: 65):

> According to old-timers, the yield in Ku Daeng has been steadily decreasing over the years. One old woman told us that the people worked harder when she was young. They pulled out all the weeds they found in the fields, using both hands, whereas nowadays the workers use only one hand. In 'her time' the yield was nearly twice what it is today. Another villager said that the farmers watched the insects more when he was young, thereby reducing crop damage. He added that people today are too lazy to take proper care of their crops. Furthermore, cooperation and leadership are lacking with regard to regulation of the water supply. A few people, nowadays, attend to the work of building the irrigation system, but when it is finished, everybody uses the water to his own advantage without consideration for his neighbors, the man concluded. The decrease in productivity is undoubtedly due to over-cultivation of the soil. This seems to be true for the country as a whole. According to one informant, fertilizer has been distributed by the govern-

ment. Favorable results have failed to materialize, however, and this was blamed on inadequate instructions received with the fertilizer.

25. Gourou (1956: 345) says: "They have rediscovered cherished habits and they obey also the lessons of experience; they have observed that permanent rice fields, without manure, gave a lesser output per day of work than ladang [swiddens]." It should be mentioned, however, that although unfertilized wet rice fields may have lower yields than swiddens, still they can support infinitely greater populations, since they give consistent yields over a long period of time. The Tonkin delta can support 800 persons per square mile, or over 100 times that of the Lamet area.

26. A touque is a five-gallon kerosene tin, approximately equal to a kalon, or container, usually a basket, with a capacity of twelve kilos of paddy (unhusked rice). Wa is a geometrically varying measure based on the circumference of a mound of rice; it approximates the length of an arm span. The Yao mut is similar to the Lao kalon. Some observers claim that this word is derived from the English gallon and has been adopted into Lao from Thai.

27. This is an extremely conservative estimate.

28. Dobby (quoted in Bartlett 1957: 385) estimates that a cutover area needs to stand unused for seven to ten years. Smalley says seven to eight years is the usual period the Khmu allow between cultivation of their hai, in the Luang Prabang area. But ideally they would prefer a longer cycle. Smalley in 1961 found that the Khmu in the area of Luang Prabang were making their fields closer to the road and at less distance from the village. They were also reducing the number of years of fallows. Reasons given were the unsettled political conditions and the desirability of convenient access to the firewood left after the slash-and-burn process which was in heavy demand in Luang Prabang town.

29. The great degree of variation becomes apparent in another excerpt from Gourou (quoted in Bartlett 1957: 565): "The 'ray' system does not permit a high density of population, but it conserves soil since erosion attacks only slightly land that is not cultivated and on which, after the second year, trees grow again, and since the reconstitution of the forest hinders laterization. . . . practiced with the unconscious wisdom of the Indochinese mountain people, the ray cultivation is a sufficient-

ly prudent technique of soil utilization in broken country." Pelzer (1958: 128) also stresses an important positive point: ". . . one of the valuable features of swidden agriculture is that normally the plow is not one of the tools used . . . the plow can be a very destructive tool when not properly handled . . . and is definitely inferior to the dibble stick and hoe on steep slopes." Many other sources could be cited, but included here are comments of two anthropologists and an agronomist who have made intensive studies of swidden cultivators in widely separated areas. Conklin (1957: 138) in discussing the agricultural swidden practices of the Hanunóo on the island of Mindoro in the Philippines states: "Within the context of Hanunóo culture, fallowing is more accurately viewed as a period in which most vegetation is prepared for the next swidden cycle by controlled natural reforestation and forest enrichment. Areas in low forest fallow are protected from destruction. It is difficult to set a minimum period of fallowing as necessary for the continued, productive use of swidden land by re-clearing. Many variables are at work. A reasonable limit seems to be somewhere between 8 and 15 years, depending on the total ecology of the local situation. Swidden farmers are usually well aware of these limitations." J.D. Freeman (1955: 29-30) concludes his study of the Iban with the following remarks: "Under Sarawak conditions, if virgin rain forest is felled, fired and farmed for one season only, and then allowed to recuperate, adequate regeneration takes place. Furthermore, if thereafter the resulting second jungle is brought into cultivation at sufficiently rare intervals and never for more than one season, the land may be utilized virtually indefinitely without serious degradation taking place."

30. In this connection see Omer C. Stewart, "Fire As the First Great Force Employed by Man," in Man's Role in Changing the Face of the Earth, ed. William L. Thomas (Chicago, University of Chicago Press, 1956), pp. 115-33; and Charles F. Cooper, "The Ecology of Fire," Scientific American, April 1961, pp. 150-60.

31. H.A.M. Wirtz, commenting on the preliminary version of this study, stated (in Tropical Abstracts 1959, pp. 356-57) that the hai holds an important complementary place in the rural economy where wet-rice cultivation is normally predominant and that shifting cultivation should not be abolished under all conditions as soon as possible. However, Wirtz continues, the Meo are responsible for severe deforestation on a large scale in Laos' highest mountains. Large steep

areas which should be forest reservations have been replaced by coarse grasses which are burned off every dry season, thus preventing natural reforestation.

In this connection it is possible that there are significant differences in the ways in which the Meo cultivate their hai as compared to groups such as the Lamet, although superficially there are many parallels. Barney states that a specific field may be used for three or four successive years, while Bernatzik observes that for the Akha as well as the Meo, fields lie fallow from eight to ten years. This is said to be a necessity since rice is planted for two years in succession in the same field. Izikowitz implies that most fields are used only a year at a time and also indicates a somewhat longer fallow period. This problem cannot really be resolved until we have more exact and extensive data for the "great forest destroying Meo." Specifically, how long do they really use their land? One, two, three, four or more years in succession? And for which crops? How do they feel about land use? Do they have any conservation practices? Are their extensive migrations ecologically, politically, or psychologically inspired, or to what extent are their motives mixed? How far do they move each time?

32. These estimates are rough and part of the fields remains fallow so it is probable that the total area in rice fields is between 400,000 and 500,000 hectares. The low hai and na yields Wirtz estimates may balance out the overestimated acreage. Since accurate surveys do not exist, it is only possible to make guesses based on various sets of statistics supplemented by particular backgrounds. An official Lao government publication (_Annuaire statistique du Laos, quatrième volume, 1953 à 1957, présentation provisoire_, 1961, p. 62) presents a figure of 670,000 hectares of rice lands and a production of 560,000 tons for 1957. One infers that more recent figures may not be available to the government itself. No breakdown into na and hai is given. There is also significant variation in the figures, e.g. for 1956, 10,000 hectares were supposedly under cultivation with an identical total yield. Clearly the surveys upon which these data are based are something less than adequate.

33. Holdings along the river bank have been enriched each year by silt from the river's annual rise.

34. Cf. Abadie (1924) and Savina (1930).

35. This is similar to the Xieng Khouang Meo. Rice and opium are given the most effort, with corn, as a livestock feed,

third. Potatoes are often used as fertilizer in the opium fields, while pumpkins may be raised as fodder for horses (Barney 1957a: 30-32).

36. A person who supplies a gun or a dog gets a double portion.

37. Dooley (1958: 106-07) describes a man who was gored by a wild boar and another who was mauled by a bear.

38. This distribution applies to meat which results from the hunt as well as to sacrificial meat.

39. Use of guns was for a time forbidden by the French colonial government. Since independence this prohibition is no longer in effect and many Khmu, and especially Meo, have guns, often of their own manufacture. The Lao police confiscate Meo guns found being used on one another. In northern Laos many of the police stations look like weapons museums, piled high with flintlocks.

40. In his The Spirits of the Yellow Leaves (1951) Bernatzik describes a hunting and gathering group on the Lao-Thai border, but the group is small and marginal and the description incomplete.

41. Though paddy land is scarce, pasturage is adequate and fodder is no problem for most owners of livestock. Roadside areas, grassy wooded areas, waterholes, and any unclaimed rice stubble are considered public for cattle grazing.

42. Farmers in northern Laos do not have wagons, due to the traditional lack of roads.

43. A similar situation prevails among the Meo, who have acquired a taste for condensed milk. In fact, Lao government officials have requested help in developing dairy cattle breeding in Xieng Khouang.

44. The Lao unit of currency; in 1957 the official rate was 35 to $1. By 1959 a free market rate of 80 to 1 prevailed.

45. It might be thought that the Lao as Buddhists would not sacrifice livestock. Buddhism, however, is only one aspect of Lao religion. As in many other Asian countries, Buddhism and animism exist side by side without significant conflict. The average rural Lao did not see any inconsistency in the official

prohibition of slaughtering of animals for three days during the 2,500th anniversary of Buddhism and, a few months earlier, sacrificing to the phi to ensure a water supply for the rice fields.

46. This order of events may be questioned. It is interesting here that the informant emphasizes the buffalo as a prerequisite to building the house. The cash expenditures are very significant and represent proceeds from rice sales or coolie labor.

47. Lévy (1959: 162) reports: "At Luang Prabang, two buffalos, white and black, are offered each year to the guardian spirit called Phi Seua Muong . . . . This sacrifice has not taken place in Luang Prabang for a number of years . . . . Yet, buffalo meat constitutes the plat de résistance during all ceremonies in honor of the spirits . . . . Formerly in Luang Prabang the King personally contributed money to the maintenance of this sacrifice, memories of which are still vivid."

48. The question was raised as to why one village sacrificed only chickens while the other used buffalo. The reply was that the desire of the respective phi was being complied with in each case.

49. In Laos many mountain peoples expressed dislike for life in the valleys.

50. From Kwang Ming Jih Pao (Peking), February 10, 1956 (translated by Union Research Service, Hong Kong, 2, 278). This chou, or special district, one of four in Yunnan, is located in the southwestern part of the province, with a total area of 25,000 square kilometers.

51. From Survey of China Mainland Press (U.S. Consulate General, Hong Kong) No. 1848, p. 9.

52. It is possible that this is the Lawa and thus closely related to the Khmu.

53. This belief exists among the Lao of Luang Prabang province, in that they often hesitate to cut down a forest for fear it will offend the resident phi, while a group of Yao in Muong Sing stated that their village phi would not approve if they came to live in the valley.

54. It would be very interesting to know how these statistics were

determined since it is unlikely that records of sacrifices were kept in every village.

55. Hung-chi (Red Flag), No. 5, March 1, 1959, as translated in China Mainland Magazines (U.S. Consulate General, Hong Kong), May 18, 1959, No. 163, p. 13.

56. Reliable figures do not exist but a 1943 estimate listed 350,000 head of cattle and 400,000 buffalo for all Laos.

57. In 1959 Laos had one fully trained agronomist, educated in France (ingénieur d'agriculture); fifteen agents (contrôleur d'agriculture), with varying degrees of education in Indochina and France; fifty-two other types of personnel with lesser training (agents de culture et de vulgarisation).

NOTES TO PART III

1. The crosscultural definitions of terms such as "surplus" have long concerned anthropologists. By "limiting biological factors" we merely mean that if people do not consume a certain minimum amount of food they cannot continue to exist.

2. Similar expressions occur in Thai and Chinese.

3. It has been estimated that in parts of Nam Tha province, chiefly Muong Nam Tha and Muong Sing, about five per cent of the rice is fed to horses and ten per cent to pigs, with some also used as chicken feed (Duclos 1959b: 8).

4. For Northeast Thailand .75 is given as a desirable minimum, although only 12 out of 69 households surveyed in one village near Ubol reached this amount (Madge 1957: 48).

5. In Vientiane canned French and Australian cheese is available, and some Vietnamese restaurants sell a Vietnamese specialty of sugared buffalo milk.

6. In the towns the more important Lao officials sometimes reside in two-story French-style villas which, although having the status of a European house, are very poorly suited to the climate. Prosperous urban Lao often have ceiling fans in their main rooms.

7. Small low folding chairs are often used since the Lao are more accustomed to squatting than sitting.

8. Among both the Khmu and Lao the couple usually resides with the wife's parents for a while after marriage, although neolocal residence is also common.

9. Among the Lao the men usually weave the wall panels. When a house is completed the Lao invite the bonzes to bless it; the Khmu sacrifice livestock to the spirits.

10. Khmu men weave baskets, many of which are purchased by the Lao.

11. This applies to all lowland areas -- except during the winter months. At the altitude at which the Meo live nights are cool throughout the year, one result being that pneumonia and other respiratory diseases are common.

12. Except in certain areas such as Muong Sai where Lao traits are being adopted to an increasing extent, and even there weav-

ing is usually done only by the more prosperous individuals and is a symbol of prestige as well as acculturation (Smalley 1959).

13. The silver is obtained from French colonial piasters or Burmese rupees which are melted down. Making bars from old coins is a small industry in Luang Prabang town.

14. Since they are removable they do not cause physical deformity as is seen in the use of neck-rings by the Paduang of Burma.

15. Lam means interpreter in Thai and Lao.

16. This is the pattern in Luang Prabang province. In some parts of northern Laos where there are no Lao the function of the lam may be assumed by tribal Tai. For example, in Muong Sing in northern Nam Tha a descendent of the hereditary "prince" of the Tai Lu acts as lam for the Kha Ko of the area. The position of lam is relative to the power-political position of the various ethnic groups in a given area. The late Prince Phetsarath acted as lam to a group of Lu living in northern Luang Prabang, a position he inherited. Here is clearly seen the hereditary and governmental aspects of the position of lam, which has certain feudal overtones. In this case Phetsarath purchased certain Lu products and helped the Lu improve their agricultural technique; in return some of them acted as his retainers. By the late 1950's, however, only fragments of the pattern remained.

17. The institution of lam has been given an orthodox Marxist interpretation by a Communist observer (Burchett 1957: 236-37): "Among the mountain people -- except the Lao Xung [Meo] -- almost every village has a 'professional' Lao Lum [Lao] who settles in as a doctor or a lawyer might into a village community in Europe. Because he has learned to read and write in the pagoda and has a higher social status, he sets up as 'general advisor.' He arbitrates in quarrels between villagers and offers to settle intervillage disputes by collecting a fee from both sides. He provokes disputes in order to settle them. He lends money at exorbitant interest rates. On holidays he makes some insignificant present to each household and collects an important contribution of rice, meat, or alcohol in return. The principle was imposed that the mountain villagers 'owed' a living to any Lao Lum who condescended to live with them. 'As a tree has leaves, so a Lao Thenh must have the Lao Lum' says a Lao Thenh proverb." Burchett goes on to describe the ways in which the French increased inequalities

and exploited the mountain peoples. Although some Lao may have lived in mountain villages, the function of the lam was more expediently served when the mountain people brought their trade goods to him. There is no question that the Lao and others often exploited the less culturally developed tribal peoples but to ignore the very real symbiotic functions of the interrelationships does violence to the facts. A recent Pathet Lao declaration calls for abolition of the lam system.

18. Seidenfaden (1958: 134) provides the following information on these people: "The Hôs or Panthays who used every cold season to come down to the markets of the towns of Northern Siam with their caravans of pack mules loaded with walnuts, chestnuts, velvet cloth, brass utensils, etc. are Muhammadans from Tali at the large inland lake of Erh-hai in western Yunnan. The Hôs are the descendents of Kublai Khan's Arab and Tartar soldiers who married Min-chia girls (besides also both Tai and Chinese ones). The Hôs, who have suffered terribly at the hands of the Chinese . . . are some of the world's greatest peddlers, first-class muleteers and opium smugglers."

19. Robequain (1925) does not mention them, stating that tools from Xieng Khouang villages supplied Luang Prabang; about a decade later Izikowitz refers to blacksmith villages in Luang Prabang and says they originated in Xieng Khouang.

20. Bernatzik (1947: 223-28) gives a detailed description of Meo and Akha trade in northern Thailand: "The Hô supply the Meo with iron, metal pots and pans, flints, matches and sulphur for making of gun powder. They sometimes obtain nitrate from bat droppings. The caravans also bring cowrie shells, buttons, silk, small mirrors, thread, needles, and magic amulets. They also supposedly trade in children for adoption and women. In return the Meo offer raw opium, stags' and rhinocerous' horns (greatly valued in the making of traditional Chinese medicines), and ivory. Much of this trade is on a barter basis, but currency is also used. If a Meo does not have silver coins he may use opium as the medium of exchange . . . . The Akha trade with the Shan in Burma, selling opium, cotton, pepper, pigs, and also honey and wax. In exchange they obtain salt and silver ornaments. One of their main items of trade is raw cotton and in suitable regions they also breed buffalo to trade to the Lao. They also carry on some opium trade with the Chinese merchants who live in Lao villages."

21. Their use is relatively recent. Most of the motors are of American manufacture and have been obtained under the Amer-

ican aid program.

22. At Thadeua, about ten miles downstream from Vientiane, a modern international ferry slip has been built with American aid. Also supplied under this program were three pusher tugs and two barges. This ferry system began operations in January 1958 and links Vientiane to Nong Khai, from which point the Thai Railway System connects with Bangkok. At Thadeua a terminal customs warehouse was also constructed with American aid. In connection with transport facilities, mention should also be made of a receiving and forwarding warehouse established with American aid at the port of Bangkok for handling cargoes destined for Laos from world-wide shippers.

23. Another important development has been a regional survey of the Mekong river basin, a project sponsored by the United Nations' Economic Council for Asia and the Far East, with headquarters in Bangkok. The project is aimed at developing the Mekong river and its tributaries for navigation, irrigation, flood-control, and hydroelectric purposes.

24. A connecting road from Nam Tha to Ban Houei Sai was planned as well as one from Nam Tha to Muong Sing. This area is now under Pathet Lao control but there are reports that the Chinese completed these roads.

25. The route is extremely rough and is best negotiated by jeep or truck. It is necessary to carry fuel for the entire trip. In contrast southern Laos has some all-weather roads.

26. This took place in 1957; by 1959 they had expanded their operations by transporting 6 1/2 tons of potatoes to Vientiane.

27. The French military base near Savannakhet is named Seno.

28. In 1956 Laos had about 1,800 miles of roads, about half of which were all-weather. The rest were usable only during the dry season, mainly because of the lack of bridges destroyed by wars or weather. About 250 miles of road were blacktopped but most required improvement. The most important road for Laos begins at Saigon, crosses into Cambodia, and runs due north through the main towns of Laos. In recent years the American and French governments in cooperation with the Lao government have built new bridges and repaired and improved existing ones. The magnitude of the requirements is revealed in the need, for example, for 952 bridges in seven provinces, about 25 of which should be sizable struc-

tures ranging from 150 to 900 feet long. Much reconstruction has been damaged or impeded as a result of recent fighting.

29. Sam Neua was supplied from Hanoi during French rule, and this link has presumably been restored by the Pathet Lao, who regained control in 1961.

30. "As regards the public domain, we maintained the custom which is consecrated by the local laws and usages. By virtue of these usages and these laws, the state is sole proprietor of the land and everything under it, without any exception, no matter how it is being exploited or what establishments have been made there, either on the surface or underneath.

    The inhabitants of the land are, in the last analysis, only usufructuaries who have the right of enjoyment of the land which they occupy and cultivate. The state may expropriate any occupant at any time by paying him a sum equal to the value of plantations or constructions made by him on the expropriated ground.

    The right of enjoyment of land is subject to certain conditions. The first of these is that the land occupied shall really be occupied and kept in a state of cultivation. Any property which has been abandoned or not cultivated for more than three years is defined as free ground and reverts to the state, which may cede it to any new usufructuary who is desirous of working it. Any inhabitant who clears free ground and places it under cultivation becomes the legitimate proprietor of the products and harvests which he obtains therefrom.

    What is true for individuals is equally true for certain races who are accustomed to living a patriarchal life. These groups which hold their work and their profits in common are regarded as a single civil person"; Notice sur le Laos Français, quoted in Reinach 1901: 242.

31. Gaudillot and Condominas (1959: 3, 18) list a total of 54 hectares owned by 16 prominent Lao, of which the largest holding is 13.5 hectares owned by former Prime Minister Phoui Sananikone.

32. About 1350 A.D. a Khmer colony, including artisans, was reported to have been established in Luang Prabang (Robequain 1925: 711).

33. In 1960 the Lao Commission for Rural Affairs began to import steel bars for distribution to villagers as part of a rural self-help program (Vientiane World, April 9, 1960).

34. The weavers at this village of Ban Panhom are not Lao but Tai Lu who were originally brought to the area several generations ago by the ancestors of the late Viceroy.

35. These flintlocks are reputed to have been modeled on those given the Chinese centuries ago by Jesuit missionaries (Dooley 1958: 129).

36. For comparison, in Bang Chan near Bangkok a marginal farmer is defined as one who produces less than 11,100 pounds (well over 400 myn), and the average is 23,400 (Sharp 1953: 164).

37. See profiles of three shoeshine boys in Vientiane, in Halpern 1964b: 164-67.

38. This dance reached Luang Prabang only within the last several years. Known in Thailand as _ram wong_, it is adapted from the folk dance _ram tone_ from the southern part of Northeast Thailand.

39. One woman in Vientiane was reported to be one million kip in debt, having mortgaged her inherited property to secure loans. It was claimed that she might lose up to 50,000 kip in a typical evening.

40. "The government of Indo-China which is both the preparer and seller of chandoo or opium for smoking is the party which would gain most from obtaining the raw drug on French territory. It is still dependent on British India for this product, and can still acquire it only on extremely disadvantageous terms.

    Since much time must still pass, however, before the Meos and the Yaos give up their age-old methods, it would be essential for the intensive cultivation of the opium poppy to be undertaken by Europeans on behalf of the administration. This would be possible if there were a guaranteed labor supply in the form of Chinese coolies, who would be enlisted primarily for the greater part of the work, and of native specialists who would deal only with scarification of the capsules, harvesting the opium and the first stage of its preparation.

    These delicate operations are the ones which the Meos and Yaos like best, but they dislike plowing, fertilizing, weeding and irrigation, all of which tasks are indispensable for obtaining a high yield of capsules and consequently of the raw drug. It would therefore be best to entrust this heavy work to foreign coolies, and it is probable that after a certain time they too would be capable of extracting opium. Impelled by their example, the natives would doubtless then be seen to break with their prejudices and devote themselves also to intensive cultivation so as to reap its full benefits.

The role of the administration would then be at an end, and it would gradually diminish its intervention as free cultivation of the poppies increased (Reinach 1901: 310)."

In an appendix Reinach describes his experiments and concludes that it should be possible to get a yield of up to 50 kilos a hectare if the proper methods are followed. As far as the present writer is aware the "improvement" was never put into effect and cultivation today appears to be carried out in the traditional way.

41. The Meo regard these silver bars as having their own phi. They sacrifice chickens on them in order to attract the spirits of other silver bars. The standard 400-gram bar is called kan and is worth about 1,000 kip. In Nam Tha silver coins are valued over paper money at a ratio of 1.8 to 1 (Duclos 1959b: 10).

42. Iwata (1961) reports a Yao village near Vang Vieng which was considering the purchase of an automobile for the transport of goods to the Vientiane market.

43. The strict suppression measures enforced by Thailand are said to have virtually closed most of the historic opium trade routes leading to the Gulf of Siam.

44. Life, January 25, 1960, pp. 91-92.

45. Time, February 29, 1960, p. 25.

46. Robequain (1925) noted that there was a great clandestine opium traffic in Luang Prabang (from Yunnan, Burma, and the Meo of Xieng Khouang) and that almost all the Lao of the town smoked opium. It appears there must have been a shift to Xieng Khouang since that time. Although there may have been some undercover trade in the late 1950's, it did not attract general notice.

47. Inheritance here probably means livestock and land.

48. A few Khmu have refused to heed Lao calls for forced labor and the Lao villagers concerned have let the matter drop.

49. This is a convenient location for the Communists, who are

said to have manipulated the tale to their advantage.

50. A more detailed discussion will be found in the section, "Patterns of Tribal Authority," in Halpern 1964b: 71 ff.

51. F.K. Lehman (personal communication).

52. Vientiane World, June 25, 1960.

53. For a discussion of these questions, see my article, "Laos and America--A Retrospective View."

54. They have their own gasoline generators, since the local charcoal-fueled power plant operates only during the day or when high officials are visiting.

55. This figure evidently does not include about 9,000 nai bans and tassengs who receive about 1,800 kip a year from the government and are part-time employees whose earnings are supplementary.

56. Prior to French rule the Lao were organized into a series of petty kingdoms with elaborate gradations of rank and an inherited royalty, but their consumption patterns were fairly uniform. There was not enough of an economic surplus to permit widely varying standards of living, although, of course, status distinctions were strongly felt. See Halpern 1964b: 63 ff. for discussion of traditional Lao hierarchy.

57. There has been an abundance of news and comment on the political situation in Laos but little information on social and economic developments occurring in those areas under Pathet Lao control. Some insight into what the future may be is given in reports dealing with the adjoining areas of North Vietnam, particularly those regions populated in large part by minority groups which exist on both sides of the border. Regardless of the precise future course of political and military events it seems clear that barring a major war the Pathet Lao will maintain control over most of the areas they now hold. At the same time, since they are financially and militarily dependent on North Vietnam, it would appear to the point to refer briefly to North Vietnamese policies for development in mountainous tribal areas. In 1959 the following objectives were set forth:

> "The main task remains agricultural development; at the same time, we must guide and encourage collective handicraft and private industry along the path of socialistic improvement.

To bolster the production of agriculture, handicraft, industry and forestry, we will have to strengthen and develop the part played by the State in the field of domestic trade, as well as by the sales and purchasing cooperatives, so that we may become predominant in the market.

"We will have to build new roads in remote areas and to centers of agricultural and forest production. Besides reinforcing and developing a system of large and medium-sized roads in remote areas, we will have to mobilize the people so that they may build more roads linking townships or hamlets, and develop the rudimentary transportation.

"We will have to take charge of all revenues accruing from mineral exploitation and forestry products of our zone, in order to guarantee the basic material conditions for the increasing needs and rate of development of our zone.

"We will have to have textbooks appropriate to every class of people, and to every level, so that we may have a systematic and extensive training organization. We will also raise the quality of our medical service and have a plan for the gradual elimination of pneumonia, malaria, and a number of common diseases in the population"(from Independent Vietnam and Thai Nguyen as quoted and translated in U.S. Joint Publications Research Service, No. 1881, September 10, 1959, pp. 18-27).

However, some problems were also mentioned:

". . . it goes without saying that the difficulties encountered are not insignificant. The level of a socialistic awareness of the people in the region is generally still rather low; the level of the administrative authorities is also low. There is a lack of cadres, conservative thoughts are still deeply entrenched in the mind of the cadres, the population is scattered" (from "Four Years of Progress in the Tai-Meo Autonomous Zone," Nhan Dan, May 11, 1959 as translated in U.S. Joint Publications Research Service, No. 1881, September 10, 1959, p. 4).

By 1963 detailed plans had been made and some accomplishments claimed in the Viet Bac Autonomous Zone (composed of 54 per cent Tai peoples and 7 per cent Meo). Average per capita food production was said to have been raised from 357 kilos a year in 1955 to 467 kilos in 1962, increasing the total value of annual agricultural production by 8.4 per cent (since no precise statistics were given it is hard to evaluate these figures; also, the comment is made that there were food shortages between harvest periods). Of significance is the claim that aid has been given to some 7,000 upland families for resettlement in lower areas. One recent report lists current difficulties:

"Although socialist reform has been basically completed, the new-style production relations have not been effectively consolidated. Many cooperatives are still embarrassed by their production plans and methods of distribution. This has impaired their internal unity and lessened their members' enthusiasm.

"In the commercial field, the purchase of agricultural and forestry products and foodstuffs and the supply of industrial goods have not yet been carried out properly, thus failing to meet the people's needs and to stimulate production. Market control still depends chiefly on bureaucratic administrative measures rather than on education and encouragement.

"In addition, the industrial branch has failed to satisfy agricultural requirements on time or adequately, and rural areas have failed to supply sufficient raw materials and agricultural products for cities" (from "Implementation of the Policy of Zonal Autonomy with Regard to Various Nationalities in the Viet Bac Zone," Hoc Tap, No. 7 as translated in U.S. Joint Publications Research Service, 20, No. 739).

In addition to resettling some mountain peoples the North Vietnamese are evidently pursuing policies similar to those of the Chinese in Yunnan and of the South Vietnamese in resettling people from the lowlands in upland tribal areas. This is apparently seen as having the double advantage of relieving population pressure and opening new lands to cultivation -- as well as increasing state control in these normally less accessible areas:

"The task for 1964 is the following . . . . strive to mobilize the people of the delta region to participate in the economic development of the mountain areas in a positive and steady manner. In 1964 we must mobilize about 240,000 men working in agriculture, forestry, local industry, communication and water utilization. Concerning land reclamation alone, we need to expand the area by about 63,000 hectares. All upland cooperatives need to step up small-scale land reclamation through admitting more people from the delta region into their cooperatives as a supplementary manpower source as alternating and merging cells, teams and households" (from Nhan Dan, December 26, 1963 as translated in U.S. Joint Publications Research Service, 23, No. 627, p. 30).

It is very possible that sparsely populated Phong Saly and Sam Neua are to be included in such schemes, since the population pressures in North Vietnam and China cannot but help affect the future of the areas controlled by their Pathet Lao protégés. The push of population into underpopulated Laos is a long-term historical trend accelerated by current military developments.

58. In recent years the American aid program has sponsored a large number of various types of village aid programs. These have been greatly hampered by lack of adequate Laotian personnel. An attempt has been made to concentrate the impact of extension services in environmental sanitation, agricultural practices, and animal husbandry, together with the construction of schools, wells, dams, irrigation systems, community centers, markets, connecting roads, bridges, and dispensaries in central "cluster" sites in those areas to which Americans continue to have access. Attempts have been made to involve the villagers in this process. In 1964 it was planned to construct 150 classrooms, repair 110 schools, and build 50 dams and irrigation systems, 30 community centers, and 10 markets. Other activities were planned in teacher training and road building, plus a project with farmers in the areas of all the Mekong river towns for increasing vegetable production and thereby decreasing food imports from Thailand. All this is in addition to the relief programs for displaced refugees whose numbers are increasing daily (according to a report in the New York Times, May 17, 1964, and information provided by the Agency for International Development.)

BIBLIOGRAPHY

Abadie, Maurice

1924 Les races du Haut-Tonkin de Phong-Tho à Lang Son, Paris, Société d'Editions Géographiques, Maritimes et Coloniales.

Anuman, Phya Rajadhon

1956 The Life of the Farmer in Thailand, New Haven, Southeast Asia Studies, Yale University. (Reprinted as Part I in William J. Gedney, trans. and ed., Life and Ritual in Old Siam, New Haven, HRAF Press, 1961.)

1958 Five Papers on Thai Custom, Southeast Asia Program Data Paper No. 28, Ithaca, Cornell University.

Ayabe, Tsuneo

1955 "Taizoku ni okeru Shakai Tōgō no Ichi Sokumen [An Aspect of Social Integration among the Thai]," Nihon Jinruigakkai: Nihon Minzokugaku Kyokai Rengo Taikai, 10.

1956 "Indochina Hantō Tōhokubu Chiiki ni okeru Fukei Ujizoku Seidō [The Patrilineage System of Northern Indochina]," Nihon Jinruigakkai: Nihon Minzokugaku Kyokai Rengo Taikai, 11.

1958 "Laozoku Shinzoku no Ichirei [A Case Study of the Lao Kinship System]," Nihon Jinruigakkai: Nihon Minzokugaku Kyokai Rengo Taikai, 13.

1959a "A Study of the Patrilineage System on the Mainland of Southeast Asia," Japanese Science Review, 10, 80-89.

1959b "The Village Structure of the Lowland Lao: The Case of Ban Pha Khao," Japanese Journal of Ethnology, 23.

1959c "Keifuteki Shōkankei yori mita Laozoku no Ichi to Henyō [Changing Aspects of the Lao People from a Genealogical Point of View]," Namposhi Kenkyū, 1, 17-36.

1959d "Sei, Shogo, Keisho, Tekunonimi no Kankei [Family Name, Title, Appellation and Teknonymy]," Nihon Jinruigakkai: Nihon Minzokugaku Kyokai Rengo Taikai, 14.

1959e "Teichi-Laozoku no Sonrakukōzō [Village Structure of the Lowland Lao]," Minzokugaku Kenkyū, 23, 86-117.

1960 "Nokumin no Seikatsu: Laozoku no Baai [Lao Farmer's Life]," Gendai Bunkajinruigaku Koza, 1.

1961 The Village of Ban Pha Khao, Vientiane Province, Laos Project Paper No. 14, ed. Joel M. Halpern, Los Angeles, University of California, mimeographed.

Ayme, G.

1931 Monographie du V[e] Territoire Militaire, Paris, Exposition Coloniale Internationale.

Baal, J. van

1961 "Erring Acculturation," American Anthropologist, 62, 108-21.

Barney, George L.

1957a "Christianity: Innovation in Meo Culture: A Case Study in Missionization," master's thesis, University of Minnesota. (Available in part in The Meo of Xieng Khouang Province, Laos Project Paper No. 13, ed. Joel M. Halpern, Los Angeles, University of California, mimeographed.)

1957b "The Meo: An Incipient Church," Practical Anthropology, 4.

Bartlett, Harley H.

1957 Fire in Relation to Primitive Agriculture and Grazing in the Tropics, Ann Arbor, University of Michigan.

Benedict, Ruth

1952 Thai Culture and Behavior, Data Paper No. 4, Southeast Asia Program, Ithaca, Cornell University.

Bernatzik, Hugo Adolf

1947 Akha und Meau: Probleme der angewandten Völkerkunde in Hinterindien, 2 vols. Innsbruck, Wagnerische Universitäts Buchdrückerei. (Citations from HRAF translation.)

BIBLIOGRAPHY

Bertholet, C.J.L. and Benchadiswat

1958 — *Housing and Food Patterns in Eleven Villages in Northeast Thailand*, Ubol, UNESCO Fundamental Education Centre.

Bock, Carl

1884 — *Temples and Elephants*, London.

Boutin, Andre

1937 — "Monographie de la province des Houa-Phan," *Bulletin des Amis du Laos*, *1*.

Burchett, Wilfred

1957 — *Mekong Upstream*, Hanoi, Red River Publishing House.

Chang, Chi Jen

1956 — "The Minority Groups of Yunnan and Chinese Political Expansion into Southeast Asia," doctoral dissertation, University of Michigan.

Chen, Han-seng

1949 — *Frontier Land Systems in Southernmost China*, New York, Institute of Pacific Relations.

Colonna, M.

1938 — "Monographie de la province de Saravane," *Bulletin des Amis du Laos*, *2*.

Condominas, Georges

1951 — "Aspects of a Minority Problem in Indochina," *Pacific Affairs*, *24*, 77-82.

Conklin, Harold C.

1957 — *Hanunóo Agriculture*, FAO Forestry Development Paper No. 12, Rome, United Nations.

Dobby, Ernest H.G.

1954 — *Southeast Asia*, London, University of London Press.

Dooley, Thomas A.

1958 — *The Edge of Tomorrow*, New York, Farrar, Straus and Cudahy.

1960 — *The Night They Burned the Mountain*, New York, Farrar, Straus and Cudahy.

Duclos, B. Havard

1959a Contribution à l'Etude économique de la province de Luang Prabang, Vientiane, mimeographed.

1959b Etude économique agricole de la province du Houa Khong [Haut Mekong or Nam Tha], Vientiane, mimeographed.

1959c Etude économique de la province de Phong Saly, Vientiane, mimeographed.

Embree, John F. and Lillian Ota Dotson

1950 Bibliography of the Peoples and Cultures of Mainland Southeast Asia, New Haven, Southeast Asia Studies, Yale University.

Embree, John F. and William L. Thomas, Jr.

1950 Ethnic Groups of Northern Southeast Asia, New Haven, Southeast Asia Studies, Yale University.

Faure, Marie-Daniel

1959 "The Boun Khoun-Khao [Harvest Festival]," in René de Berval, ed., Kingdom of Laos, Saigon, France-Asie.

Fisher, Charles

1964 South-East Asia: A Social, Economic and Political Geography, London, Methuen.

Fox, Len

1958 Friendly Vietnam, Hanoi, Foreign Language Publishing House.

Fraisse, Andre

1951 "Les villages du plateau de Bolovens," Bulletin de la Société des Etudes Indochinoises, 26, 52-72.

Franck, Harry A.

1926 East of Siam: Ramblings in the Five Divisions of French Indochina, New York, Century.

Freeman, J.D.

1955 Iban Agriculture: A Report on the Shifting Cultivation of Hill Rice by the Iban of Sarawak, London, H. M. Stationery.

Gaudillot, Claude and Georges Condominas

1959 La Plaine de Vientiane: Rapport d'étude, Tomes I-III, Royaume du Laos, Commissariat au Plan, Octobre 1959, Paris, Bureau pour le Développement de la Production Agricole.

Ginsburg, Norton and Fred Eggan

1955 Laos, Subcontractor's Monograph, New Haven, Human Relations Area Files, Inc.

Gourou, Pierre

1945 Land Utilization in French Indochina, 3 vols. New York, Institute of Pacific Relations.

1951 "Land Utilization in Upland Areas of Indochina," in Development of Upland Areas of the Far East, 2, New York, Institute of Pacific Relations.

1956 "The Quality of Land Use of Tropical Cultivators," in William L. Thomas, Jr., ed., Man's Role in Changing the Face of the Earth, Chicago, University of Chicago Press.

Graham, David Crockett

1954 Song and Stories of the Ch'uan Miao, Smithsonian Miscellaneous Collections, 123, No. 1, Washington, Smithsonian Institution.

Hall, D.G.E.

1955 A History of South-East Asia, London, Macmillan.

Halpern, Joel M.

1958a Aspects of Village Life and Culture Change in Laos, New York, Council on Economic and Cultural Affairs.

1958b "Trade Patterns in Northern Laos," Eastern Anthropologist, 12, 119-24.

1960a The Lao Elite: A Study of Tradition and Innovation, RM-2636-RC, Santa Monica, RAND Corporation.

1960b "Laos and Her Tribal Problems," Michigan Alumnus Quarterly Review, 67, 59-67.

1960c The Role of the Chinese in Lao Society, P-2161, Santa Monica, RAND Corporation.

1961 "American Policy in Laos," _Michigan Alumnus Quarterly Review_, _67_, 213-19.

1963 "Traditional Medicine and the Role of the Phi in Laos," _Eastern Anthropologist_, _16_, 191-200.

1964a "Capital, Savings and Credit among Lao Peasants," in Raymond Firth and B. S. Yamey, eds., _Capital, Savings and Credit in Peasant Societies_, George Allen & Unwin.

1964b _Government, Politics, and Social Structure in Laos: A Study of Tradition and Innovation_, Monograph Series No. 4, New Haven, Southeast Asia Studies, Yale University.

Halpern, Joel M., ed.

1961 _Laos Project Papers_, Los Angeles, Department of Anthropology, University of California.

This series of mimeographed studies was written by Joel M. Halpern except where otherwise noted.

No. 1 The Role of the Chinese in Lao Society

No. 2 Capital, Savings and Credit among Lao and Serb Peasants: A Contrast in Cultural Values

No. 3 Population Statistics and Associated Data

No. 4 Geographic, Demographic and Ethnic Background on Laos

No. 5 An Annotated Bibliography on the Peoples of Laos and Northern Thailand

No. 6 American Policy in Laos

No. 7 Laotian Educational Statistics

No. 8 Government Statistics

No. 9 Laotian Agricultural Statistics

No. 10 Laotian Health Statistics

No. 11 Economic and Related Statistics on Laos

No. 12 Village Life in Vientiane Province, 1956-57 (by Howard K. Kaufman)

No. 13 The Meo of Xieng Khouang Province (by George L. Barney)

No. 14 The Village of Ban Pha Khao, Vientiane Province (by Tsuneo Ayabe), translation.

No. 15 Ethnic Groups in the Valley of the Nam Song and the Nam Lik (by Keiji Iwata), translation.

No. 16 Minority Groups in Northern Laos, Especially the Yao (by Keiji Iwata), translation.

No. 17 The Natural Economy of Laos

No. 18 Laos Profiles

No. 19 The Rural and Urban Economies

No. 20 Laotian Health Problems

No. 21 Government, Politics and Social Structure of Laos: A Study in Tradition and Innovation

No. 22 Laotian Bibliography

1962 Laotian Bibliography, Berkeley, Center for Southeast Asian Studies, University of California.

Halpern, Joel M. and Barbara Halpern

1964 "Laos and America--A Retrospective View," South Atlantic Quarterly, 63, 175-87.

Hamada, Hideo

1959 "Laos Xieng-Khouang Kogen no Laojin to Miyaozoku no Nogyo [Agriculture among Lao and Meo in Xieng Khouang Province]," Minzokugaku Kenkyū, 23, 25-43.

Hickey, Gerald C.

1958 "Social Systems of Northern Viet Nam: A Study of Systems in Contact," doctoral dissertation, University of Chicago.

Holloway, A. H.

1957 — Basic Data for Planning a Public Health Program in the Kingdom of Laos, Vientiane, United States Operations Mission to Laos.

Iwata, Keiji

1958 — "Suwa Diaw Kan [Sua Diaw Kan]," Nihon Jinruigakkai: Nihon Minzokugaku Kyokai Rengo Taikai, 13.

1959a — "Ethnic Groups in the Valley of the Nam Song and Nam Lik: Their Geographic Distribution and Some Aspects of Social Change," Japanese Journal of Ethnology, 23.

1959b — "Nam Song, Nam Liku Ryuiki ni okeru Shōshuzoku no Bunpu to Ido [Ethnic Groups in the Valley of the Nam Song and Nam Lik: Their Geographical Distribution and Some Aspects of Social Change]," Minzokugaku Kenkyū, 23, 63-79.

1960a — "Boloban Kogen no Jinbun Chiri [Descriptive Geography of the Boloven Plateau]," Jinbun Kenkyū, 11, 46-70.

1960b — "Hokubu Laos no Shosu Minzoku [Minority Groups in Northern Laos]," Shilin, 1.

1961a — Ethnic Groups in the Valley of the Nam Song and Nam Lik, Laos Project Paper No. 15, ed. Joel M. Halpern, Los Angeles, University of California, mimeographed.

1961b — Minority Groups in Northern Laos, Especially the Yao, Laos Project Paper No. 16, ed. Joel M. Halpern, Los Angeles, University of California, mimeographed.

Izikowitz, Karl Gustav

1941 — Fastening the Soul: Some Religious Traits among the Lamet, Göteborg, Elanders boktryckeri aktiebolag.

1951 — Lamet: Hill Peasants in French Indochina, Etnologiska Studier No. 17, Göteborg, Etnografiska Museet.

Janlekha, Kamol Odd

1955 — A Study of the Economy of a Rice-growing Village in Central Thailand, Bangkok, Division of Agricultural Economics, Ministry of Agriculture.

BIBLIOGRAPHY

Jin-Bee, Aoi

1958 "The Distribution of Present-Day Man in the Tropics: Historical and Ecological Perspective," in Proceedings of the Ninth Pacific Science Congress, 1957, 20, Bangkok, Department of Science.

Jumsai, M.L. Manich

1959 Results of the Country Survey to Collect Materials for Textbook Production, Vientiane, UNESCO, mimeographed.

Kaufman, Howard K.

1961 Village Life in Vientiane Province, 1956-57, Laos Project Paper No. 12, ed. Joel M. Halpern, Los Angeles, University of California, mimeographed.

1963 "Nationalism and the Problems of Refugee and Ethnic Minority Resettlement," in Proceedings of the Ninth Pacific Science Congress, 1957, 3, 170-74.

Kingshill, Konrad

1960 Ku Daeng--The Red Tomb: A Village Study in Northern Thailand, Chiengmai, Thailand, The Prince Royal's College.

Klausner, William J.

1956 Report on the Village of Nong Khon near Ubon, Thailand, Bangkok, United States Operations Mission to Thailand, mimeographed.

Lafont, Pierre-Bernard

1957 "Slash and Burn Cultivation Methods among the Mountain Peoples of Central Viet-Nam," paper read at the Ninth Pacific Science Congress, Bangkok, mimeographed.

1959 Aperçus sur le Laos, Vientiane, Comité de l'Alliance Française au Laos.

1960 Review of J. M. Halpern, Aspects of Village Life and Culture Change in Laos, Bulletin de l'Ecole Française d'Extrême-Orient, 50, 184-90.

Laos

1957 About Laos, Washington, Press and Information Service, Royal Embassy of Laos.

1958 Bulletin statistique du Laos, No. 4, Vientiane, Ministère des Finances de l'Economie Nationale et du Plan.

1959 Plan du développement économique et social, Royaume du Laos, Vientiane.

LeBar, Frank M. and Adrienne Suddard, eds.

1960 Laos: Its People, Its Society, Its Culture, New Haven, HRAF Press.

Lévy, Paul

1959 "The Sacrifice of the Buffalo and the Forecast of the Weather in Vientiane," in René de Berval, ed., Kingdom of Laos, Saigon, France-Asie.

Lewis, Elaine T.

1957 "The Hill Peoples of Kengtung State (Burma)," Practical Anthropology, 4.

Lunet de Lajonquière, E. I.

1906 Ethnographie du Tonkin septentrional, Paris, Leroux.

Madge, Charles

1957 Survey before Development in Thai Villages, Series on Community Organization and Development, New York, United Nations, mimeographed.

Mickey, Margaret P.

1947 "The Cowrie Shell Miao of Kweichow," Papers of the Peabody Museum of American Archaeology and Ethnology, 32, 1-80.

Pelzer, Karl J.

1958 "Land Utilization in the Humid Tropics: Agriculture," in Proceedings of the Ninth Pacific Science Congress, 1957, 20, Bangkok, Secretariat Ninth Pacific Science Congress.

Pietrantoni, Eric

1953 "La population du Laos de 1915 à 1945," Bulletin de la Société des Etudes Indochinoises, 28.

1957 "La population du Laos en 1943 dans son milieu géographique," Bulletin de la Société des Etudes Indochinoises, 32, 223-43.

BIBLIOGRAPHY

Reinach, Lucien de

1901 Le Laos, 2 vols. Paris, A. Charles, Librairie-Editeur. (Translated by the Human Relations Area Files, Indochina Source No. 149.)

Robequain, Charles

1925 "Notes sur Luang Prabang," Revue du Institut Géographique Alpine, 13, 707-38.

Roux, Henri

1924 "Deux tribus de la région de Phongsaly (Laos septentrional)," Bulletin de l'Ecole Française d'Extrême-Orient, 24, 373-500.

Roux, Henri and Tran Van Chu

1927 "Les Tsa Khmu," Bulletin de l'Ecole Française d'Extrême-Orient, 27, 169-222.

1954 "Quelques minorités ethniques du Nord-Indochine," France-Asie, 10, 135-419.

Savina, F. M.

1930 Histoire des Miao, 2d ed. Hongkong, Imprimerie de la Société des Missions-étrangères de Paris.

Seidenfaden, Erik

1958 The Thai Peoples, Bangkok, Siam Society.

Serene, Raoul

1959 "Fishing and the Ang Festivities," in Réne de Berval, ed., Kingdom of Laos, Saigon, France-Asie.

Sharp, Lauriston et al.

1953 Siamese Rice Village: A Preliminary Study of Bang Chan 1948-1949, Bangkok, Cornell Research Center.

Sinavong, Boun Than

1963 "Agrarian Rites in Laos," in Proceedings of the Ninth Pacific Science Congress, 1957, 3, 103-06.

Smalley, William A.

1952 Unpublished Khmu texts from the environs of Luang Prabang, Laos, as transcribed during 1952-54.

1956 "The Gospel and the Cultures of Laos," Practical Anthropology, 3, 47-57.

1959 "Some Questions about Missionary Medicine," Practical Anthropology, 6.

1961a Outline of Khmu' Structure, New Haven, American Oriental Society.

1961b "Ethnographic Notes on the Khmu' of Northern Laos," unpublished manuscript dated December 15.

Srisvasdi, Bun-chay

1950 Thirty Races in Chieng Rai [in Thai], Bangkok. (Citations from HRAF translation, Source No. 39.)

Thailand

1957 Thailand: Past and Present, Bangkok, Publicity Committee, Ninth Pacific Science Congress.

1958 Agricultural Statistics of Thailand, 1957, Bangkok, Division of Agricultural Economics, Ministry of Agriculture.

Truxton, Addison Strong

1958 "The Integration of the Karen Peoples of Burma and Thailand into Their Respective National Cultures: A Study in the Dynamics of Culture Contact," master's thesis, Cornell University.

Wales, H.G. Quaritch

1931 Siamese State Ceremonies, London, B. Quaritch.

Wang, Shu-tang

1955 China: Land of Many Nationalities, Peking, Foreign Languages Press.

Wiens, Herold J.

1954 China's March toward the Tropics, Hamden, Connecticut, Shoe String Press.

Wirtz, H.A.M.

1958 Rapport intérimaire au Gouvernement Royal du Laos sur l'économie agricole du Laos et le développement des services agricoles, Rome, Food and Agriculture Organization, United Nations.

Young, Oliver Gordon

1961 The Hilltribes of Northern Thailand, Bangkok, United States Operations Mission to Thailand.

LIST OF TABLES

TABLE 1. POPULATION DENSITIES IN LAOS (1901-61) AND IN NEIGHBORING AREAS

Area	People per square mile	Source
Laos (1901)	4.7	Reinach 1901: 92
North	2.9	
South	7.0	
Laos (1943)	13.0	Pietrantoni 1957: 225
North	7.4	
South	17.4	
Central[a]	16.9	
Laos (1947)	12.8	Based on a population of 1,169,000
Laos (1957)	15	Statistical Yearbook of the United Nations 1957: 25 (population given as 1,450,000)
Laos (1957)	33	About Laos (Lao Embassy, Washington, 1957), population given as 3,000,000
Laos (1959)	19	Lafont 1959: 11
Laos (1961)	20	Fisher 1964: 177 (population given as 1,850,000)
Mekong valley in Laos along Thai border	180	Gaudillot and Condominas 1959: 1, 25-26
Vientiane plain	137 (77)[b]	Area Handbook on Laos (HRAF Subcontractor's Monograph No. 23, 1955), p. 112
Lamet tribe in Nam Tha province	6.8	Izikowitz 1951: 38
Northeast Thailand	94	Madge 1957: 12
Village near Bangkok	320	Sharp 1953: 24

[a] Vientiane, Khammouane, and Savannakhet provinces.

[b] Second figure is without urban Vientiane area.

TABLE 2. POPULATION DENSITIES IN SOUTHEAST ASIA

Area	People per square mile
Laos	21
Thailand	140
Cambodia	83
North Vietnam	280
South Vietnam	225
Burma	88

Source: _United Nations Demographic Yearbook for 1963_, pp. 131-34.

TABLE 3. GROWTH IN AVERAGE POPULATION PER VILLAGE, 1911-59

Year	Number of villages	Rural population	Average per village
1911	6,315	639,000	101
1918	6,631	739,000	110
1921	7,948	800,000	106
1943	8,888	987,000	116
1959[a]	10,053	1,526,500	152

[a] Conservative population estimate.

Source: Pietrantoni 1957: 240 and Lao government statistics.

TABLE 4. VILLAGE SIZE AND POPULATION CONCENTRATION IN VIENTIANE, ATTOPEU, AND XIENG KHOUANG PROVINCES, 1959

Village population	Vientiane: Number of villages	%	Population in thousands	%	Attopeu: Number of villages	%	Population in thousands	%	Xieng Khouang: Number of villages	%	Population in thousands	%
-100	341	44.1	21.2	16.4	187	56.9	12.6	25.9	799	67.8	49.4	46.7
100-199	222	28.7	32.9	25.5	83	25.2	11.3	23.2	332	28.2	43.8	41.4
200-299	108	13.9	26.6	20.6	25	7.6	6.0	12.3	37	3.1	8.7	8.2
300-399	52	6.7	17.9	13.9	12	3.6	4.1	8.4	8		2.7	2.6
400-499	22	2.8	9.7	7.5	8	2.4	3.6	7.4	1		0.4	0.4
500-599	10	1.3	5.4	4.2	5		2.8	5.7		0.8		
600-699	4		2.6		1		0.7	1.4	1		0.7	0.7
700-799	7		5.2		2		1.4	2.9				
800-899	4	2.5	3.3	11.9	2	4.3	1.6	3.3				
900-	4		4.2		4		4.6	9.4				
Totals[a]	774	100.0	129.0	100.0	329	100.0	48.7	99.9	1178	100.0	105.7	100.0
Average village size	166				148				90			

[a] Vientiane is officially estimated to be 99 per cent Lao; Attopeu, 70 per cent Kha; and Xieng Khouang 40 per cent Meo and Yao.

Source: Lao Bureau of Statistics, 1959.

TABLE 5. POPULATION OF LAOS, 1955

Province	Number of villages	Number of inhabitants	Average population per village[a]
Savannakhet[b]	1,100	221,504	201
Vientiane[b]	785	187,815	239
Saravane	994	153,448	154
Luang Prabang	1,958	131,165	67
Champassak[b]	541	114,950	212
Khammouane[b]	887	111,971	126
Sayaboury[b]	523	98,786	189
Xieng Khouang	940	86,828	92
Sam Neua	873	65,000	74
Nam Tha	583	55,720	96
Phong Saly	616	50,000	81
Attopeu	297	43,315	146
Totals	10,097	1,320,502	131

[a] Includes major towns as well as villages.

[b] Provinces in which 80 per cent or more of the population is Lao or Tai.

Source: All data are from Lao government sources for 1953-55, except for Phong Saly and Sam Neua provinces, where estimates based on earlier figures are used.

TABLE 6. ETHNOLINGUISTIC GROUPS OF LAOS

Proto-Indochinese

(dwell on mountain slopes between the Tai and Meo)

Kha Mou (Khmu)[a]	Kha Alak
Kha Seng	Kha Kattang
Kha Bit	Kha Tahoi
Kha Lamet	Kha Teu
Kha Phoutheng[a]	Kha Kouy[b]
Kha Bô	
Kha Sô	Love
Kha Souei[b]	Halang

Khmer

(valley dwellers in southern Laos)

Thai

Lao (dwell in valleys along streams)	Phoutai
Tai (dwell in mountain valleys)	Tai Lu
White Tai (Tai Kao)	Nyang
Black Tai (Tai Dam)	Youanne
Red Tai (Tai Deng)	Phouen
Tai Neua	Phong

Meo-Yao (Miao-Man), Lanten[c]

(dwell on the mountain tops -- rarely below 3,000 feet -- and like the Tai are divided into subgroups bearing names indicating the color of their distinctive costume)

Sino-Tibetan

Lolo (Kha Ko also known as Akha)
Xapho
Phunoi (Kha Pai)
Mossu (subdivided into Black and Red groups also known as Lahu)

[a] Considered by Smalley to be identical; he also feels that Kha Mou is a false etymology and that the proper expression, often used by the Lao, is Kha Khmu.

[b] Smalley suggests that Kha Souei and Kha Kouy may be different names for the same group.

[c] Though their exact linguistic associations are not known, these groups have been strongly influenced by Chinese culture. The subgroups of the Meo appear to have mutually intelligible dialects: the Striped and Black Meo seem to be similar linguistically and the important phonological and lexical differences of the White Meo evidently do not hinder mutual intelligibility.

Source: This table represents a partial listing of groups and is based on Lafont 1959: 13.

TABLE 7. CERTAIN IDENTIFYING CHARACTERISTICS OF SELECTED ETHNIC GROUPS IN NORTHERN LAOS

Group	Women's dress[a]	House type	Other comments
Lao	Silk sarong-type skirts with gold or silver woven trim; often of multicolored cotton in villages	Usually of woven bamboo, with open verandah and thatch roof; on stilts	Center of village is pagoda (wat), usually largest and best-constructed building; abbot of wat has highest prestige; kinship loosely structured; village headman first among equals only
Lu	Indigo-dyed skirts with multicolored striped insets; unmarried girls wear pink turbans	Often of plank construction and larger than those of the Lao	Household groups usually larger than those of Lao; Lu concentrated in valley of Nam Ou and in Muong Sing, where remnants of a princely state exist
Black Tai (Tai Dam)	Name derived from fitted black blouses and long silk skirts of women; married women wear chignon high on center of forehead	Usually of woven bamboo, on the ground in Vietnamese fashion; in Nam Tha on stilts with plank construction	Related to White (Kao) and Red (Deng) Tai, originally ruled by hereditary princes; main center is Dien Bien Phu, now part of the D.R.V.; highly structured religious system with patrilineal cult of ancestors
Khmu	Simple striped cotton skirts woven by the Lao; often wear turbans	Bamboo houses in small villages in upland areas; poorer than those of the Lao	Trade forest products and game to Lao; practice tattooing and betel-chewing to a greater extent today than do the Lao; animal sacrifice important; aboriginal inhabitants, animists
Meo	Both sexes wear loose black trousers and silver neck-rings; Meo Kao women wear embroidered aprons; Meo Dam are identified by short, full batik-printed linen skirts and black leg wrappings; the Meo Lai (Striped Meo) have strips of colored cloth appliqued on sleeves	Large plank houses built on ground; interior subdivided into family units; animal corrals nearby	Headman has important position; extended families patriarchal and patrilineal; recent immigrants from Yunnan; noted for opium cultivation, livestock; mountaintop villages moved every few decades

[a] In most cases there are fewer differences in men's dress.

TABLE 8. CULTURAL CHARACTERISTICS OF SIX ETHNIC GROUPS OF NORTHERN LAOS

P = Present L = Limited
S = Secondary A = Absent

	Lao	Black Tai	Meo	Yao	Khmu	Lamet
Irrigated rice cultivation	P	P	L	A	L	A
Slash-and-burn agriculture	S	S	P	P	P	P
Opium cultivation	A	A	P	P	S	A
Knowledge of writing	P	P	S[a]	S[a]	A	A
Village political organization	S	P	P	P	S	S
Extravillage political organization	P	P	L	L	A	A
Organized extravillage political hierarchy	P	L	L[b]	A	A	A
Patrilineal family structure	A	P	P	P	A	A
Buddhism	P	A	A	A	L	A
Class groups within village	L	P	S	S	L	L
Class groupings beyond village	P	P	A	A	A	A
Formally educated officials, civil servants, and technicians	P	S	L	L	A	A
Represented in politically organized units in Chinese People's Republic or Democratic Republic of Vietnam	P	P	P	P	A	A

[a] Use Chinese script.

[b] Have a representative in the Lao National Assembly.

TABLE 9. ETHNIC COMPOSITION OF THE POPULATION OF LAOS, 1911-55

Group	1911	%	1921	%	1931	%	1936	%	Kingdom of Luang Prabang[d] 1942	%	All of Laos 1942	%	1955[e]	%
Lao	276,801	44.8	429,000	53.1	485,000	52.3	565,000	57.2	168,050	34.8	441,450	43.6 / 60.9	856,000-865,000 (Lao-Tai)	77-74
Tai	124,238	20.1	122,000	15.1	113,000	12.2	100,000	10.1	108,490	22.4	175,170	17.3		
Kha	195,996	31.7	221,000	27.4	268,000	28.9	247,000	25.0	141,400	29.2	300,138	29.6	210,000-258,000[f]	19-22
Meo-Yao	15,205	2.5	25,000	3.1	39,000	4.2	47,000	4.8	47,240	9.8	49,240	4.9	52,300-52,900	4-4
Vietnamese	4,109	.7	9,000		19,000	2.0	27,000	2.7	15,400	3.2	39,470	3.9	8,000[g]	
Chinese	486				3,000	.3			2,440	.5	6,100	.6	32,350[g]	
European	226[a] 163[b]		353 8[c]		1,000	.1			560	.1	900	.1	8,000[h]	
Cambodian	1,270		1,300				2,000							
Indian and Pakistani	6				200								500[g]	
Total	618,500	99.8	807,661	98.7	928,200	100.0	988,000	99.8	483,580	100.0	1,012,468	100.0	1,167,150-1,223,850	100

a French.
b Métis.
c Other Europeans.
d Principally Luang Prabang province and part of Sayaboury.

e Excludes Phong Saly and Sam Neua; present calculations based on projection of available estimates.
f Kha appear to be seriously underestimated.
g 1959 estimates; 41,121 non-Lao Asians were registered in Laos in 1959.
h Includes French military base at Seno and American community (500) in Vientiane (1959).

Source: Lao Ministry of the Interior, Annuaire Statistique du Laos and Annuaire Statistique de l'Indochine.

TABLE 10. PERCENTAGE OF URBAN POPULATION IN LAOS AND OTHER AREAS, 1950
(localities of 20,000 or more inhabitants)

Country	Percentage of population in urban areas
Asia (ECAFE region)	13
World total	21
Africa	9
North America	42
Europe	35
Burma	10
Laos (1959)[a]	4
Vietnam	8
Philippines	13
India	12
Thailand	8
Nepal	4

[a] Based on maximum estimate for city of Vientiane, the only truly urban area in Laos. In reality Laos is the least urban country in all of Asia: using maximum population estimates Laos has only five cities of over 5,000 population compared, for example, to Nepal's ten. Minimum estimates would give a figure of 3 per cent urbanization for Laos.

Source: Economic Bulletin for Asia and the Far East, 10 (1959), 18.

TABLE 11. POPULATION ESTIMATES FOR SELECTED TOWNS, 1901-58

Town	1901	1930	1943	1958
Luang Prabang	5,900	5,400	4,950	11,000
Xieng Khouang	150	1,400	2,100	3,500
Vientiane	2,700	15,800	23,200	68,000
Savannakhet	300	4,500	5,500	8,500
Saravane	650	-	-	2,350
Attopeu	900	-	-	2,750
Pakse	-	3,400	7,300	8,000
Thakhek	-	3,400	8,100	5,500

Source: For 1901, Reinach 1901: 200-17; for 1930 and 1943, Pietrantoni 1957: 230; for 1958, Lao government statistics.

TABLE 12. POPULATION GROWTH IN SELECTED TOWNS AND PROVINCES, 1943-59

	Town	Province	Town	Province	Town	Province
	1943		Estimated 1959		Per cent Increase	
Xieng Khouang	2,100	85,000	3,500	150,000	66.7	76.5
Vientiane	23,200	126,000	68,000[a]	215,000	193.1	70.6
Savannakhet	5,500	186,000	8,500	310,000	54.5	66.7

[a] Gaudillot and Condominas (1959: 1, 34) cite the figure 71,857 for Vientiane but state that only 53,958 are urban.

Source: Pietrantoni 1957; Lao government statistics.

TABLE 13. ANNUAL RICE YIELDS IN KILOS PER HECTARE[a]

Swiddens (hai)

Ethnic group and location	Yield	Source
Averages for provinces of Laos	814-3,347 (range)	Laos Project Paper No. 9 (1961), Table 10
Lamet, Nam Tha province	1,335 (average)	
	1,100-1,670 (range)	Izikowitz 1951: 287-88
Meo, Xieng Khouang[b]	3,840	Hamada 1959
Mountain tribes of central Vietnam[c]	2,300 (1st yr.)	
	1,500 (2nd yr.)	
	500 (3rd yr.)	Lafont 1957: 1
Hanunóo, Philippines	1,524 (conservative average)	
	689-2,488 (range)	Conklin 1957: 119

Flooded or irrigated fields (na)

Ethnic group and location	Yield	Source
All of Laos	932 (average)	Laos Project Paper No. 9 (1961), Table 4
Tai and other groups		
Nam Tha district, Nam Tha province	2,020 (average)	Duclos 1959b
Muong Sing district, Nam Tha province	1,921 (average)	Duclos 1959b
Phong Saly district, Phong Saly province	633 (average)	Duclos 1959c
Ou Neua district, Phong Saly province	431 (average)	Duclos 1959c
Ou Tay district, Phong Saly province	397 (average)	Duclos 1959c
Boun Neua district, Phong Saly province	425 (average)	Duclos 1959c
Lao		
Champassak (highest provincial average)	1,231	Laos Project Paper No. 9 (1961), Table 10
Muong Ngoi district, Luang Prabang province	1,600 (average)	Duclos 1959a
Muong Sai district, Luang Prabang province	1,755 (average)	Duclos 1959a
Luang Prabang district, Luang Prabang province	1,443-2,063 (average)	Laos Project Paper No. 9 (1961)
Lao, Xieng Khouang province[b]	1,667-10,833 (range)	Hamada 1959
Meo, Xieng Khouang province[b]	1,600-4,500 (range)	Hamada 1959
Laos, Ministry of Agriculture test plots	1,700-4,500 (range)	Lao Ministry of Agriculture (1959)

(continued)

TABLE 13. ANNUAL RICE YIELDS IN KILOS PER HECTARE (continued)

Ethnic group and location	Yield	Source
Lao (continued)		
Ubol province, Northeast Thailand	225-1,125 (range)	Madge 1957: 50
Petchaboon province, Northeast Thailand	3,150 (average)	Madge 1957: 50
Chiengmai province, North Thailand	1,900-3,190 (range)	Kingshill 1960: 65
Bangkok plain	2,200	Sharp 1953: 163, 166
Others		
Preyveng province, Cambodia[d]	826	Statistical Yearbook of Cambodia, 1937-57
Kratie province, Cambodia[d]	1,889	Statistical Yearbook of Cambodia, 1937-57
Average of all provinces, Cambodia	1,118	Statistical Yearbook of Cambodia, 1937-57
Indochina	1,050 (average)	Ginsburg 1955: 205
North Vietnam	2,500 (average)	Radio Hanoi, November 28, 1959
Dien Bien Phu (North Vietnam)	3,600 (average)	Radio Hanoi, November 28, 1959
Thaun Chao (Tai-Meo Autonomous Region, North Vietnam)	3,700-4,600 (range)	Radio Hanoi, November 28, 1959

[a] These are but rough comparisons of relative fertility since only the rice yield is considered. Many crops are grown together with rice in the hai fields. Conversely, in certain areas such as Chiengmai and the Bangkok region, double rice cropping is often practiced in the na fields. There is an additional problem in using these figures since it is not always clear when paddy (unhusked rice) is referred to and when milled rice is meant. The loss in the milling stage is variously calculated. In the United States a 20 per cent loss is estimated; Duclos gives 34 per cent and Izikowitz calculates 37 per cent in Laos. Estimates provided to the author in Laos ranged around 25 per cent. In this table Duclos' estimate has been used to convert paddy to rice where necessary. It should also be noted that even the term paddy itself may refer to rice.

[b] Although within the range of possibility, Hamada's estimates appear to be high.

[c] These figures are for the first to third years of consecutive use. If the field is used again after five to seven years of lying fallow, the yield for the first year is 1,500 and for the second, 750 kilos of rice per hectare.

[d] The range of provincial averages.

TABLE 14. ESTIMATED RICE PRODUCTION IN TWENTY SELECTED VILLAGES, 1954
(na fields only)

Village and province	Number of households	Number of parcels	Number of parcels per household	Estimated cultivation area (in hectares)	Average parcel size (in square meters)	Average holding per household (in hectares)	Village yield in kilos of (husked) rice	Yield per household in kilos of (husked) rice	Yield per hectare in kilos of (husked) rice
Luang Prabang province									
Ban Song Tay	57	1,954	34.3	66.1	338.1	1.16	95,360	1,673	1,443
Muong Khay	63	2,189	34.7	91.1	416.3	1.45	188,000	2,984	2,063
Ban Pak Sy	56	2,790	49.8	58.4	209.4	1.04	106,300	1,898	1,866
Ban Khoy	6	238	39.7	5.9	246.8	.98	13,200	2,200	2,247
Ban Paklong	13	278	21.4	7.0	252.2	.54	13,000	1,000	1,854
Total	195	7,449	-	228.8	292.5	-	415,860	-	-
Average	39	1,489	38.2	45.7	315.1	1.17	83,172	2,133	1,820
Vientiane province									
Ban Nong Heo	40	923	23.1	56.5	611.8	1.41	66,480	1,662	1,177
Ban Hom	42	689	16.4	68.1	988.5	1.62	57,000	1,357	836
Nong Pa Nay	27	664	24.6	74.2	1,118.2	2.75	24,960	924	336
Ban Phak Khao	43	934	21.7	83.7	896.0	1.95	56,076	1,304	670
Ban Peuk	53	1,057	19.6	48.9	463.1	.92	108,600	2,049	2,218
Total	205	4,267	-	331.5	815.5	-	313,116	-	-
Average	14	853	20.8	66.3	776.8	1.62	62,623	1,527	945
Champassak province									
Ban Luong Khao	12	443	36.9	22.6	511.0	1.88	27,600	2,300	1,219
Ban Si Kheut	21	835	39.8	37.8	453.1	1.80	44,520	2,120	1,171
Dong Thank Khonoy	35	2,251	64.3	138.9	617.2	3.97	92,440	2,641	665
Ban Khang	82	5,363	65.4	177.8	331.6	2.17	266,292	3,247	1,500
Pha Nong Khy	38	1,840	48.4	61.7	335.1	1.62	109,440	2,880	1,775
Total	188	10,732	-	438.9	449.6	-	540,292	-	-
Average	37	2,146	57.1	87.8	409.0	2.33	108,058	2,874	1,231
Savannakhet province (Muong Champone)									
Ban Kho	61	2,142	35.1	47.5	221.6	.78	91,920	1,507	1,936
Dong Mone	109	1,927	17.7	72.7	377.3	.67	91,368	838	1,251
Ban Phay	133	4,178	31.4	141.4	338.3	1.06	92,820	698	657
Ban Nakhon	81	2,130	26.3	67.6	317.4	.83	107,292	1,325	1,587
Ban Back	124	3,800	30.6	140.1	761.2	1.13	108,000	871	771
Total	508	14,177	-	469.2	403.2	-	491,400	-	-
Average	101	2,835	27.9	93.8	331.0	.92	98,280	967	1,047

Source: Lao Ministry of Agriculture.

TABLE 15. LAND HOLDINGS IN MUONG KHAY AND SONG TAY, LUANG PRABANG DISTRICT, 1954[a]

	Muong Khay, Tasseng Muong Khay		Song Tay, Tasseng Pak Lung	
Hectares	Number of households	Per cent of total	Number of households	Per cent of total
0 - .49	1	1.6	1	1.8
.50- .99	9	14.3	20	35.1
1.00-1.49	32	50.8	23	40.4
1.50-1.99	6	9.5	7	12.3
2.00-2.49	11	17.5	6	10.5
2.50-2.99	3	4.8		
8.00 and over	1	1.6		
Total	63	100.1	57	100.1

[a] There are, on the average, 1.16 hectares of na land per household in Song Tay, and 1.45 in Muong Khay. In 1958 there were 83 houses and 414 people in Muong Khay and 88 and 406 respectively in Song Tay. By comparison, in Bang Chan near Bangkok 14 per cent of the farms are over 10 hectares.

Source: Lao Ministry of Agriculture.

TABLE 16. NUMBER OF PARCELS OF LAND PER HOUSEHOLD IN MUONG KHAY AND SONG TAY, 1954[a]

	Muong Khay		Song Tay	
Number of parcels	Number of households	Per cent of total	Number of households	Per cent of total
Ten and under	-		-	
11 - 20	10	15.9	12	21.1
21 - 30	25	39.7	18	31.6
31 - 40	12	19.0	11	19.3
41 - 50	8	12.7	9	15.8
51 - 60	5	7.9	6	10.5
61 - 70	1	1.6	1	1.8
71 - 80	-	-	-	-
81 - 90	1	1.6	-	-
91 -100	-	-	-	-
101 and over	1	1.6	-	-
Total	63	100.0	57	100.1

[a] The average number of parcels per household in Song Tay is 34.3; in Muong Khay, 34.7.

Source: Lao Ministry of Agriculture.

TABLE 17. ESTIMATED ANNUAL RICE YIELDS IN KILOS PER HOUSEHOLD[a]

Swiddens

Ethnic group and location	Yield	Source[b]
Khmu, Luang Prabang province	9,600-12,000 (range of highest estimates)	
	3,600 (considered a good harvest)	
	1,200- 2,400 (average)	
	Under 1,200 (poor yield)	
Lao, Luang Prabang province	2,400- 6,000 (range)	
	3,600 (average)	
Meo, Luang Prabang province	3,600 (average)	
Yao, Luang Prabang province	2,400- 4,800 (range)	
Lamet, Nam Tha province	2,255- 2,900 (range)	Izikowitz 1951: 288
Meo, Xieng Khouang province	9,600 (estimate)	Hamada 1959

Flooded and irrigated fields

Ethnic group and location	Yield	Source[b]
Lao, Luang Prabang province	12,000 (maximum)	
	2,400- 6,000 (average range)	
	Under 2,400 (marginal)	
Lao, Luang Prabang province (see Table 18)	1,673- 2,984 (average range)	
Tai, Nam Tha province	2,855 (average)	Duclos 1959b: 6
Lao, Xieng Khouang province	3,600- 8,700 (range)	Hamada 1959
Meo, Xieng Khouang province	4,000-10,000 (range)	Hamada 1959
Lao, Vientiane province	2,700- 3,600 (average range)	Kaufman 1961: 3
Lao, Vientiane province	3,504 (average)	Ayabe 1959b
Lao, Northeast Thailand	840- 2,828 (average range)	Madge 1957: 50
Thai, Bangkok plain	1,400-39,600 (range)	Sharp 1953: 164
	11,900 (average)	
	Under 5,500 (marginal)	

[a] In northern Laos, yields per proprietor can apparently range from 60 to 10,400 kilos. The yields from swiddens and irrigated rice fields are not strictly comparable because many supplementary crops are raised with the rice in the swiddens, while corn is often raised in other hai fields. In addition, groups such as the Lao of Luang Prabang province frequently cultivate both na and hai fields. As regards the na cases cited, with the exception of Luang Prabang and Nam Tha provinces, no hai fields are used. Single cropping is the rule in Laos. As in Table 13 an attempt has been made to correct unhusked rice figures.

[b] Unless otherwise cited, the author's field data are used.

TABLE 18. RICE PRODUCTION IN KILOS PER PROPRIETOR IN TWO VILLAGES OF LUANG PRABANG DISTRICT, 1954[a]

	Muong Khay, Tasseng Muong Khay		Song Tay, Tasseng Pak Lung	
Paddy production	Number of households	Per cent of total	Number of households	Per cent of total
200 - 499	1	1.6	7	12.3
500 - 999	3	4.8	17	29.8
1000 - 1499	3	4.8	4	7.0
1500 - 1999	6	9.5	6	10.5
2000 - 2499	7	11.1	10	17.5
2500 - 2999	10	15.9	2	3.5
3000 - 3499	15	23.8	4	7.0
3500 - 3999	6	9.5	2	3.5
4000 - 4999	6	9.5	3	5.3
5000 - 5999	1	1.6	1	1.8
6000	2	3.2	1	1.8
7000	1	1.6		
8000	1	1.6		
12,000	1	1.6		
Total	63	100.1	57	100.0

[a] In Song Tay the average yield per household is 1,673 kilos and per hectare, 1,443; the figures are 2,984 and 2,063 respectively in Muong Khay. Hai fields are not included.

Source: Lao Ministry of Agriculture.

TABLE 19. EXAMPLES OF LIVESTOCK SACRIFICE AMONG THE PEOPLES OF NORTHERN LAOS[a]

Ethnic group	Occasion	Animal sacrificed
Lao	To appease house, village, or field spirits	Chicken
	Harvest festival "to glorify the soul of the rice" and other agricultural ceremonies	Buffalo, ox, chicken
Lao, Khmu, Tai	Buffalo sacrifice early in rainy season, common to many peoples in Southeast Asia	Buffalo
Black Tai	To "god of the soil" at planting time	Buffao, pig, duck, or chicken
	Harvest festival to honor the "god of the soil"	Buffalo
	Funeral	First day: duck; second day: chicken
Khmu	To honor "messiah" who will bring a new promised life	Pigs and chickens
	Illness	Chicken
	Death	All animals of the deceased for the funeral feast
	Spirit of the village	Pig, ox, chicken
Kha Ko (Akha)	For a pregnant woman to bear a boy	Chicken
	To offset the bad effect of twins or defective children	Goat or dog
	Death (offerings for the soul depends on sex and status)	Ox, goat, dog, pig
Lamet	Marriage	Roosters or pig
	To aid in conception, when pregnancy is ascertained, and when first child is born	Pig
	Illness, particularly of head of household	Buffalo or pig
	Before a funeral procession	Several pigs
Meo	To get rid of evil _phi_	Varies
	Illness "due to bad _phi_"	Cow or lesser livestock
	Death: for each day corpse remains in the house	Chicken, or preferably pig
	Death: every child of deceased, on day before burial	"At least one cow"
	If _phi_ of deceased parents come to visit and ask for food	"Depends on wishes of the _phi_"
	To _phi_ of the house, if girl's parents discover daughter sleeping with a boy	Pig or dog
	To _phi_ of silver bars, to increase household's wealth in silver	Chicken

[a] Lamet examples are from Izikowitz (1951), Black Tai from Hickey (1958), and Akha cases from Srisvasdi (1950). All others are from author's field notes.

TABLE 20. AVAILABILITY AND PRICE OF FRUITS AND VEGETABLES IN NORTHERN LAOS[a]

Item	Price in kip per kilo	Comments
Bamboo shoots	10	An important food item gathered by all groups; an important trade item for the Khmu
Bananas (common variety)	10-25	Eaten fresh or fried
Bananas ("egg" variety)	20	Small, with sweet flavor
Banana leaves	-	Arranged in packets by the Khmu; sold as wrapping material for other goods
Banana stalks	15	Pickled and eaten
Bean sprouts	15	Common vegetable
Beans (runner)	20	Available most of the year
Beans (string)	30	Plentiful in summer months
Betel nut (from areca palm)	100 per touque[b]	
Betel leaves	-	Spread with lime paste as wrapping for the nut
Cabbage	10-30	Grown by Lao and Meo; plentiful in February-March; more expensive at other times
Chili peppers	30-50	Important in diet of all groups
Chinese mustard	-	Grown by Meo
Citronella grass	5 per bunch	Gathered by Khmu; for brewing tea
Coconut (young)	15 each	Eaten as a sweet
Coconut (old)	30 each	Milk and meat important supplementary foods; used in cooking
Coffee	35	Fairly common village plant; grown particularly in the area of Nam Bac
Coriander	8	Plentiful in July
Corn	5 per three ears	Grown by Meo but usually sold directly to other Meo as livestock feed; occasionally grown and sold on market by the Lao
Cucumbers	13-50	Plentiful in summer but avail able most of the year; large seedy variety less expensive than long thin "Thai" type
Custard apple	4-5 each	On market in July
Eggplant	10-50	Available most of year; plentiful July-October; grown by Lao and some Khmu
Garlic	10-50	In season in February; expensive in July

(continued)

TABLE 20. AVAILABILITY AND PRICE OF FRUITS AND VEGETABLES IN NORTHERN LAOS (continued)

Item	Price in kip per kilo	Comments
Ginger	15	Common spice among Lao
Lemon	4-6	Frequent in Lao villages
Lichees	15	A wild variety; plentiful in July
Limes	10	Small, hard; plentiful in July
Mangoes	50	Favorite July fruit
Melons	15-35 each	Common summer fruit
Mint	15	Eaten chopped in many lao dishes
Mushrooms (black)	30	Gathered in the forest by Khmu
Onions (fresh)	15-30	Plentiful in February; expensive in July
Onions (dried)	100	Sold dried in the summer
Oranges	30	Small, bitter, from Nam Bac region
Papaya	10-30	Sold by Lao; a favorite fruit
Peaches	1-3 each	Gathered by Meo and Khmu in July
Peanuts	-	Sold shelled and unshelled
Pineapple	15 each	In season in July; price fluctuates from 5 to 30
Pomelo	10 each	In season in July
Potatoes (white)	10-20	Grown by Meo
Potatoes (sweet)	10-33	Grown by Khmu and other groups
Rice (glutinous)	90-110 per kalon[c] (Nov.-Feb.) 120-130 per kalon (Mar.-June) 140-150 per kalon (July-Oct.)	Main Lao food staple
Scallions	15	Grown by Lao and Khmu; plentiful in July-August
Sugar cane	-	Grown in Lao and some Meo villages
Tamarind	20	Used for jam; plentiful in May-June
Tea	5 per 50 grams (imported)	Grown by Lamet as well and on Nam Tha market in June
Tobacco[d]	50	Grown by some Lao and Khmu
Tomatoes	30-40	Available March-June
Vine leaves	8	Eaten by Lao as salad greens
Watermelon	10-20 each	Grown by Lao and Tai Dam

[a] These figures refer to Luang Prabang town and are average prices obtained in 1957.
[b] About eight kilos.
[c] For husked rice, approximately 16 kilos.
[d] On Nam Tha market.

TABLE 21. LIVESTOCK, FISH, AND FOWL PRODUCTS IN NORTHERN LAOS[a]

Item	Price in kip	Comments
Bats	12-15 each	Eaten by Lao, dried and fried
Beef		Not commonly available outside Vientiane
Birds	7-8 each	Eaten by Lao in soup or fried with vegetables
Buffalo	3000-4000 per animal (average)	Purchased for agricultural work or sacrifice
Buffalo meat	40-50 per kilo	More expensive trimmed; an important meat source for all groups
Buffalo bones	30 per kilo	For soup
Buffalo blood	12-20 per kilo	Sold in jellied form
Buffalo skin	30-40 per kilo	Sold dried; boiled and eaten by Lao
Buffalo viscera	40 per kilo	Used in preparation of many dishes
Chicken	80-120 each	Medium-sized (by local standards); plucked
	30-60 each (Nam Tha)	
Chicken eggs	5-6 each	Usually about fifty per cent rotten[b]
Cicadas	-	Seasonal delicacies, eaten by Lao, sold grilled on bamboo skewers
Crickets	-	" " "
Cow	3500 per animal	Price for large Meo cow
	1100-1200 for a calf (Muong Sing)	Kept by Lao and other groups for prestige and sacrifice
Deer	1500-3500 (Nam Tha)	Hunted and sold by the Khmu
Doves	30-50 each	Lao delicacy, eaten roasted

(continued)

TABLE 21. LIVESTOCK, FISH, AND FOWL PRODUCTS IN NORTHERN LAOS (continued)

Item	Price in kip	Comments
Duck	150 each	For live duck weighing about 2 kilos
	70-80 each (Nam Tha and Muong Sing)	
Duck eggs	6 each	In many areas more commonly used than chicken eggs
Fish (fresh)	80-120 per kilo	Supply irregular; caviar a delicacy
Fish (dried)	200 per kilo	Imported from Thailand
Lard	50 per kilo	Used by Lao as supplement to fish oil for cooking needs
Pig	1000 per animal	For Meo pig weighing 25 kilos
Pig blood	15-20 per kilo	Sold in jellied form
Pig intestines	50 per kilo	Used by Lao and Chinese for making sausage
Pig skin	25 per kilo	Sun-dried, a Lao delicacy
	50 per kilo	Dried and fried in lard, eaten as snack
Pork	60-80 per kilo	More expensive trimmed; a primary meat source for all groups
	35 (Muong Sai)	
	25 (Muong Sing and Nam Tha)	

[a] Data pertains to Luang Prabang (1957) unless otherwise noted; prices for areas other than Vientiane or Luang Prabang are based on Duclos (1959b and 1959c).

[b] This appears to be by intention, since the Lao prefer "fermented" eggs to fresh ones, considering them a fortifying food.

TABLE 22. SOME HOME-PREPARED FOODS SOLD ON THE LUANG PRABANG MARKET

Item	Price in kip	Description
Khao poun	15-20 per kilo	Lao noodles: a fine rice vermicelli
Khao poun	5-20 per serving, depending on quality of ingredients	The noodles served in a sauce of meat, fish, and grated coconut cooked in coconut milk and flavored with onions and garlic; raw chopped bean sprouts, mint, and banana flower stamens are sprinkled on top
Padek	300 per 12 kilos	Fish mixed with salt, rice, and rice bran and allowed to ferment; keeps for 6 to 12 months; purchased by Lao and Khmu
Som mou	100 per kilo	Chopped pork, pig skin, salt, saltpeter, onions, and steamed rice packed into banana-leaf wrappers and allowed to ferment for several days
Sai ou	100 per kilo	Similar ingredients as above, but no saltpeter as preservative; instead stuffed in pig intestines and smoked to make sausage
Khao lam	4-5 per bamboo section	Glutinous rice mixed with coconut milk and a little sugar and steamed inside a section of bamboo
Voun	2 per square	A candy made of coconut milk cooked with gelatin and tinted a bright pink color; after setting, it is cut in squares

TABLE 23. CLOTHING COMMONLY PURCHASED BY LAO, KHMU, AND MEO VILLAGERS IN LUANG PRABANG

Group	Item	Price in kip	Comments
Lao, Khmu	Long pants	150[a] 180-200[b] 250-400[c]	Minimum price, manufactured in Hong Kong
Lao	Socks (nylon)	60-70[b] 50-70[c]	Worn mainly by urban Lao
Lao, Khmu	Short pants	100[a]	Minimum price, manufactured in Hong Kong
Lao, Khmu	Man's shirt	100-150[a] 120-150[b] 120-250[c]	Minimum price, manufactured in Hong Kong
Lao, Khmu	Long-sleeved man's shirt	150-200[b] 160-300[c]	Used largely by urban Lao
Lao, Khmu	Man's hat	80-250[a]	Prestige item for wealthier villagers
Lao, Khmu	Undershirt	50[a]	Often worn instead of shirt
Lao, Khmu	Canvas sneakers	70-250[a] 120-180[c]	Worn by prosperous villagers on special occasions
Lao	Man's long sarong	100-200[a] 50-60[c]	Of bright plaid silk, woven in Cambodia
Lao, Khmu	<u>Pakhoma</u>	70-100[a] 60-80[b] 50-60[c]	Short cotton sarong, worn by Lao men for bathing; worn by some Khmu; also used as sash and as container for personal effects

(continued)

TABLE 23. CLOTHING COMMONLY PURCHASED BY LAO, KHMU, AND MEO VILLAGERS IN LUANG PRABANG (continued)

Group	Item	Price in kip	Comments
Lao	Handkerchief	20-30[b] 15-25[c]	Luxury item
Lao, Khmu	Woman's skirt[a]	100-200[a] 150+[b]	Locally hand-woven cotton[d]
Lao	Woman's skirt[a]	500-900+[a] 1,000-3,000[c]	Good quality hand-woven silk[d,e]
Lao	Skirt border[a]	150,300,450+[a]	Of cotton, silver, or gold respectively; the characteristic elaborate border trim on Lao skirts[d]
Lao	Blouse	150-300[a]	Of cotton or nylon, manufactured in Hong Kong
Lao	Scarf	200-400[a] 700-1,000[c]	Locally hand-woven cotton or silk, worn draped across bosom and over one shoulder[d]
Khmu	Small towel	50[a] 70-100[b]	Used by women as turban
Meo	Black cotton fabric	50-80[c] 80 per meter[a]	Used by all Meo for characteristic trousers and short jackets; fabric manufactured in Hong Kong
Meo	Red cotton fabric	80 per meter[a]	Manufactured in Hong Kong; used for Meo men's long sashes

[a] 1957 prices in Luang Prabang.
[b] 1959 prices in Luang Prabang.
[c] 1959 prices in Vientiane, where items are often of better quality and available in larger variety.
[d] Woven in villages near Luang Prabang.
[e] Woven in Vientiane.

TABLE 24. EXAMPLES OF SELF-EMPLOYMENT, WAGES, SERVICE CHARGES, AND CEREMONIAL EXPENSES IN LUANG PRABANG TOWN AND PROVINCE, 1957[a]

Paid by	Paid to	Price or income in kip	For
SELF-EMPLOYMENT			
Lao village woman	Self	100-150 per day	Procuring and selling fresh produce in town market
Lao village woman	Self	80 per day	Booth along road in village[c]
Lao village woman	Self	150 per day	Store in home[c]
Lao village blacksmith	Self	100-300 per day	Making agricultural tools (seasonal)
Lao weaver (woman)	Self	50 per day	Weaving cloth and Lao skirts and scarves
Lao (or occasional Khmu) pedicab driver	Self	150-200 per day (holiday; 500)	Transporting goods and passengers within town
Lao barber	Self	100-200 per day	In Vientiane (1959)
WAGES			
Government	Lao villagers	70 per person per day without food	Work on local small construction project
Lao merchant in town	Lao villager	25-30 per day with food	Work as coolie (temporary)
Lao farmer	Lao villager	1 *kalon* paddy (value 60 kip)	Day's agricultural labor
		40 per day with food	Day's agricultural labor (Vientiane area, 1959)
Lao farmer	Lao villager	2000 per year	Seasonal agricultural labor
Lao farmer	Lao (man)	1000 kilos rice	Seasonal agricultural labor[c]
Lao farmer	Lao (man)	16 kilos per day	Seasonal agricultural labor
		60-100 per day[b]	
Lao farmer	Thai or Lao	1000 600	Harvest season[c] Transplanting season[c]
Lao farmer	Lao (woman)	750 kilos rice	Seasonal agricultural labor

(continued)

TABLE 24. EXAMPLES OF SELF-EMPLOYMENT, WAGES, SERVICE CHARGES, AND CEREMONIAL EXPENSES IN LUANG PRABANG TOWN AND PROVINCE, 1957 (continued)

Paid by	Paid to	Price or income in kip	For
Government	Khmu villagers	Young boy or woman, 50-80 per day; man, 80-100 per day (without food, 60-100 per day)[b]	Coolie road work (seasonal)
Lao villager	Khmu villager	50 per day plus 1 meal	Day's agricultural labor
Lao villager	Khmu villager	3 kilos salt per day (value 24 kip)	Day's agricultural labor (in northern Luang Prabang province)
Lao villager	Khmu villager	Meals and sometimes old clothes	Corvée, for harvesting, house-building, etc.[d]
Lao urban elite	Lao or Khmu	500-1000 per month plus food, clothing, shelter	Domestic servant
Chinese merchant	Lao or Khmu	800-1000 per month plus food, shelter	Labor as coolie
Chinese merchant	Lao	3500 per month (no food or lodging)	Unskilled labor in Vientiane
Government	Khmu	2000 per month	Labor as coolie in town power plant (difficult work)
Government	Lao _nai ban_	1200 per year	Duties as village headman
Government	Lao clerk	4000 per month	Routine office duties
Government	Lao teacher	5000 per month	Teaching elementary school
Government	Lao official	15,000 per month	Senior military or civil position
Vietnamese or Chinese contractor	Vietnamese skilled laborers	300 per day 200-500 per day[b]	Carpentry work
SERVICE CHARGES			
Lao farmer	Lao, Tai, or Chinese mill owner	12 per _myn_ or 12 kilos 5 per kalon or 16 kilos in Muong Sai[i]	Milling rice for sale

(continued)

TABLE 24. EXAMPLES OF SELF-EMPLOYMENT, WAGES, SERVICE CHARGES, AND CEREMONIAL EXPENSES IN LUANG PRABANG TOWN AND PROVINCE, 1957 (continued)

Paid by	Paid to	Price or income in kip	For
Lao villagers	Lao or Vietnamese jeep "taxi" owner	About 2 per km.	Personal transportation
Lao villager	Lao midwife	5 kilos rice (value 50 kip)	Delivery of infant
Lao villager	Barber	20 30[b]	Haircut
Lao villager	Lao village or urban landowner	20-35 per cent of crop	Rental of land
Lao villager	Lao village or urban landowner	50 per cent of crop	Rental of land when land-owner supplies buffalo and rice seedlings and repairs dikes
Lao villager	Lao village or urban landowner	30-50 per cent of crop	Rental of land[c]
CEREMONIAL EXPENSES			
Lao	Bonze	200-300 (1000 maximum)	Special recitation of scriptures
Lao village family	General expenses	About 1500	Ceremony for ordination of a bonze[c]
Lao urban family	General expenses	10-50,000	Ceremony for ordination of a bonze
Meo groom's family	Family of bride	2500-15,000 equivalent in silver bars	Bride price[e]
Lamet groom's family	Family of bride	1-6 buffalo	Bride price[f]
Urban Lao groom's family	Family of bride	10-100,000	Bride price[e]
Lao village bride's family	General expenses	2000	Wedding[c]
Lao urban bride's family	General expenses	10-20,000	Wedding[h]
Lao village family	*Wat* and general expenses	800	Funeral[c]
Lao urban family	*Wat* and general expenses	30,000	Funeral
Urban Lao	*Wat* and general expenses	10-200,000	*Boun*[g]

[a] Unless otherwise noted.
[b] Luang Prabang, 1959.
[c] These examples are from Vientiane province (Kaufman: 1961).
[d] Corvée is technically illegal but still widely practiced.
[e] Among the Meo and Lamet the bride price is compensation to the bride's family for loss of a worker; among the Lao it is used for expenses of the marriage celebration and for purchasing household effects.
[f] Silk fabric, jewelry, porcelain bowls, and gongs are also used.
[g] A personal religious *boun*, sometimes given by an individual woman, to gain merit; can sometimes be very elaborate and expensive.
[h] This is for people of moderate circumstances; for an official of middle rank 100,000 kip or more would be common.
[i] Data from Duclos 1959.

TABLE 25. SELECTED EXAMPLES OF BARTER TRADE[a]

Item bartered	By	To	In exchange for
Rice	Lao (Vientiane)	Lao and local merchants	Salt, fish, tools, clothing
Salt[b]	Lao (Northeast Thailand)	Other Lao	Rice
Opium	Meo	Lao merchants and others	Salt, cloth, silver and iron bars
Rice, cotton, forest products baskets, game	Khmu	Lao village traders	Cloth, blankets, salt tools, utensils, _padek_
Rice	Lamet	Tai Lu or Lao village traders	Clothing, pottery tools
Cloth, cotton, fish	Lanten[c]	Tai Lu[d]	Salt
Silk	Tai Dam	Meo, Yao	Opium[e]

a Payment in kind, by exchange of services for goods, is also made.

b Certain villages in the Ubol area specialize in making salt by evaporation. There are also salt deposits exploited by Lao villagers near the Nam Lik river and at Ban Keun in the vicinity of Vientiane.

c A tribal group in Nam Tha province.

d Work in salt mines near Yunnanese border (at Botene 30 kilometers northeast of Nam Tha).

e According to Duclos the rate in 1959 was a half kilo of raw opium for one kilo of silk. The latter was valued at 600-900 kip per kilo.

TABLE 26. PRICES OF SOME AGRICULTURAL AND FOREST PRODUCTS OF NORTHERN LAOS, 1957

Item	Sold or traded by	Price in kip	Comments
Alcohol (rice)	Tai	20 per beer bottle (Nam Tha)	4-6 bottles per 16 kilos of rice
	Tai Neua	15-20 per beer bottle (Muong Sing)	
Bamboo[a]	Khmu	4-5	For pole about 2-4 meters long
Basketry products	Khmu		Data from Pak Beng[b]
Sleeping mat		40	2x3 meters
Basket		15	For carrying rice
Basket		5	For steaming rice
Small covered basket		30	For serving cooked rice
Large tray		20	For winnowing rice
Low stool		20	Usually used when eating
Low platform table		50	Used as serving and eating surface
Beeswax	Lamet, Khmu		Sold to Lao for making candles
Benzoin[c]	Khmu	140 per _kalon_[d]	Purchased in small quantities by Lao merchants and resold in bulk to French and Chinese exporters at 4000 per _kalon_
Charcoal[e]	Khmu	2-8 per kilo	Price depends on season, quality and quantity in which sold; often further processed by Lao and resold
Cotton	Lao, Khmu, Kha Ko (Muong Sing)	10-15 per kilo 150-200 per 12 kilos	Relatively small amounts grown by the Lao, who weave for them-selves and trade cloth to tribal groups
Firewood	Meo, Khmu		For Luang Prabang market -- used for cooking and heating; in countryside Lao cut their own; sold by Lao in Vientiane
Lac	Khmu	5-10 per kilo	Purchased by Lao merchants and resold to French exporter; used in varnishes and shellac, great variation in supply

(continued)

TABLE 26. PRICES OF SOME AGRICULTURAL AND FOREST PRODUCTS OF NORTHERN LAOS, 1957 (continued)

Item	Sold or traded by	Price in kip	Comments
Opium	Meo (also some Khmu and other groups)	1200-5000 per kilo (for raw opium sold by the Meo)[f]	Depends on season, quality, demand, and area; major cash crop for Meo; its sale is technically illegal in Luang Prabang province but it is available on the open market in Xieng Khouang
		5-15,000 per kilo (for "cooked" or crudely refined)	
		40,000 per kilo	Price in Bangkok (illegal)
Salt	Various groups	10 per 700-gram packet (Nam Tha)	Produced at Botene in northern Nam Tha province and also in the Muong Sai area
		13-15 per 700-gram packet (Muong Sing)	
		15-25 per 700-gram packet (Luang Prabang)	
Silk	Tai Dam	600-900 per kilo (Nam Tha)	Also produced in most Lao villages for individual household needs
Sugar	Lao	5 per 300-gram packet	Coarse, dark, very crude; ground in village mills
Minerals	Lao		Reportedly gold is sold by Khmu in Pak Beng area and semiprecious stones in the Houei Sai region; both are in northern Luang Prabang province

[a] This is a special non-rotting variety; other kinds are cheaper.
[b] Trading center on the Mekong in northern Luang Prabang province.
[c] These prices were high in 1957 due to the exclusion of production from the Pathet Lao-held provinces of Sam Neua and Phong Saly.
[d] A container, usually a basket, equal to about 12 kilos of unhusked rice or 16 kilos of milled rice; often equivalent to the amount in a five-gallon tin.
[e] Used for cooking purposes (in braziers) and by blacksmiths; a considerable part goes to power the electric power plant in Luang Prabang town. Also an important market product of farmers in the Vientiane area.
[f] According to Hamada the price was 5,200 kip per kilo in Xieng Khouang in 1957.

TABLE 27. FORMS OF TRAVEL IN NORTHERN AND CENTRAL LAOS, 1959

Form	Use
LAND	
Feet	Used by all groups for short trips, and up to several weeks' walking if no other type of transportation available
Horse	Used by Meo, particularly for trading
Elephant	For travel and transport of goods through jungle, particularly in Sayaboury province
Buffalo cart	Used by Lao villagers in Vientiane province; non-existent farther north
Jeep, truck[a]	Owned by Chinese, Vietnamese, and some Lao merchants, for transport of villagers and goods, especially in Luang Prabang
Buses	Used in Vientiane area, none in Luang Prabang
Bicycle[b]	Used extensively in towns and occasionally in nearby villages
Pedicab	For passengers and goods in the vicinity of the major towns such as Luang Prabang and Vientiane
WATER	
Pirogue	Common among Lao villagers for transport of people and light goods
Pirogue with outboard motor	Used on a small scale by some Lao merchants
Motorized barge	Operated by Chinese and Lao for larger scale river transport of goods and some passengers
Bamboo raft	Made by Lao and Khmu villagers for one-way trip downstream; at destination raft is disassembled and bamboo is sold
AIR	
Air Laos	Carries passengers and freight; used extensively by government, military personnel, merchants, and Europeans; uses DC-3's and Otters
Helicopters	Use limited to the military
Veha Akat	Company utilizes "Beavers" and "Dragons"; makes nonschedul flights to more remote areas of northern Laos (there are several other small private airlines)

[a] Many high Lao officials have private cars -- Opels, Citroens, and Mercedes Benz. Motor scooters are also used. Taxis are common in Vientiane. In a few cases private automobiles are found in some villages around Vientiane.

[b] According to Gaudillot and Condominas (1959: 164-65) bicycles are becoming increasingly important on the Vientiane plain; in one village there is one per 30 inhabitants and in another one per 150. In some places they outnumber the carts. In the village of Pha Kh (pop. 402) near Vientiane, Ayabe (1961: 53) noted 31 bicycles, 29 carts, 2 motorcycles, a 2 automobiles.

TABLE 28. PACK-HORSE TRANSPORTATION IN NAM THA PROVINCE, 1959

Route	Kilo-meters	Dry-season load (60 kilos)			Wet-season load (50 kilos)		
		Days	Kip	Per kilo	Days	Kip	Per kilo
Muong Sing-Xieng Kok	74	3	500	8.3	15	750	15
Muong Sing-Nam Tha	52	2	400	6.6	7	450	9
Muong Sing-Muong Mugne	100	7	1,000	16.6	-	Route closed	-
Muong Sing-Xieng Keng	40	2.5	600	10	13	7-800	14-16

Source: Duclos 1959b: 18.

TABLE 29. SOME RURAL-URBAN DIFFERENCES AMONG THE LAO

VILLAGER	PROSPEROUS TOWN DWELLER
Works at agricultural labor	Works in an office or store
Has largely subsistence economy, with small amount of cash	Is salaried or gets other cash income
Is illiterate or rarely has more than three years of schooling	Has had six years or more of schooling
Speaks only Lao	Fair to good speaking knowledge of French
With rare exceptions, has traveled only within his own province	At least moderate travel within Laos and possibly abroad
Has no contact with Europeans, only occasional contact with Chinese or Vietnamese	Some contact with Europeans, frequent contact with Chinese and Vietnamese
House is traditional bamboo and thatch, possibly with some wood, on piles; sleeps on bamboo mat, uses low stools, simple kerosene lamp or candlelight illumination	House may be of concrete construction in European style, usually has electricity; home has chairs, tables and beds
Usually has only one wife	May have two or three wives
All domestic work usually done by members of own household	May have one or more servants
May own a bicycle	Owns a bicycle; may own a jeep or other type of automobile
Clothing is mostly homespun, plus cheap manufactured items; often has no shoes, little jewelry	Clothing is both European and traditional Lao; women have gold and silver jewelry
Has little knowledge or interest in government affairs	Often has considerable interest in government and politics and reads a newspaper
Distrusts, resents, and sometimes fears townspeople	Often shows disdain for villagers, treats them with condescension
Relies for recreation on traditional village celebrations, rice wine	Often attends movies, plays tennis, drinks beer, listens to radio
Treats monks with great respect and often joins the priesthood (usually on a temporary basis)	Religion and participation in pagoda activities plays a smaller role in his life
Relies primarily on traditional curing techniques from monks or village curers	Uses both Western and traditional medical techniques

TABLE 30. SELECTED ITEMS AVAILABLE IN SHOPS IN LUANG PRABANG AND VIENTIANE

ITEM	PRICE IN KIP	MARKET[a]	COMMENTS
Ammunition (shotgun shells)	-		Meo among best customers; sulphur and saltpeter also available, for mixing with charcoal at home -- used by Meo for gunpowder and by Lao for rockets
Asparagus (canned)	100 per tin	LP 57	Delmonte brand, 1 lb. 13 oz. tin, occasionally bought by Lao and Europeans
Aspirin tablets	-		Used for all illnesses by Lao, and by Meo and Khmu who can afford it; made in Thailand
Batteries (flashlight)	15 each 2 for 25 2 for 20-25	LP 57 LP 59 V 59	American brands, imported via Hong Kong and used by Lao and Meo
Beer	75 per quart	LP 57	For Tsingtao brand (from mainland China)
	35 per pint 25 per pint 35 per pint	LP 57 V 59 LP 59	For Carlsberg brand (Danish) and San Miguel (Philippines); some American brands also available; consumed chiefly by soldiers and by prosperous urban Lao
Bicycle	4-6000 4-5000	LP 57 LP 59	Mostly Japanese brands, used by urban Lao and some villagers near town; used bicycles (English and French brands: BSA, Aiglon, Trophee) are also available
Blanket	90-150	LP 57	For thin cotton type
	600	LP 57	For woolen blankets; these are an important trade item for the Meo, who prefer red ones
Bread	20 per loaf 4 per small roll 40 per loaf	LP 57 LP 57 LP 59	Baked by Vietnamese with imported wheat flour (from Australia); consumed chiefly by Europeans and urbanized Lao
Candles	10 per small pkge. 4-5 per box of 8	LP 57 LP 59- V 59	Manufactured in Vientiane; important item in all Lao ceremonies
Cigarettes	15-30 per pkge. 15 (Job-Saigon) 15 (Robin Hood-Hong Kong) 23 (Lucky Strike-US)	LP 57 LP 59 LP 59 LP 59	Price varies according to brand; cheapest and most popular is Mic brand made in Saigon; domestic varieties also available since 1959
Cigarette lighter	150 +	LP 57	Prestige item for Khmu and some Lao
Coffee (powdered)	70 per can 60 per can	LP 57 LP 59	For 2 oz. Nescafe; luxury item for prosperous Lao and Meo villagers
Crackers	160-180 per tin	LP 57	Jacob brand, imported via Hong Kong; urban luxury item
Drum (bronze)	3-6000	LP 57	Formerly used in Khmu ceremonials, now chiefly a tourist item

(continued)

TABLE 30. SELECTED ITEMS AVAILABLE IN SHOPS IN LUANG PRABANG AND VIENTIANE (continued)

ITEM	PRICE IN KIP	MARKET[a]	COMMENTS
Enamel mug	30 40-60 30-50 150-180 (plastic) 180-200 (plastic)	LP 57 LP 59 V 59 LP 59 V 59	Assorted sizes and shapes used by Lao and Meo and some Khmu
Flashlight	100	LP 57	Commonly used by Lao and Meo
Flour (wheat)	40 per kilo	LP 59	Imported from various sources
Gasoline	300-500 per five-gallon tin	LP 59	Imported from Bangkok
Gum (chewing)	10 per box	LP 59	Chicklets (U.S.)
Gun	3-7000	LP 57	For handmade flintlock smooth bore, made by Meo
	10,000+	LP 57	For manufactured shotgun; guns used by some Lao and Meo
Hair ornament (gold)	1-1,200	LP 57	Made by local goldsmith and worn by more prosperous Lao women
Ices	20	LP 59	Sold by street vendors
Ink	25 per bottle 35 per bottle 20 per bottle	LP 57 LP 59 V 59	Scrip brand (U.S.) used by urban and rural school children Quink (U.S.)
Iron bar	800 per 16 kilo bar 100 per 4 kilo bar 100 per 4 kilo bar	LP 57 LP 57 LP 59	A basic trade item, bought by Lao and Meo blacksmiths
Iron digging tip	20-25 30	LP 57 LP 59	Used by all groups, on digging sticks; made in Lao villages near town
Kerosene	300 per five-gallon tin 350-400 per five-gallon tin	LP 57 LP 59	Bought by all groups, for use in home lamps
Knife (pocket)	20-40 30-40	LP 59 V 59	Very popular item
Lamp (kerosene)	25 15 5	LP 57 LP 59 LP 59	Common among all groups, made of used evaporated milk cans (small size)
Lichees (canned)	70 per tin	LP 57	Made in mainland China; 1 lb. tin; urban Lao delicacy
Lime			Bought by Lao and Khmu for use with betel chews; made locally
Matches	3 per box 2 per box 3 per box	LP 57 LP 59 V 59	Made in Thailand; bought by all groups

(continued)

TABLE 30. SELECTED ITEMS AVAILABLE IN SHOPS IN LUANG PRABANG AND VIENTIANE (continued)

ITEM	PRICE IN KIP	MARKET[a]	COMMENTS
Milk	30 per tin (Ziel U.S.)	LP 57	For condensed sugared brands; popular as a luxury item among prosperous Lao and Meo
	25 per tin (Ziel U.S.)	LP 59	
	140 per tin	LP 57	For 1 lb. of powdered Klim brand
Mosquito netting	80-120	LP 57	For enough to cover two people; commonly used in most Lao villages near towns
Needles	15-20 per pkge.	LP 57	Bought by Lao and Meo
Newspapers and books		V 59	Available at separate stores specializing in Thai, French, and English materials in Vientiane
Orangeade	15-20 per bottle	LP 57	Greenspot brand, from Thailand; a popular urban drink
	25 (chilled)	V 59	
Ovaltine	100 per can	LP 57	Popular drink in town, especially in cool months
	90 per can	LP 59	
	75 per can	V 59	
Paper (pad)	30-50	LP 59	In 1959 there was at least one stationery store in Vientiane with variety of items
Perfume	50 per bottle	LP 57	"Evening in Hong Kong" used by some Lao women, even in villages, as luxury item
Polish (shoe)	25 per tin	LP 57	Kiwi brand, used by military and government officials
Pots (aluminum)	80-150	LP 57	Depending on size; most come with covers, are popular with Lao and Meo villagers; manufactured in Hong Kong
Pots (clay)	10-50	LP 57	Depending on size; made in Lao village near town, poor quality; necessary for all groups for steaming rice
	5-10 (small)	LP 59	
	30-40 (large)	LP 59	
Prunes	60 per box	LP 57	Luxury item, imported from California
Radio	About 10,000	LP 57	Rare in Lao villages
	10,000	LP 59	In 1960 transistor models were available in Vientiane
	4,500	V 59	Four-tube Phillips
Raincoat	300-450	LP 57	Depending on quality; plastic ones cheaper, manufactured in Hong Kong; common among urban Lao
	200 (plastic)	LP 59	
	300 (rubberized)	V 59	
	200-350	V 59	
Raisins	60 per box	LP 57	Luxury item, imported from California (1 lb.)

(continued)

TABLE 30. SELECTED ITEMS AVAILABLE IN SHOPS IN LUANG PRABANG AND VIENTIANE (continued)

ITEM	PRICE IN KIP	MARKET[a]	COMMENTS
Roofing material	90-120 90	LP 57 LP 59	Price per square meter, for galvanized tin sheets, varies with supply; used by prosperous Lao and a few village schools
Salt	15-25 per kilo 15	LP 57 LP 59	Coarse, sold in bricks; after rice, most basic commodity for all groups
Saltpeter			Used in making gunpowder and also as a preservative for certain foods
Sardines (canned)	15-25 per tin	LP 57	Thai, French, and other brands, bought as a delicacy by some urban and rural Lao
Sauce (fish)	30 per liter	LP 57	OK brand, made in Thailand and imported in large earthenware crocks
Sauce (soy)	60 per liter	LP 57	A popular ingredient in many Lao dishes; European-style Maggi brand (French adaptation) also available at slightly higher price
Silver bars	1000 per 1400-gram bar	LP 57	Preferred unit of currency among mountain peoples, e.g. in Nam Tha 1 kip in silver is equivalent to 1.8 kip in paper currency
Silver bowl	About 1600	LP 57	For small size, handmade and embossed by local silversmiths; common in Lao homes for ceremonial purposes
Silver jewelry	700-3000	LP 57	Solid silver bracelets, solid neck-rings (Yao) and hollow neckrings (Meo); this type of jewelry is made in the villages and is not commonly found in Luang Prabang shops
Soap	10-20 per bar 12 per bar (Lux) 15-20 per bar (Palmolive)	LP 57 LP 59 V 59	Price varies with brand; Lux most expensive; commonly used in Lao villages
Soap powder	30-40 per box 25 per box	LP 57 V 59	For 7 1/4 oz. size; Fab brand, widely used for washing clothes, even in Lao villages
Sugar	30-50 per box	LP 57	For 1 lb. box Taikoo brand cubes, made in Hong Kong
Sugar	30-50 per kilo 35 per kilo	LP 57 LP 59	Coarse, yellow, and moist; crudely refined in southern Laos; locally produced bricks are also available
Suitcase	100 400-1000 400-1300	LP 57 LP 59 V 59	Made of cardboard and plywood, used by Lao for storing extra clothes

(continued)

TABLE 30. SELECTED ITEMS AVAILABLE IN SHOPS IN LUANG PRABANG AND VIENTIANE (continued)

ITEM	PRICE IN KIP	MARKET[a]	COMMENTS
Sulphur			Used in making gunpowder and fireworks
Tea	45 per lb.	LP 59	Luxury item, from England; local herb varieties also available
Thermos bottle	100 600-1200 (for ice)	LP 57 V 59	Common in town, for keeping water hot; a prestige item in Lao and Meo villages; also used extensively by monks; most brands made in Hong Kong; wide-necked variety used in towns for storing ice cubes
Toothbrush	20 5-10	LP 57 V 59	Used by educated Lao; worn as a necklace ornament by some Meo
Thread	20 per spool	LP 57	Imported from Hong Kong, commonly bought by Lao and Meo villagers
Umbrella	75-150	LP 57	Less expensive are oiled paper and bamboo types, made locally; large black fabric ones, made in Hong Kong, are also used, mainly as sun-shield by Meo and other groups
Wristwatch	1000 (average) 1000-4800	LP 57 LP 59	Mainly a jewelry item, imported from Hong Kong and Japan
Whiskey			A rice whiskey made in Vientiane and popular among urban Lao

[a] LP 57 = Luang Prabang 1957
LP 59 = Luang Prabang 1959
V 59 = Vientiane 1959

TABLE 31. SOME DIFFERENCES BETWEEN A POOR AND A RELATIVELY PROSPEROUS KHMU[a]

	POOR	PROSPEROUS
FAMILY	Has one wife	Possibly has second wife, larger household
HOUSE	Is small, of bamboo and thatch, of flimsy construction	Is larger, with woven bamboo walls and possibly plank flooring and split bamboo roofing
FURNISHINGS	Has bare essentials: woven sleeping mats, clay cooking pots, baskets for serving and eating	Has stuffed sleeping pads, mosquito netting, enamel plates, kerosene lamp, possibly a suitcase for storing clothes
CLOTHING	Has one set of shirt and short pants, in worn condition	Has one set of work clothing and a cheap Western-style shirt and trousers, probably not new
AGRICULTURE	To supplement produce of own hai, must work for other Khmu or Lao to get enough to eat	Has surplus rice production, with some for sale; also has vegetable garden
LIVESTOCK	Has a few chickens	Has a few pigs and chickens, and possibly a buffalo
MISCELLANEOUS	Possibly speaks a little broken Lao	Probably speaks fairly adequate Lao
	Chief personal possession is a crossbow	Possibly possesses a gun, wristwatch, shoes, cigarette lighter

[a] Items not listed in Khmu order of importance.

TABLE 32. DEGREES OF URBANIZATION IN VIENTIANE, LUANG PRABANG, AND NAM THA, 1959[a]

Facility	Vientiane	Luang Prabang	Nam Tha
Airfield	All-weather, with maintenance facilities	All-weather	Not usable during height of rainy season
Roads	Connections to other provinces; blacktop in town	Paved in town; connecting roads closed in rainy season	A few miles of local dirt road; no connections to other provinces
Communications	Radio, telegraph, limited local phones	Radio, telegraph	Radio only
Electricity	Diesel power plant	Charcoal-powered plant, operates only in evenings	No civilian facilities
Banks	Lao, Chinese, French	Lao government finance office	None
Industries	Various small industries producing consumer goods	More limited than Vientiane	Only handicrafts and rice mills
Population	Lao; Thai; and extensive Chinese, Vietnamese, European and Indian communities	Lao; small Chinese and Vietnamese communities; a few Europeans and Indians; tribal peoples	Lao; tribal peoples; a few Chinese and Vietnamese; one Indian; no resident Europeans
Hospitals	Modest but fully staffed hospital	One Lao and one French military physician; limited facilities	A clinic with a practical nurse
Schools	Lycée	Collège (9 years)	Elementary (6 years)
Transportation of goods	By ferry from railhead in Thailand as well as by air, road, and river	By air, road, and river	By air, horse caravan, and pirogue
Shops	Great variety, e.g. auto and travel agencies, bookstores	Food, clothing, drugs, and general supplies only	General supplies
Hotels	Government-owned and privately owned	One government-owned bungalow	One small rooming house
Government	All agencies	All provincial bureaus	Army, police, clinic, and school

[a] Both Vientiane and Luang Prabang are old administrative centers. Nam Tha was only recently made a provincial capital. Its facilities are analogous to those existing in provinces such as Phong Saly, Sam Neua, Sayaboury, and Attopeu where, with the exception of Sayaboury, the majority of the population is composed of non-Lao tribal peoples.

TABLE 33. SUMMARY OF INDUSTRIES EXISTING IN VIENTIANE, 1958

Category	Number
Sawmills	11
Carpenter shops	12
Garages	21
Rice mills	11
Print shops	7
Ice works	3
Charcoal, charcoal brick works	160
Hotels	5
Moving picture theatres	5
Construction firms	50
Airlines	4
Carbonated water plants	3
Candles	3
Beauty products	3
Alcoholic beverages	3
Raw sugar	2
Soap works	2
Fruit syrups	1
Automatic laundry	1
Tobacco products	1
Metal parts supplier (for construction)	1

Source: Lao Ministry of Finance.

TABLE 34. LAO PATTERNS OF CONSUMPTION, 1958

Items	Distribution value, urban and rural areas[a]	Coefficient of 1000 in Lao urban survey[b]		
		Group	Subgroup	Article
FOOD		558		
Cereal products			122	
Lao rice (glutinous)	(4)			73
Nonglutinous rice[b]	(3)			21
Chinese noodles	(3)			2
Lao noodles	(4)			10
Bread	(2)			16
Meat			93	
Beef (1st quality)[c]	(3)			15
Beef (2nd quality)[c]	(3)			23
Buffalo (fillet)	(3)			23
Pork	(3)			10
Pork with lard	(3)			13
Pork chops	(3)			5
Pig's feet	(3)			2
Pig's head	(3)			2
Poultry			32	
Medium-sized chicken (live)	(3)			20
Medium-sized duck (live)	(3)			12
Sausage and tripe			22	
Chinese sausage	(3)			2
Liver paste	(3)			2
Som mou (a fermented pork dish)	(3)			8
Pork liver	(3)			5
Pork intestines	(3)			5
Fish, fresh and dried[d]			39	
Pa bouk, average size	(3)			8
Pa kho, average size	(3)			8
Pa pak	(3)			3
Pa eun	(3)			2
Pa kho, dried	(3)			10
Salted fish	(2)			8
Canned goods			6	
Sardines	(1)			5
Abalone	(1)			1
Milk, eggs, and fats			67	
Chicken eggs	(3)			7
Duck eggs	(3)			8
Fresh milk, (buffalo)[e]	(2)			2
Powdered milk	(2)			8
Condensed milk (Nestle)	(2)			10
Salted tinned butter	(1)			2
Tinned cheese	(1)			1
Bacon	(2)			2
Peanut oil	(2)			4
Lard	(3)			16
Dried coconut	(4)			7

(continued)

TABLE 34. LAO PATTERNS OF CONSUMPTION, 1958 (continued)

Items	Distribution value, urban and rural areas[a]	Coefficient of 1000 in Lao urban survey[b]		
		Group	Subgroup	Article
Vegetables, fresh, dried, and canned			41	
Lettuce	(4)			5
Cabbage	(4)			5
Water vines	(4)			7
Tomato	(4)			3
Green beans	(4)			5
Potato	(4)			5
Fresh shallots	(4)			3
Garlic	(4)			1
Dried onion	(4)			1
Dried shallots	(4)			1
Black mushrooms	(4)			1
Canned green peas	(1)			1
Canned beans	(1)			1
Dried large pimento	(4)			2
Fruit			27	
Banana (kouei ngao)	(4)			10
Banana (kouei hom)	(4)			8
Orange	(4)			6
Canned lichees	(2)			1
Canned pears (1 kg. tin)	(1)			1
Orange marmalade (250 gr.)	(1)			1
Grocery items			46	
Chocolate bar	(2)			1
Tea (250 gr. pkg.)	(2)			1
Green coffee	(3)			5
Salt	(4)			5
Nam pa (pickling brine) 1st quality	(2)			10
Padek (whole preserved fish) 2nd quality	(3)			10
Vinegar	(2)			2
Tapioca	(2)			1
Local sugar	(3)			2
Granulated sugar	(1)			7
Snacks outside the home			26	
"Soupe Chinoise"	(2)			10
Black coffee	(2)			8
Coffee with milk	(2)			4
Ovaltine	(2)			3
Cakes	(2)			1
Beverages			37	
Lemonade, Seven-Up	(2)			4
Beer (Carlsberg)	(2)			8
Carbonated water	(2)			2
Aperitif (Dubonnet)	(1)			2
Aperitif (martini)	(1)			2
Cointreau	(1)			1
Cognac	(1)			4
Lao rice alcohol	(4)			10
Red wine	(1)			4

(continued)

TABLE 34. LAO PATTERNS OF CONSUMPTION, 1958 (continued)

Items	Distribution value, urban and rural areas[a]	Coefficient of 1000 in Lao urban survey[b]		
		Group	Subgroup	Article
DWELLING		138		
Rent (2 rooms)	(2)		37	37
Lighting and heating	(2)		63	
Electricity	(2)			15
40-watt bulb	(2)			5
25-watt bulb	(2)			5
Firewood	(4)			15
Charcoal	(4)			10
Kerosene	(3)			11
Wood alcohol	(2)			2
Household furnishings			14	
Table	(3)			3
Chair	(3)			3
Sleeping mat for two	(4)			3
Cotton blanket for one	(3)			3
Linoleum	(2)			1
Oilcloth	(2)			1
Eating utensils			13	
Enamel dish	(3)			6
Glass	(3)			7
Household utensils			7	
Aluminum fork and spoon	(3)			2
Medium-sized wash basin	(3)			1
Medium-sized casserole	(2)			2
Small coffee grinder	(2)			1
Lao broom	(4)			1
Small items			4	
40-watt bulb	(2)			1
Pliers	(3)			1
Hammer	(3)			1
Electrical wire	(2)			1
DOMESTIC HELP		32		
Servant (without food)	(2)			7
Cook (without food)	(2)			5
Nursemaid (food and lodging)	(2)			5
General servant (food and lodging)	(3)			15
PERSONAL CARE		80		
Household products			21	
Laundry soap (1 kg.)	(2)			10
Detergent (Fab)	(3)			10
Wax	(2)			1

(continued)

TABLE 34. LAO PATTERNS OF CONSUMPTION, 1958 (continued)

Items	Distribution value, urban and rural areas[a]	Coefficient of 1000 in Lao urban survey[b]		
		Group	Subgroup	Article
Toilet articles			7	
Facial soap (Lux)	(3)			3
Toothpaste (Colgate)	(2)			2
Eau de cologne	(2)			1
Razor blades	(2)			1
Laundry			9	
Laundering one set of cotton underwear	(1)			7
Laundering one shirt	(1)			2
Hairdresser			10	
Haircut (men)	(4)			5
Shampoo (men)	(1)			2
Haircut (ladies)	(1)			1
Permanent wave	(2)			2
Notions			4	
Sewing needles	(4)			1
Knitting needles	(2)			1
Sewing thread	(4)			1
Snaps, hooks-and-eyes	(3)			1
Medical care			29	
Office visit to urban doctor	(2)			13
Aspirin	(3)			4
Quinine	(3)			5
Ganidan (dysentery drug)	(2)			5
Absorbent cotton	(2)			2
TRANSPORTATION		23		
Taxi	(3)			2
Pedicabs	(3)			10
Gasoline	(2)			9
Oil (30- or 40-weight)	(2)			1
CLOTHING		111		
Personal garments and yard goods			55	
Plastic raincoat (man's)	(2)			4
Shirt	(4)			8
Poplin (2nd quality)	(4)			18
Calico	(4)			15
Household linens, clothing			56	
Small towel	(3)			10
Handkerchief (2nd quality)	(3)			4
Double sheet	(3)			8
Underpants	(2)			4
Undershirt	(4)			4
Leather shoes	(2)			10
Sandals	(3)			10
Umbrella	(3)			4
Parasol	(4)			2

(continued)

TABLE 34. LAO PATTERNS OF CONSUMPTION, 1958 (continued)

Items	Distribution value, urban and rural areas[a]	Coefficient of 1000 in Lao urban survey[b] Group	Subgroup	Article
MISCELLANEOUS		58		
Entertainment			9	
Movies (2nd class seat)	(2)			7
Theatre (2nd class seat)	(2)			1
Sports event	(2)			1
Reading matter			8	
"Journal d'Extrême-Orient"	(1)			2
"Paris Match"	(1)			2
Miscellaneous publications	(2)			4
Postoffice			5	
Stamps for international postage	(1)			2
Sending printed matter	(2)			1
Sending parcels	(2)			1
Other items				1
Stationery			5	
Ball-point pen	(2)			1
32-page notebook	(2)			2
Airmail envelopes (50)	(2)			2
Smoking items			31	
Matches	(3)			3
Cigarettes	(3)			20
Tobacco	(3)			8

[a] Key for "distribution value" column:
(1) Used by urban elites almost exclusively.
(2) Occurs mainly in towns or considered an unusual luxury in villages.
(3) Known in villages but use or availability limited by cultural or economic factors.
(4) Utilized in both urban and rural areas.
These are obviously rough classifications and there is considerable overlap.

[b] The relative weighting in this urban cost of living survey was determined by officials of the Bureau of Statistics of the Ministry of the Plan in Vientiane. It is estimated that approximately 1.5 per cent of urban income goes for gifts to monks. Also missing from this survey are gambling expenses.

[c] More common among Meo than Lao villagers.

[d] Limited mainly to villages along rivers.

[e] Milk or milk products traditionally have not been used in Southeast Asia.

Source: Ministère du Plan, Service de la Statistique du Laos, Les dépenses de la consommation familiale des fonctionnaires à Vientiane, August 1958.

LIST OF PUBLICATIONS

Southeast Asia Studies . Yale University

BIBLIOGRAPHY SERIES

2. Embree, John F. and Lillian Ota Dotson. _Bibliography of the Peoples and Cultures of Mainland Southeast Asia_. 1950.

   xxxiii, 821, xii pages; maps. Out of print.

   (Photographic reprint available from University Microfilms, Inc. OP No. 6654. $31.15.)

4. Hart, Donn V. _An Annotated Guide to Current Philippine Periodicals_. 1957.

   xxi, 116 pages. Out of print.

   (Photographic reprint available from University Microfilms, Inc. OP No. 16,716. $8.30.)

5. Irikura, James K. _Southeast Asia: Selected Annotated Bibliography of Japanese Publications_. Published by arrangement with the Human Relations Area Files, Inc. 1956.

   xii, 544 pages. $8.50.

6. Kennedy, Raymond. _Bibliography of Indonesian Peoples and Cultures_. (Thomas W. Maretzki and H. Th. Fischer, eds.) Published by arrangement with the Human Relations Area Files, Inc. 1955; second revised edition, 1962.

   xxii, 207 pages; maps. $8.50.

7. Pelzer, Karl J. _Selected Bibliography on the Geography of Southeast Asia_. 3 vols. Published by arrangement with the Human Relations Area Files, Inc.

   Part I. _Southeast Asia: General_. 1949.
   43 pages. Out of print.

   Part II. Philippines. 1950. 76 pages. Out of print.

   (Photographic reprint of Parts I and II available from University Microfilms, Inc. OP No. 11,000. Paper-bound, $7.00; library-bound, $9.25.)

   Part III. _Malaya_. 1955. 162 pages. $1.75.

8. Trager, Frank N. Furnivall of Burma: An Annotated Bibliography of the Works of John S. Furnivall. 1963.

ii, 55 pages. $1.75.

9. Anderson, Gerald H. Christianity in Southeast Asia: A Bibliographical Guide. Published by the Missionary Research Library with the assistance of Southeast Asia Studies. (in press)

CULTURAL REPORT SERIES

1. Coughlin, Richard J. The Position of Women in Vietnam. 1950.

43 pages. Out of print.

(Photographic reprint available from University Microfilms, Inc. OP No. 17,125. $3.10.)

3. Hart, Donn V. The Philippine Plaza Complex: A Focal Point in Culture Change. 1955; second printing, 1961.

55 pages; charts. $1.50.

4. Koentjaraningrat, R. M. A Preliminary Description of the Javanese Kinship System. 1957.

111 pages. Out of print.

(Photographic reprint available from University Microfilms, Inc. OP No. 17,124. $4.20.)

5. Cunningham, Clark E. The Postwar Migration of the Toba-Bataks to East Sumatra. 1958; second printing, 1962.

xii, 187 pages. $4.50.

6. Koop, John C. The Eurasian Population in Burma. 1961.

66 pages. $2.00.

7. Hart, Donn V. The Cebuan Filipino Dwelling in Caticugan: Its Construction and Cultural Aspects. 1959.

148 pages; charts; drawings; photographs. Out of print.

(Photographic reprint available from University Microfilms, Inc. OP No. 17,126. $5.55.)

8. Skinner, G. William, ed. Local, Ethnic and National Loyalties in Village Indonesia: A Symposium. 1959.

68 pages. $2.00.

10. Cooley, Frank L. Ambonese Adat: A General Description. 1962.

99 pages; map; photographs. $4.00.

11. Alisjahbana, S. Takdir. Indonesian Language and Literature: Two Essays. 1962.

40 pages. $1.75.

12. Jay, Robert R. Religion and Politics in Rural Central Java. 1963.

viii, 117 pages; charts; maps. $3.75.

TRANSLATION SERIES

1. Langrand, Gustave. Social and Religious Organization of a Vietnamese Village. [Summary translation.] 1950.

33 pages. Out of print.

(Photographic reprint available from University Microfilms, Inc. OP No. 14,590. Paper-bound, $2.50; library-bound, $4.50.)

2. Maspero, Georges. The Kingdom of Champa. [Chapter I. Le Royaume Du Champa.] 1949.

56 pages. Out of print.

(Photographic reprint available from University Microfilms, Inc. OP No. 14,603. Paper-bound, $3.60; library-bound, $6.35.)

3. Nguyen Van Vinh. Savings and Mutual Lending Societies (Ho). 1949.

Out of print.

(Photographic reprint available from University Microfilms, Inc. OP No. 14,158. Paper-bound, $2.50; library-bound, $4.50.)

4. Odaka, Junio. Economic Organization of the Li Tribes of Hainan Island. 1950.

92 pages. Out of print.

(Photographic reprint available from University Microfilms, Inc. OP No. 17,127. $6.05.)

5. Rajadhon, Phya Anuman. The Life of the Farmer in Thailand. 1956.

Out of print.

(Reprinted as Part I in William J. Gedney, trans. and ed., Life and Ritual in Old Siam, HRAF Press, 1961. 191 pages. $4.50.)

MONOGRAPH SERIES

1. Higgins, Benjamin H., et al. Entrepreneurship and Labor Skills in Indonesian Economic Development: A Symposium. 1961.

138 pages. $4.00.

2. McHale, Thomas R. and Mary C. McHale. Early American-Philippine Trade: The Journal of Nathaniel Bowditch in Manila, 1796. 1962.

65 pages. $3.25.

3. Paauw, Douglas S., ed. Prospects for East Sumatran Plantation Industries: A Symposium. 1962.

xiii, 68 pages; maps. $2.75.

4. Halpern, Joel M. Government, Politics, and Social Structure in Laos: A Study of Tradition and Innovation. 1964.

xii, 202 pages; map; tables. $4.50.

5. Halpern, Joel M. Economy and Society of Laos: A Brief Survey. 1964.

xii, 234 pages; drawings; maps; photographs; tables; bibliography.

6. Landé, Carl H. Leaders, Factions, and Parties: The Structure of Philippine Politics. (in press)

SPECIAL PUBLICATIONS

Maung Maung. Aung San of Burma. Published for Yale University Southeast Asia Studies by Martinus Nijhoff, The Hague. 1962.

162 pages. $5.75.

United States Economic Survey Team to Indonesia. Indonesia: Perspective and Proposals for United States Economic Aid: A Report to the President of the United States. 1963.

xi, 205 pages; tables. $4.50.

McVey, Ruth T., ed. Indonesia. Published by arrangement with HRAF Press. 1963.

xx, 600 pages; maps; charts; tables. $12.00.

Southeast Asia Studies publications are distributed by:

The Cellar Book Shop
P. O. Box 6
College Park Station
Detroit, Michigan 48221

Publications by arrangement with the Human Relations Area Files, Inc. or with HRAF Press are also available from:

Taplinger Publishing Co.
119 West 57th Street
New York, New York 10019

Photographic reprints may be ordered from:

University Microfilms, Inc.
313 N. First Street
Ann Arbor, Michigan 48107